CRIME AGAINST CHILDREN

CRIME AGAINST CHILDREN

By

Rajneesh Gugnani

2008

CYBER TECH PUBLICATIONS
4264/3, Ansari Road, Daryaganj, New Delhi-110002 (India)
Ph.: 011-23244078. Fax: 011-23280028
E-Mail: cyberpublicationsdelhi@yahoo.com

CRIME AGAINST CHILDREN

Rajneesh Gugnani

First Edition 2008

Published by :

G.S. Rawat for Cyber Tech Publications
4264/3, Ansari Road, Daryaganj, New Delhi-110002 (India)
Ph.: 011-23244078. Fax: 011-23280028
E-Mail: cyberpublicationsdelhi@yahoo.com

Printed at : **Amit Enterprises**, Maujpur, Delhi, (9810878184)

Preface

Crime is an act, or commission of an act, that is forbidden or the omission of a duty that is commanded by a public law and that makes the offender liable to punishment by that law. The challenge of crime to society changes with the advance of civilisation, particularly as technology continues to increase. Societal and scientific concepts of crime are related to antisocial behaviour of criminals.

It is a common fact that the general public and government officials have very limited understanding of the true nature and extent of crime. Any serious study looking into the understanding and control of crimes against children like sex, homicide, etc. should be insighted from a wide variety of disciplines for it to be advantageous in providing justice to the needed one.

Even in this digital age of cyberspace, no state possesses defensible borders to crimes especially against children as they are innocent and naive. The new century therefore should bring greater technological innovation and a law enforcement community prepared for the criminals who commit crimes against the children. The purpose of this book is to provide challenging and practical advice to the general public and government officials to stand against the venerable activities of criminals which result in crucial offences and losses to human community. It is intended be an academic study of crime trends, criminal justice and crime prevention.

I have made every possible effort to bring all the facts and required tables in the text to make it informative and to aware the masses against this social abuse. Hope this work of mine would be very informative and alarming against the present situation. Your valuable suggestions and complaints are always welcome.

—*Author*

Contents

1

INTRODUCTION

Children have always been vulnerable to victimization. Their trusting natures and naivete make them perfect targets for perpetrators-both people they know and those they don't. As children grow into adolescents, they remain vulnerable to victimization. Youth are often curious and eager to try new things. Many youth struggle with issues of rebellion and independence and seek attention and affection from people outside the home, often by using computers. Today, an estimated 10 million children are using the Internet. By 2005, approximately 77 million kids will be on-line. With so many children on-line, today's predators can easily find and exploit them. For predators, the Internet is a new, effective, and more anonymous way to seek out and groom children for criminal purposes such as producing and distributing child pornography, contacting and stalking children for the purpose of engaging in sexual acts, and exploiting children for sexual tourism for personal and commercial purposes.

The nature of Internet crimes presents complex new challenges for law enforcement agencies and victim service providers with regard to investigating crimes, collecting evidence, identifying and apprehending offenders, and assisting child victims and their families. For example, victims and perpetrators are often separated geographically, which may hamper investigation efforts. Also, victims are often ashamed and reluctant to come forward, which makes identifying offenders difficult. These challenges are being addressed by federal and local law enforcement agencies, but there is still much to learn about preventing, identifying, and investigating

Internet-based crimes against children. This chapter is based on the experiences of professionals now working with child victims of Internet crimes and their families. It highlights some of the challenges law enforcement and victim service professionals face in addressing Internet crimes against children and focuses attention on child victims of these crimes by examining who they are and how best to respond to their needs and the needs of their families.

INTERNET CRIMES AGAINST CHILDREN

New computer technology presents complex challenges for law enforcement agencies and victim service providers. These professionals must protect Internet users as they conduct investigations, secure evidence, identify and apprehend offenders, and help child victims and their families. Based on the knowledge and experience of those working with child victims, this Bulletin focuses attention on child victims of Internet-based crimes, highlighting the challenges for law enforcement personnel and victim service providers, examining who the child victims are, and determining how best to respond to these victims' needs and the needs of their families.

The growth of technology has changed our lives dramatically. Computers were viewed as a luxury or even an extravagance 30 years ago. We relied on television, newspapers, and radio as primary sources of news and information. Cables, modems, and on-line services were virtually nonexistent.

Today, computers are prevalent in businesses, homes, schools, libraries, and even airports. The World Wide Web provides instant access to news, reference information, shopping, banking, stock trading, auctions, and travel information and reservations. People routinely use the Internet to take college courses, play games, listen to music, and view videos. Chat rooms and e-mails are now replacing telephones as our favorite means of long-distance communication.

The proliferation of computer technology obviously has enhanced our lives in many ways, such as enabling improved productivity and efficiency at work, school, and home. Anyone with access to a computer and modem now has unparalleled recreational and educational opportunities. Unfortunately, criminals are also using modern technology-to prey on innocent victims. Computers and the Internet have made the predator's job easier. Historically, child predators found their victims in public places where children tend to gather-school yards, playgrounds, and shopping malls. Today, with so many children on-line, the Internet provides predators a new place-cyberspace-to target children for criminal acts. This approach eliminates many of the risks predators face when making contact in person.

Scope of the Problem

The sheer number of young people using computers today makes our concern for them well founded. Recent years have seen a great increase in access to and use of the Internet. By the end of 1998, more than 40 percent of all American homes had computers, and 25 percent had Internet access. This trend is expected to continue. Children and teenagers are one of the fastest growing groups of Internet users. An estimated 10 million kids are on-line today. By the year 2002, this figure is expected to increase to 45 million, and by 2005 to 77 million. With so many youth on-line and vulnerable to predators, it is extremely important for parents, law enforcement officials, prosecutors, and victim service providers to know as much as possible about Internet crimes against children so they can prevent victimization and prosecute offenders.

Who is Vulnerable?

Traditionally, both intrafamilial offenders and strangers have found that young children and teenagers are perfect targets for criminal acts because they are often trusting, naive, curious, adventuresome, and eager for attention and affection. However, the most attractive factor to predators is that children and teenagers historically have not been viewed as credible witnesses. Today, the danger to children is even greater because the Internet provides predators anonymity. Whether the victimization occurs in person or over the Internet, the process is the same-the perpetrator uses information to target a child victim. For example, the predator may initiate an on-line friendship with a young person, sharing hobbies and interests.

This may lead to the exchange of gifts and pictures. Just like the traditional predator who targets children in person, the on-line predator usually is willing to spend considerable time befriending and grooming a child. The predator wants to build the child's trust, which will allow the predator to get what he or she ultimately wants from the child.

Although no family is immune to the possibility that their child may be exploited and harassed on the Internet, a few factors make some children more vulnerable than others. Older children tend to be at greater risk because they often use the computer unsupervised and are more likely to engage in on-line discussions of a personal nature. Some victims become unwitting participants as they actively participate in chat rooms, trade e-mail messages, and send pictures on-line. Troubled or rebellious teens who are seeking emancipation from parental authority can be susceptible to Internet predators. The risk of victimization is greater for emotionally vulnerable youth who may be dealing with issues of sexual identity. These young people may be willing to engage in conversation that is both titillating and exciting but appears innocent and harmless. Unfortunately, Internet interactions that initially appear innocent can gradually lead to sexually explicit conduct.

Types of Internet Victimization

Internet crimes are often thought of as victimless. Nothing could be further from the truth. Children and teenagers can and do become victims of Internet crimes. Predators contact teenagers and children over the Internet and victimize them by:

- Enticing them through on-line contact for the purpose of engaging them in sexual acts.
- Using the Internet for the production, manufacture, and distribution of child pornography.
- Using the Internet to expose youth to child pornography and encourage them to exchange pornography.
- Enticing and exploiting children for the purpose of sexual tourism (travel with the intent to engage in sexual behavior) for commercial gain and/or personal gratification.

Unique Characteristics of Cyber Crimes

Several characteristics distinguish Internet crimes from other crimes committed against children:

Physical contact between the child and the perpetrator does not need to occur for a child to become a victim or for a crime to be committed. Innocent pictures or images of children can be digitally transformed into pornographic material and distributed across the Internet without the victims' knowledge.

The Internet provides a source for repeated, long-term victimization of a child that can last for years, often without the victim's knowledge. Once a child's picture is displayed on the Internet, it can remain there forever. Images can stay on the Internet indefinitely without damage to the quality of the image.

These crimes transcend jurisdictional boundaries, often involving multiple victims from different communities, states, and countries. The geographic location of a child is not a primary concern for perpetrators who target victims over the Internet. Often, perpetrators travel hundreds of miles to different states and countries to engage in sexual acts with children they met over the Internet. Many of these cases involve local, state, federal, and international law enforcement entities in multiple jurisdictions.

Many victims of Internet crimes do not disclose their victimization or even realize that they have been victims of a crime. Whereas children who experience physical or sexual abuse may disclose the abuse to a friend, teacher, or parent, many victims of Internet crimes remain anonymous until pictures or images are discovered by law enforcement during an investigation. The presumed anonymity of Internet activities often provides a false sense of security and secrecy for both the perpetrator and the victim.

Youth Internet Safety Survey

Although it was clear that young people are using the Internet in ever-increasing numbers, no research existed on how many youth encounter unwanted sexual solicitations and exposure to sexual material and harassment on-line. To obtain a clearer picture of the scope of the problem, the National Center for Missing & Exploited Children (NCMEC) provided funding to Dr. David Finkelhor, Director of the Crimes Against Children Research Center at the University of New Hampshire, to conduct a research survey in 1999 on Internet victimization of youth. His research provides the best profile of this problem to date.

Crimes Against Children Research Center staff interviewed a nationally representative sample of 1,501 youth, aged 10 to 17, who used the Internet regularly. "Regular use" was defined as using the Internet at least once a month for the past 6 months on a computer at home, at school, in a library, at someone else's home, or in some other place.

Survey Areas

The survey looked at four types of on-line victimization of youth, which Finkelhor defined as:

- *Sexual Solicitation and Approaches*: Requests to engage in sexual activities or sexual talk or to give personal sexual information that were unwanted or, whether wanted or not, made by an adult.
- *Aggressive Sexual Solicitation*: Sexual solicitations involving off-line contact with the perpetrator through mail, by telephone, or in person, or attempts or requests for offline contact.
- *Unwanted Exposure to Sexual Material*: When on-line, opening e-mail, or opening e-mail links, and not seeking or expecting sexual material, being exposed to pictures of naked people or people having sex.
- *Harassment*: Threats or other offensive content (not sexual solicitation) sent on-line to the youth or posted on-line for others to see.

The survey also explored Internet safety practices used by youth and their families, what factors may put some youth more at risk for victimization than others, and the families' knowledge of how to report on-line solicitations and harassment.

Statistical Findings

The survey results offered the following statistical highlights:

- One in 5 youth received a sexual approach or solicitation over the Internet in the past year.
- One in 33 youth received an aggressive sexual solicitation in the past year. This means a predator asked a young person to meet somewhere, called a young person on the phone, and/or sent the young person correspondence, money, or gifts through the U.S. Postal Service.
- One in 4 youth had an unwanted exposure in the past year to pictures of naked people or people having sex.
- One in 17 youth was threatened or harassed in the past year.
- Most young people who reported these incidents were not very disturbed about them, but a few found them distressing.
- Only a fraction of all episodes was reported to authorities such as the police, an Internet service provider, or a hotline.
- About 25 percent of the youth who encountered a sexual approach or solicitation told a parent. Almost 40 percent of those reporting an unwanted exposure to sexual material told a parent.
- Only 17 percent of youth and 11 percent of parents could name a specific authority, such as the Federal Bureau of Investigation (FBI), CyberTipline, or an Internet service provider, to which they could report an Internet crime, although more indicated they were vaguely aware of such authorities.
- In households with home Internet access, one-third of parents said they had filtering or blocking software on their computers.

Other Findings

The survey results confirm what is already known: although the Internet is a wonderfully fun and educational tool, it can also be very dangerous. According to the survey, one in five youth who regularly use the Internet received sexual solicitations or approaches during a 1-year period. The survey also found that offenses and offenders are more diverse than previously thought. In addition to pedophiles, other predators use the Internet. Nearly half (48 percent) of the offenders were other youth, and one-fourth of the aggressive episodes were initiated by females. Further, 77 percent of targeted youth were age 14 or older-not an age characteristically targeted by pedophiles. Although the youth stopped most solicitations by leaving the Web site, logging off, or blocking the sender, the survey confirmed current thinking that some youth are particularly vulnerable to on-line advances.

Most youth reported not being distressed by sexual exposures on-line. However, a significant 23 percent reported being very or extremely upset, 20 percent reported being very or extremely embarrassed, and 20 percent reported at least one symptom of stress. These findings point to the need for more research on the effects on youth of unwanted exposure to sexual materials and the indicators of potentially exploitative adult-youth relationships.

The large number of solicitations that went unreported by youth and families was of particular interest. This underreporting is attributed to feelings of embarrassment or guilt, ignorance that the incident was a reportable act, ignorance of how to report it, and perhaps resignation to a certain level of inappropriate behavior in the world.

Possibly due to the nature and small sample size of the survey, there were no reported incidences of traveler cases. The survey also revealed no incidences of completed Internet seduction or sexual exploitation, including trafficking of child pornography. Despite the findings of this survey, law enforcement agencies report increasing incidents of Internet crimes against children.

Recommendations

Among the many findings of Finkelhor's survey, the most significant is that we are only beginning to realize the extent of the complex and increasingly prevalent phenomenon of

Internet-based crimes against children. We have much to learn about the magnitude of the problem, the characteristics of its victims and perpetrators, its impact on children, and strategies for prevention and intervention.

INFORMATION AND INTERVENTION RESOURCES

National Center for Missing and Exploited Children

The National Center for Missing & Exploited Children is a comprehensive resource for families, victim service practitioners, and law enforcement personnel. NCMEC is supported by the U.S. Department of Justice's Office of Juvenile Justice and Delinquency Prevention (OJJDP) and functions as a clearinghouse and resource center for collecting and distributing information about missing, runaway, and sexually exploited children, including exploitation resulting from Internet solicitations. In partnership with the U.S. Postal Inspection Service, U.S. Customs Service, and FBI, NCMEC operates the CyberTipline, an on-line form for reporting suspected child sexual exploitation (www.missingkids.com/cybertip), and the Child Pornography Tipline (1-800-843-5678). Through the CyberTipline and the telephone hotline, NCMEC

- Receives reports 24 hours a day, 7 days a week, of child sexual exploitation and the production and distribution of pornography on the Internet. Calls to the toll-free Child Pornography Tipline can be received from the United States, Canada, Mexico, and the United Kingdom.
- Receives reports of offenses such as child pornography, child sex tourism, on-line enticement of children for sexual acts, and child sexual molestation (outside the family). Analysts review each report and provide information to investigating law enforcement agencies.
- Provides leads on child exploitation cases to appropriate law enforcement authorities and agencies.

NCMEC case managers work directly with law enforcement personnel, offering technical assistance, resources, information, and advice on child sexual exploitation. NCMEC also has developed specialized training programs, materials, and curricula designed for law enforcement personnel. Training is available at little or no cost to local jurisdictions through OJJDP.

Internet Crimes Against Children Task Force Program

In 1998, the Missing Children's Program of OJJDP initiated its Internet Crimes Against Children (ICAC) task force program, a national effort to combat the threat of offenders who use the Internet to sexually exploit children. Through this program, state and local law enforcement agencies can acquire the skills, equipment, and personnel resources to respond effectively to ICAC offenses. The program encourages law enforcement agencies to develop specialized multijurisdictional, multiagency responses to prevent, interdict, investigate, and prosecute Internet crimes against children. As of mid-2000, 30 ICAC task forces were participating in the ICAC task force program. Each task force is composed of federal, state, and local law enforcement personnel; federal and local prosecution officials; local educators; and service providers such as mental health professionals. These task forces serve as valuable regional resources for assistance to parents, educators, prosecutors, law enforcement personnel, and others who work on child victimization issues.

FEDERAL BUREAU OF INVESTIGATION

The FBI has established the Innocent Images program to focus specifically on computer-facilitated child sexual exploitation. Each FBI Field Division has designated two Crimes Against Children Coordinators to work with state and local law enforcement officials to investigate and prosecute cases that cross jurisdictional boundaries. OVC has placed a victim witness coordinator in the Innocent Images program to focus greater attention on the needs of child victims.

U.S. Postal Inspection Service

The U.S. Postal Inspection Service protects children on-line by monitoring the transmission of child pornography through the mail. Increased amounts of pornography are being sent through U.S. mail as more illicit Web sites emerge advertising child pornographic material for sale. In response, the U.S. Postal Inspection Service is tracking down these materials. In addition, the U.S. Customs Service Cyber Smuggling Center monitors the illegal generation, importation, and proliferation of child pornography.

The Future

The future holds many challenges for those fighting Internet crimes against young people. Cases involving Internet crimes against children are complex and labor intensive for both the police and prosecutors. The time between victimization and arrest can be lengthy. These cases are usually multi-jurisdictional, which presents challenges in the investigation and prosecution of a case and can present problems for the criminal justice system, the child victim, and the family in terms of resources, travel, and court appearances.

Challenges

Child victimization on the Internet is a complex matter. The full impact of such victimization on children is not completely understood. Family dynamics often play a significant role in children's denial of a crime and their willingness to participate in the investigation and prosecution. A child's ability to acknowledge and accept the crime can be linked to family values, peer pressure, and feelings of guilt, shame, and embarrassment. Denial and recantation can be common among children who unwittingly participated in the crime. Because of these issues, the greatest challenges facing law enforcement and victim service professionals are to identify the victims, protect their privacy, and serve them without further victimization.

Until more knowledge is gathered about Internet crime and its effects on victims, law enforcement and victim service professionals will continue working on Internet child exploitation using the tactics and standard approaches that have proved effective for working with other types of child victims. These tactics and approaches are discussed below.

Precautions during Interviews

- Ensure that the interview is conducted with developmentally appropriate language. A child's ability to relate to concepts and receive messages varies depending on his or her stage of development. The interviewer must assess the child's developmental level and adapt the interview accordingly.

- Ensure that the interview is conducted in a culturally sensitive manner with culturally appropriate language. Determine which words the child is comfortable with. Is an interpreter needed? If so, use a professional interpreter and not a family member. Family members inadvertently may interject their interpretations into the translation and may prejudice the child's account.
- Be patient with victims. At first, many victims will deny their involvement. However, with continued support and encouragement, the child victim usually will divulge and discuss the victimization.
- Avoid duplicative interviews when possible. Multiple interviewers and interviews tend to confuse and intimidate children, especially younger ones, and may revictimize the child and produce inconsistent victim statements. Joint or taped interviews minimize the number of interviews required and maintain consistent phrasing of questions.
- If the victim is from another jurisdiction, work with victim witness staff in that community to ensure that victim services are provided.
- Do not show surprise or shock. Remember, the youth is probably already feeling guilt, shame, or embarrassment about what occurred.
- Be honest with the child about what he or she can expect from the investigation and prosecution of the case and about any future contact he or she may have with the perpetrator.
- Talk to the child victim about a victim impact statement and restitution if the case will be prosecuted and if it is developmentally appropriate. Regardless of the child's age, find ways to give him or her a sense of control over the situation-provide choices, no matter how small, and

help him or her prepare for the court process. Consider requesting a guardian ad litem to represent and support the child throughout the legal process. Make the child familiar with the courtroom environment. A properly prepared child may find active involvement in the case empowering.

For the Family

- Internet crimes against children impact the entire family. Family members may feel guilty for not protecting their child more effectively. They also may feel anger or shame about their child's involvement in the crime. Family members are secondary victims and need to be offered support and information to help them understand the nature of these crimes and know how to better handle their often conflicting feelings.
- Assist families victimized by Internet crime who require travel and lodging arrangements related to the legal proceedings, such as depositions and hearings.
- Prepare the family for media and press coverage. Be sensitive to the privacy needs of the victim and family. Will the victim's name appear in any public documents? If so, can these documents be sealed if the family so desires?
- Help the family understand what their child is experiencing so they can help the child and feel some sense of control over the situation.

2

CRIME AGAINST CHILDREN BY BABYSITTERS

INTRODUCTION

The Office of Juvenile Justice and Delinquency Prevention (OJJDP) is committed to improving the justice system's response to crimes against children. OJJDP recognizes that children are at increased risk for crime victimization. Not only are children the victims of many of the same crimes that victimize adults, they are subject to other crimes, like child abuse and neglect, that are specific to childhood.

The impact of these crimes on young victims can be devastating, and the violent or sexual victimization of children can often lead to an intergenerational cycle of violence and abuse. The purpose of OJJDP's Crimes Against Children Series is to improve and expand the Nation's efforts to better serve child victims by presenting the latest information about child victimization, including analyses of crime victimization statistics, studies of child victims and their special needs, and descriptions of programs and approaches that address these needs.

In recent years, parents and policymakers have become increasingly concerned with ensuring the safety of children when they are in the custody of childcare workers. Such concerns have sparked extensive debates about how childcare providers should be hired and screened and whether routine criminal background checks should be used to uncover potential offenders. These safety concerns have even prompted the use of surveillance devices to monitor workers who care for children.

Unfortunately, information that might clarify these issues is limited. For example, public data on juvenile abuse and crime victimization do not routinely present the identity of perpetrators in a way that allows identification of specific groups of offenders, such as teachers or daycare operators. Instead, perpetrators are grouped more generally, either as undifferentiated childcare providers or simply as acquaintances of the victim.

Parents are particularly concerned about babysitters, whose recruitment and screening are often informal. Nonfamilial paid babysitters have generated anxiety ever since they became a nearly universal social phenomenon in the post-World War II child-rearing environment. As mothers entered the workforce and fewer families lived with other relatives, more and more parents relied on babysitters to care for their children. Concerns about babysitters may have increased in recent years, especially in the wake of cases like that of Louise Woodward, the Boston-area au pair convicted of killing 8-month-old Matthew Eappen, who was in her full-time care.

Despite such publicity, the literature on the offenses of babysitters is scant. However, this lack of information is beginning to change. Babysitters are one of the new categories of offenders for whom specific information is now being collected within the Federal Bureau of Investigation's (FBI's) growing National Incident-Based Reporting System (NIBRS). The availability of these data for the first time, combined with public and policy interest, makes babysitter offenses worthy of analysis.

Analysis of NIBRS data on crimes against juveniles (ages 0 to 17) reveals the following information:

- Babysitters are responsible for a relatively small portion of the reported criminal offenses against children: 4.2 percent of all offenses for children under age 6-less than the percentage accounted for by family members or strangers.
- Among the reported offenses that babysitters commit, sex crimes outnumber physical assaults nearly two to one.

- Children most at risk of physical assaults by babysitters are younger (ages 1-3) than those at risk of sex crimes (ages 3-5).
- Males constitute the majority of sex-offending babysitters reported to the police (77 percent); females make up the majority of physical assaulters (64 percent).
- Juvenile offenders are responsible for nearly half the babysitter sex crimes known to police (48 percent) but only 15 percent of the physical assaults.
- Babysitter offenses rarely result in death, but victims of babysitter crimes known to police are more likely than other child crime victims to suffer an injury (75 percent versus 53 percent for victims under age 6).

The Data

NIBRS, which compiled the data that are the basis of this analysis, was created to eventually supplant the existing Uniform Crime Reports (UCR) program as the national statistical database of crimes reported to the police. NIBRS can collect considerably more detailed information about crime incidents than UCR, including the range of offenses committed, victim characteristics (including age), offender characteristics, and incident circumstances. While NIBRS is not yet national in scope and only encompasses jurisdictions in 17 States (see sidebar for further discussion of NIBRS), the combined reports for 1995, 1996, 1997, and 1998 yielded 1,427 babysitter victimizations for analysis. Given the general absence of data on this group of offenders, this large number of cases merits investigation-even though the cases are not nationally representative and the findings drawn from them are preliminary.

"Babysitter" is a term with some ambiguity. Children are cared for by a variety of people, including close and extended family, friends, family daycare operators, professional daycare centers, and schools; some of these providers may be paid while others are not. The term "babysitter" may be loosely applied to any of these providers, with the exception of schools and, possibly, daycare centers. Fortunately, the NIBRS system uses the more common meaning of the term, following the usage typical of many State child protective agencies (Margolin, 1990; U.S. Department of Health and Human Services, 2001). NIBRS considers babysitters to be those persons who temporarily care for children for pay, usually in the child's or babysitter's home.

This usage excludes preschool and commercial daycare center staff members but includes both licensed and unlicenced home-based daycare providers. NIBRS protocols, like those of many State child protective services, also exclude family offenders from the babysitter category. Offenders who commit crimes against family members are identified in NIBRS by their family relationship to the victim, and not as babysitters, because NIBRS only categorizes offenders in a single relationship category. As a result, babysitters identified by NIBRS reporting agencies are not members of the victim's family. Thus, the majority of babysitter offenders identified in NIBRS are paid nonfamily juveniles or adults caring for children in a home setting. However, NIBRS relies on local law enforcement agencies to collect data, and specification practices may vary somewhat from agency to agency.

An accurate number of children in the United States cared for by babysitters (as defined in NIBRS) is difficult to estimate. The National Child Care Survey (NCCS) estimated that, in 1990, 14 percent of the 18.5 million children under age 5 had a nonrelative in-home provider or family daycare as their primary childcare arrangement (Hofferth et al., 1991). However, NCCS and other childcare surveys tally only children's "primary arrangements." Large numbers of children whose primary arrangements involve care by their own mother, another relative, or a daycare center are also occasionally cared for by babysitters. Therefore, it seems likely that a majority of all young children are exposed to paid babysitters at some time.

The National Incident-Based Reporting System

The U.S. Department of Justice is replacing its long-established Uniform Crime Reports (UCR) program with a more comprehensive National Incident-Based Reporting System (NIBRS). While UCR monitors a limited number of index crimes and, with the exception of homicides, gathers few details on each crime event, NIBRS collects a wide range of information on victims, offenders, and circumstances for a greater variety of offenses. Offenses tracked in NIBRS include violent crimes (e.g., homicide, assault, rape, robbery), property crimes (e.g., theft, arson, vandalism, fraud, embezzlement), and crimes against society (e.g., drug offenses, gambling, prostitution). Moreover, NIBRS collects information on multiple victims, multiple offenders, and multiple crimes that may be part of the same episode.

Under the new system, as with the old, local law enforcement personnel compile information on crimes coming to their attention, and this information is aggregated in turn at the State and national levels. For a crime to be counted in the system, it simply needs to be reported and investigated. The incident does not need to be cleared or an arrest made, although unfounded reports are deleted from the record.

NIBRS holds great promise, but it is still far from a national system. Its implementation by the FBI began in 1988, and participation by States and local agencies is voluntary and incremental. By 1995, jurisdictions in 9 States had agencies contributing data; by 1997, the number was 12; and by the end of 1999, jurisdictions in 17 States submitted reports, providing coverage for 11 percent of the Nation's population and 9 percent of its crime. Only three States (Idaho, Iowa, and South Carolina) have participation from all local jurisdictions, and only one city with a population greater than 500,000 (Austin, TX) is reporting.

The crime experiences of large urban areas are particularly underrepresented. The system, therefore, is not yet nationally representative, nor do its data represent national trends or national statistics. Nevertheless, the system is assembling large amounts of crime information and providing a richness of detail about juvenile victimizations previously unavailable. The patterns and associations these data reveal are real and represent the experiences of a large number of youth. For 1998, the 17 participating States1 reported a total of 1,344,361 crimes against individuals, with 143,523 occurring against juveniles. Nevertheless, patterns may change as more jurisdictions join the system.

FINDINGS

Reporting

Babysitters were only a small portion of the offenders in NIBRS jurisdictions who committed violent crimes against children. They accounted for 0.5 percent of offenders who committed crimes against juveniles (youth under age 18) and 4.2 percent of those who committed crimes against young children (those under age 6) (figure 1). In contrast, family members (including nonparental offenders) accounted for 21.4 percent of offenders who committed crimes against all juveniles and 53.5 percent of those who committed crimes against young children. (Parental family offenders alone are 12 percent and 36 percent, respectively.) Complete strangers accounted for 11.0 percent of offenders against juveniles and 5.6 percent of offenders against young children. In assessing these figures, it would be useful to compare babysitters with other categories of professional childcare providers, such as teachers or youth workers, but such comparisons are not possible because these categories are not separately identified in NIBRS.

Figure 1: Percentage of Offenders Who Committed Violent Crimes Against Juveniles, by Relationship to the Victim

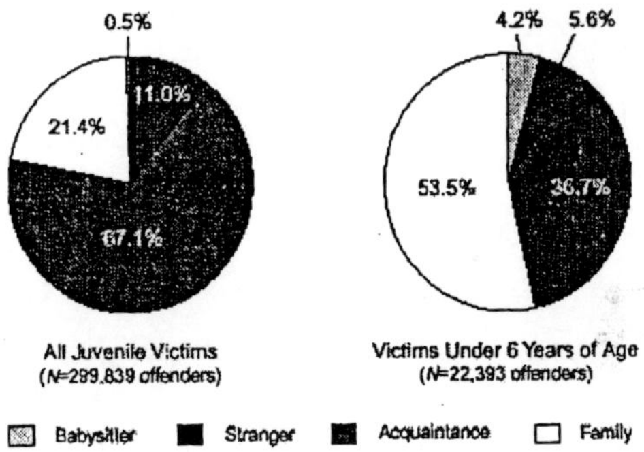

Note: The data also include nonforcible sex offenses. Data are provided only for incidents with identified offender(s). Juveniles are persons under 18 years of age.

Source: Federal Bureau of Investigation (1995, 1996, 1997, 1998), National Incident-Based Reporting System (NIBRS) computer file (17 States only), Washington, DC: U.S. Department of Justice. Tabulations undertaken by Crimes against Children Research Center.

Victim Characteristics

Children under age 6, the group most likely to be cared for by babysitters, are also those most likely to be victimized by them (figure 2). Children in this age group made up 60 percent of the victims of babysitter crimes in the NIBRS jurisdictions, although youth 12 and older were sometimes victimized. (The victims in the older age group may have included disabled youth who still require some professional childcare.)

In terms of racial distribution, juvenile victims of babysitter offenses known to police were more likely to be white (92 percent) than juvenile crime victims in general (75 percent). This racial disparity may exist because nonwhite children are less likely to be cared for by paid nonfamily babysitters due to cost factors and the greater availability of care by relatives (Casper, 1997).

Figure 2: Age of Victims of Physical Assaults and Sex Offenses Committed by Babysitters

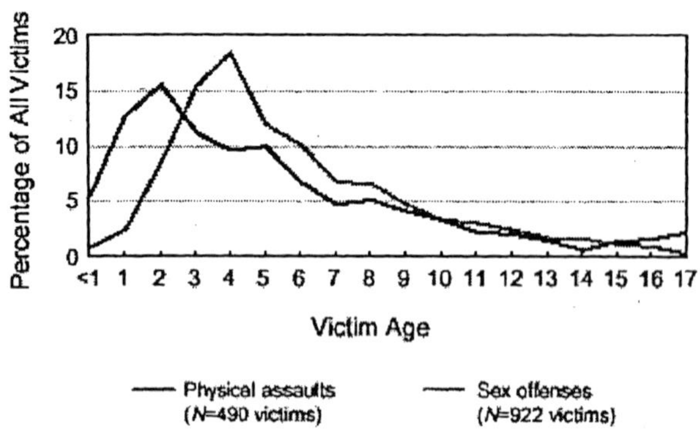

Note: Percentages calculated separately for physical assaults and sex offenses.

Source: Federal Bureau of Investigation (1995, 1996, 1997, 1998), National Incident-Based Reporting System (NIBRS) computer file (17 States only), Washington, DC: U.S. Department of Justice. Tabulations undertaken by Crimes against Children Research Center.

Among babysitter offenses that were reported to the police, sex offenses outnumbered physical assaults 65 percent to

34 percent (figure 3). Most of the sex offenses involved fondling rather than the more serious crimes of rape or sodomy (41 percent, 9 percent, and 11 percent of all babysitter offenses, respectively).

Simple assaults made up 25 percent of all reported babysitter offenses, whereas aggravated assaults accounted for 9 percent. A very small fraction of the offenses entailed a kidnapping (0.5 percent) or homicide (0.6 percent).

Figure 3: Types of Crime Committed Against Juveniles by Babysitters

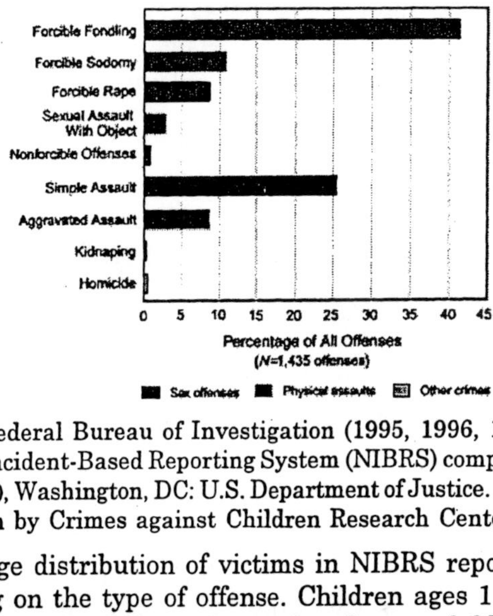

Source: Federal Bureau of Investigation (1995, 1996, 1997, 1998), National Incident-Based Reporting System (NIBRS) computer file (17 States only), Washington, DC: U.S. Department of Justice. Tabulations undertaken by Crimes against Children Research Center.

The age distribution of victims in NIBRS reports varies, depending on the type of offense. Children ages 1 to 3 faced the greatest risk of physical assault, whereas children ages 3 to 5 were most vulnerable to sex offenses (figure 4). Victim gender also varied by type of offense. More boys than girls were victims of physical assault by babysitters (54 percent versus 46 percent), whereas girls made up 65 percent of the sex offense victims.

Offender Characteristics

Overall, among babysitters, male offenders outnumbered female offenders (63 to 37 percent) in police reports. However, this percentage masks the true disproportion in the risk of male offending, in that most children are exposed to more female than male babysitters, both in terms of numbers and the amount of time spent in their care.

No reliable information is available about the overall gender ratio of babysitters, but one teen survey found that females were twice as likely as males to have had babysitting experience (Kourany, Martin, and LaBarbera, 1980).

Among adult babysitters, the ratio is considerably higher (U.S. Bureau of the Census, 2001). Therefore, the true risk of a male babysitter offending is likely much greater than the two-to-one ratio of male to female offenders found in the data.

Figure 4: Gender of Juvenile Victims of Babysitters, by Type of Offense

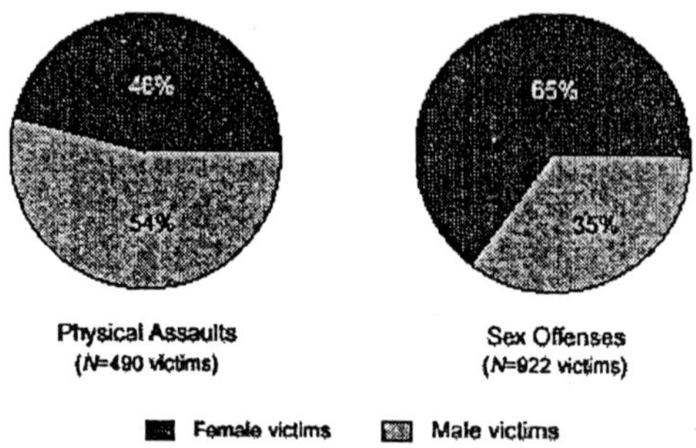

Source: Federal Bureau of Investigation (1995, 1996, 1997, 1998), National Incident-Based Reporting System (NIBRS) computer file (17 States only), Washington, DC: U.S. Department of Justice. Tabulations undertaken by Crimes against Children Research Center.

Males were disproportionately involved in sex offenses (77 percent of offenders known to police). Females committed the majority of the physical assaults (64 percent of offenders). Of babysitters who committed sex offenses, males were more likely than females to target female victims and victims ages 6 and older (figure 5). They were also more likely to be adults (58 percent), whereas female sex offenders were predominantly juveniles (67 percent), mostly ages 13 to 15.

In addition to gender of the offenders, one of the most dramatic differences between sex offenses and physical assaults reported in NIBRS jurisdictions was the offender age profile (figure 6).

Nearly half (48 percent) of the babysitter sex offenders were themselves juveniles. On the other hand, only 15 percent of the physically assaultive babysitters were under age 18.

This age pattern-teens overrepresented in the commission of sex offenses and adults in the commission of physical offenses-held true for both male and female offenders.

Figure 5: Gender and Age of Juvenile Victims of Sex Offenses Committed by Babysitters, by Offender Gender

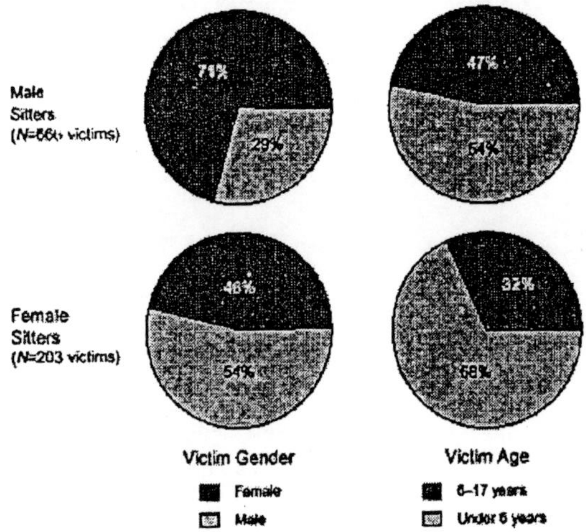

Source: Federal Bureau of Investigation (1995, 1996, 1997, 1998), National Incident-Based Reporting System (NIBRS) computer file (17 States only), Washington, DC: U.S. Department of Justice. Tabulations undertaken by Crimes against Children Research Center.

One possible explanation for this pattern may be that adult babysitters are more likely to be given responsibility for young children for longer periods (e.g., a whole day or several days a week) than teenage babysitters, and this continuous exposure creates the kind of stress and control-related conflicts that tend to trigger physical assaults on young children.

Sex offenses, by contrast, are often crimes of opportunity that occur during the more occasional exposures that children have with teen babysitters.

Injury

Death was a relatively uncommon outcome for victims of babysitter crimes in NIBRS jurisdictions (0.6 percent). However, babysitter victims were more likely to sustain injuries than juvenile victims of other offenders. Among juvenile victims of physical assault, 67 percent of those assaulted by babysitters incurred a major or minor injury, compared with 52 percent of victims of other offenders (figure 7).

Figure 6: Age of Babysitters Who Committed Physical Assaults and Sex Offenses Against Juveniles

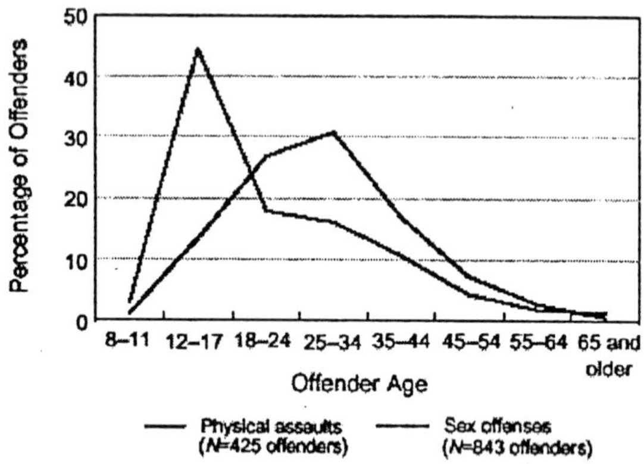

Note: Percentages calculated separately for physical assaults and sex offenses.

Source: Federal Bureau of Investigation (1995, 1996, 1997, 1998), National Incident-Based Reporting System (NIBRS) computer file (17 States only), Washington, DC: U.S. Department of Justice. Tabulations undertaken by Crimes against Children Research Center.

For assault victims under age 6, the injury discrepancy was even larger (75 percent of babysitter victims injured versus 53 percent of victims of other offenders). Sexual assault injury rates are fairly low and similar for babysitters and nonsitters alike.

Figure 7: Injuries Sustained by Juvenile Victims of Physical Assaults Committed by Babysitters and Other Offenders

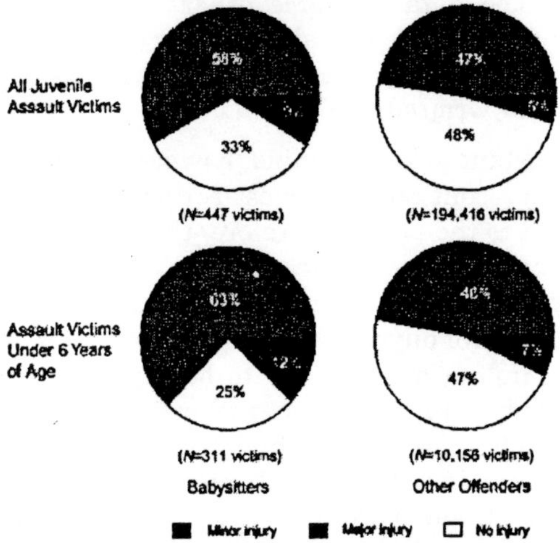

Source: Federal Bureau of Investigation (1995, 1996, 1997, 1998), National Incident-Based Reporting System (NIBRS) computer file (17 States only), Washington, DC: U.S. Department of Justice. Tabulations undertaken by Crimes against Children Research Center.

IMPLICATIONS

Police data reveal that babysitters do indeed commit serious crimes against children in their care. While NIBRS data cannot be used to estimate national crime statistics, the numbers extrapolated from NIBRS jurisdictions (which represent about 6 percent of the Nation's crimes for 1997 and 1998) suggest that roughly 7,000 to 8,000 babysitter offenses-the majority of which are sex crimes-are reported to police over the course of a year. This estimate is certainly large enough to justify that precautions be taken by parents in screening and hiring care providers.

However, the threat posed by babysitters, especially when compared with other childhood threats, should not be overemphasized. Babysitters were responsible for only 4.2 percent of the reported crimes against children under 6 years-fewer than crimes committed by family members, other acquaintances, or even strangers. Given the large number of children exposed to babysitters, this is a relatively small percentage. The data reinforce other studies that suggest primary efforts should seek to shield young children from crimes committed by family perpetrators, not childcare providers (Finkelhor and Ormrod, 2001).

It is important to keep in mind, however, that the numbers in NIBRS represent only the most serious criminal acts, the ones reported to the police; therefore, they do not fully reflect the scope of babysitter misconduct. Although sexual acts toward children are usually considered very serious and reported to police, many acts of physical assault by babysitters, even those resulting in injury, are unlikely to be reported. In addition, episodes of babysitter neglect and emotional abuse are rarely reported to police. Data from child protection agencies might document more instances of physical abuse, neglect, and emotional abuse, but parents are probably more inclined to simply terminate a babysitter's services than bother with official police or child protection reports. In addition, babysitter crimes may be disproportionately obscured because younger victims are often unable to communicate this abuse to their parents.

In short, crime reports on babysitters are only a crude guide to the perils children face in the company of babysitters. For example, the finding of NIBRS data that sex offenses by babysitters outnumber physical assaults may only reflect the kind of crime considered serious enough to be reported to police. In reality, physical assaults may be more common than sex offenses but less reported. Similarly, to the extent that physical assaults are underreported compared with sex offenses, the offenses of female babysitters may be underreported compared with those of males.

Other NIBRS findings may not be so tainted by reporting biases. Children under 6 are likely the main targets of babysitter offenses because they spend the most time with babysitters. Teenagers likely commit more of the sex offenses against children because the sexual pressures and conflicts of their adolescence may motivate them to take advantage of the children in their care. Male babysitters probably outnumber female babysitters among offenders because males outnumber females in virtually all categories of crime, including family offenses and offenses against children.

Also, despite their limitations, NIBRS data highlight the diversity of offenders and victims. It is now clear that both female and male babysitters commit sexual offenses. Sexual assaults do occur against some very young children, and some older children also are being criminally victimized by babysitters.

These data are neither comprehensive nor detailed enough to offer strong guidance about preventive efforts. However, the young age of sexual abuse victims does confirm the potential value of providing preschool children with age-appropriate awareness about inappropriate touching (Wurtele et al., 1989). The frequent appearance of adolescent sexual abusers in NIBRS babysitter data suggests that parents may need to carefully screen and train young babysitters with this in mind. The preponderance of male offenders, given the relatively small number of males in the childcare workforce, certainly contributes to the already evident dilemma of those who would increase children's exposure to nurturant males. Unfortunately, the implications of all these findings have policy complexities that require better data than NIBRS can currently provide about the particular features of offenders, victims, their families, and the process by which potential babysitters are screened and chosen.

NIBRS is still in its formative stage, and its data may prompt more questions rather than provide firm answers. However, to the extent that its data remind the public and policymakers of the diverse perils that confront children, including threats from babysitters and other care providers, NIBRS may eventually improve the entire effort of crime prevention and detection for this vulnerable population.

CHILDREN AND YOUNG PEOPLE-INFORMATION FOR PARENTS

Children and young people can be equally upset by crime and can have different reactions. Some common types of crime against children are theft or mugging, assault, racial harassment and bullying. After a crime takes place, children can feel shock, anger, a desire for revenge, fear of going out alone, or fear of returning to where an attack took place (which could include school). Your child may also have headaches, stomach pains, wet the bed, behave differently or become withdrawn.

Young children often experience feelings of guilt, and may find it difficult to tell anyone about the crime. It is important to reassure your child that they have done the right thing by talking to you. Young people may fear that parents and carers will be angry with them for having been a victim of crime, despite it not being their fault. For many young people, this can make the effects of the crime much more serious.

Children can also be affected by crimes committed against other people, for example their parents, or against family property. When this happens, they, and those around them, may not realise that their problems are related to crime. If you don't talk about the crime, they may wonder why nothing has been said and this may confuse or frighten them.

As you know your child best of all, you will know the best way to help them recover. It is important to be sensitive to their needs and feelings and let them develop at their own pace when they start to get back into old routines and activities.

Our volunteers can talk with you in confidence and provide information on practical help and reporting the crime, if this is what you want. We normally only see children under 16 with the permission of their parents or carers.

You may also like to look at our leaflet on helping your child cope with the effects of crime.

Child Witnesses

If your case is going to court, Victim Support's Witness Service can help children, you and other family members, to understand and cope with the experience. Should your child need to be a witness, a special information pack is available from the police.

3

Police Abuse and Street Children

This report was made possible through the invaluable assistance of lawyers, representatives of nongovernmental organizations working with street children in India, and the children who provided their testimony. All of them must remain anonymous out of fear of reprisals by local police.

Human Rights Watch uses the definition of "child" in Article One of the United Nations Convention on the Rights of the Child which states: "For the purposes of the present Convention, a child means every human being below the age of eighteen years unless, under the law applicable to the child, majority is attained earlier."

Section 2(h) of India's Juvenile Justice Act (1986) states that a "juvenile" is "a boy who has not attained the age of sixteen years or a girl who has not attained the age of eighteen years."

This report will use the UNICEF definition of street children as cited by Nandana Reddy in Street Children of Bangalore: A Situational Analysis (NOIDA: Government of India, 1992), p. 2.

Street children are those for whom the street (in the widest sense of the word, i.e. unoccupied dwellings, wasteland, etc.) more than their family has become their real home, a situation in which there is no protection, supervision, or direction from responsible adults, and the three operational categories:

1. *Children on the Street:* Forming the largest category, these are children who have homes; most return to their families at the end of the day.

2. *Children of the Street:* These children are a group who have chosen the street as their home and it is there that they seek shelter, livelihood, and companionship. They have occasional contacts with their families.
3. *Abandoned Children:* These children have severed all ties with their families. They are entirely on their own, not only for material survival but also psychologically.

SUMMARY

The diabolical recurrence of police torture, result[s] in a terrible scare in the minds of common citizens that their lives and liberty are under a new peril when the guardians of law gore human rights to death. The vulnerability of human rights assumes a traumatic, torturesome poignancy when the violent violation is perpetrated by the police arm of the state whose function is to protect the citizens and not to commit gruesome offences against them.

India has the largest population of street children in the world. At least eighteen million children live or work on the streets of urban India, laboring as porters at bus or railway terminals; as mechanics in informal auto-repair shops; as vendors of food, tea, or handmade articles; as street tailors; or as ragpickers, picking through garbage and selling usable materials to local buyers.

Indian street children are routinely detained illegally, beaten and tortured and sometimes killed by police. Several factors contribute to this phenomenon: police perceptions of street children, widespread corruption and a culture of police violence, the inadequacy and non-implementation of legal safeguards, and the level of impunity that law enforcement officials enjoy. The police generally view street children as vagrants and criminals. While it is true that street children are sometimes involved in petty theft, drug-trafficking, prostitution and other criminal activities, the police tend to assume that whenever a crime is committed on the street, street children are either involved themselves or know the culprit. Their proximity to a crime is considered reason enough to detain them. This abuse violates both Indian domestic law and international human rights standards. Street children are also easy targets. They are young, small, poor, ignorant of their rights and often have no family members who will come to their defense. It does not require much time or effort to detain and beat a child to extract a confession, and the children are unlikely to register formal complaints.

Police have financial incentives to resort to violence against children. Many children report that they were beaten on the street because the police wanted their money. The prospect of being sent to a remand home, the police station or jail, coupled with the threat of brutal treatment, creates a level of fear and intimidation that forces children or in some cases, their families, to pay the police or suffer the consequences.

Indian law contributes to the problem. Under the Indian Penal Code, anyone over the age of twelve is considered an adult, and ambiguities in the code concerning the ability of the child to be cognizant of a crime have made it possible for children as young as seven to be treated as adults under the law. There are no provisions in the code that prohibit the detention of juveniles in police stations or jails. The Juvenile Justice Act, which applies to all the states and Union Territories in India except Jammu and Kashmir, does prohibit the detention of "neglected" or "delinquent" juveniles in police lock-ups or jails, but these provisions are routinely ignored by police. Moreover, at the remand stage, the law makes no distinction between neglected and delinquent children, so that a six-year-old orphan on the street and a fifteen-year-old child who has committed murder are likely to be treated the same way under the law, an issue analyzed further below.

Finally, there is the de facto immunity of police from prosecution. The government of India has known about the extent of custodial abuse, including abuse of children, at least since 1979 when the National Police Commission issued a devastating indictment of police behavior. More than a decade and a half later, none of its recommendations have been adopted, and police can detain, torture and extort money from children without much fear of punishment. This report documents police abuse of Indian street children and deaths of children in police custody. It is based on investigations conducted in India during February and March 1995 and December and January 1995-96. Human Rights Watch spoke with more than one hundred street children, as well as representatives of nongovernmental organizations, social workers, human rights activists, human rights lawyers, and other individuals who work with street children in Bangalore, Bombay, Delhi, and Madras. Of the one hundred children interviewed, sixty complained of police abuse in the form of detentions, beatings, extortion, or verbal abuse. All the children interviewed reported a fear of the police. Of the sixty street children who reported police abuse, Human Rights Watch recorded twenty-two detailed testimonies.

These cases were selected because the children had better recollection of the incidents and could provide a comprehensive description of their treatment by police. The testimony of two social workers who had been abused by police for attempting to stop the police from beating children was also recorded; one of these cases involved detention and severe beating. In total, forty-one cases are presented in this report.

In addition to this first-hand information, written statements taken by lawyers from children who had been victims of police abuse, documents written by police officials concerning police abuse, case files prepared by India's National Human Rights Commission, press reports, reports by local human rights organization, reports by the United Nations, studies on street children funded by the government of India and the United Nations Children's Fund (UNICEF), and reports by local nongovernmental organizations (NGOs) provided corroborating evidence in the preparation of this report.

This report also details the deaths in custody of fifteen children from 1990 to 1994 and the death of one child in a remand home in 1996.

Human Rights Watch was able to interview only boys for this report. Access to girls was limited because most groups working with street children do not work with girls, and because cultural norms make it improper for girls to speak to strangers, especially males.

Recommendations

To the Government of India: Implement the recommendations made by the National Police Commission in 1980, specifically those that call for a mandatory judicial inquiry in cases of alleged rape, death, or grievous injury of people in police custody and the establishment of investigative bodies whose members would include civilians as well as police and judicial authorities.

Implement the Juvenile Justice Act in all states and Union Territories and amend the Juvenile Justice Act to provide for a complaints and prosecution mechanisms for cases of custodial abuse of children. These mechanisms should be constituted along the lines described in the National Police Commission's recommendations for the creation of civilian, judicial, and police complaints bodies for cases of police abuse.

Implement the recommended amendments to the Code of Criminal Procedure made by the Parliamentary Committee on Home on March 4, 1996. These recommendations include a mandatory judicial inquiry in cases of custodial death or rape and compensation to families of people who have died in custody.

Amend Sections 53 and 54 of the Code of Criminal Procedure so that medical examination (including age verification) is mandatory at the time of detention, in order to provide a medical record of the condition of the detainee. Subsequent examinations should be carried out at regularly scheduled intervals. This procedure would circumvent attempts by police officers to intimidate detainees not to complain of torture, and would also protect police from frivolous claims of torture because a complete medical record would exist for the duration of the detention. The order for a medical examination would be independent of the detainee and the police. The initial and final examinations should be done by different people to further ensure their validity.

Amend Section 197, specifically Sections 3, 3A, and 3B of the Code of Criminal Procedure to delete the provision that requires government approval for prosecution of law enforcement officials when complaints of custodial abuse or illegal detention are alleged.

Amend Section 43 of the Police Act, so that police cannot claim immunity for actions while executing a warrant in cases of illegal detention or custodial abuse.

Amend the Trade Union Act to allow children to form and participate in trade unions. The Convention on the Rights of the Child, which India has ratified, guarantees children the right of freedom of association. Review all laws relating to child labor and the Juvenile Justice Act to ensure that the implementation of these laws does not result in criminalizing children who are forced to work.

Establish a civilian review board comprised of NGO representatives, judges, and lawyers to monitor police stations. Members of the review boards should be adequately trained and provided access to lock-ups and detention registers.

Establish a high-level commission to investigate allegations of custodial abuse and killings of children.

Complaints against law enforcement personnel should be promptly and thoroughly investigated by an independent agency with subpoena power and an adequately trained investigatory staff. This agency should be directly accessible to street children.

Investigate all complaints of illegal detention, physical abuse, and killings of children by law enforcement officers, and prosecute to the full extent of the law those found responsible.

Investigate all complaints of extortion and bribes from children, their families, or NGO representatives working with street children and prosecute to the full extent of the law those found responsible.

Require the registration of each child taken to a police station, including the time, date, and reason for detention. The registers should be subject to frequent mandatory review by a judicial magistrate.

Enforce payment of compensation for people who have been victims of custodial abuse, as per the Supreme Court decision in Nilabati Behara v.State of Orissa (1993) which ordered compensation in case of custodial death under Article 32 of the Constitution of India.

Conduct a census of street children through city-wide surveys with the assistance of nongovernmental organizations (NGOs). Without an accurate estimate of the population of street children, it is difficult to plan and implement programs for their benefit.

Promptly submit the report on India's compliance with the United Nations Convention on the Rights of the Child to the Committee on the Rights of the Child.

Ratify the United Nations 1984 Convention Against Torture and Other Forms of Cruel, Inhuman, or Degrading Treatment or Punishment.

Invite the United Nations Special Rapporteur on Torture and Other Forms of Cruel, Inhuman or Degrading Treatment or Punishment and the Working Group on Arbitrary Detention to India to investigate allegations of illegal detention, abuse and deaths of children in police custody.

To the United Nations: The United Nations Special Rapporteur on Torture and Other Forms of Cruel, Inhuman or Degrading Treatment or Punishment and the Working Group on Arbitrary Detention should visit India and investigate police abuse of street children.

The United Nations Committee on the Rights of the Child should investigate the abuse and killings of street children by police in India.

The United Nations Committee on the Rights of the Child should devote one of its theme days to police violence against street children.

To Nongovernmental Organizations Working With Street Children: Maintain detailed records of incidents of violence between police and children in order to monitor and document abuses by police. Submit these records to the National Human Rights Commission on a regular basis.

OVERVIEW

Police abuse of street children is symptomatic of three problems: the increasing population of street children, the perception of street children as criminals, and the lawlessness of police. In the four cities Human Rights Watch visited, UNICEF estimated that the population of street children totaled 295,000. All observers we spoke to agreed that this population was increasing. The rising number of street children is linked to India's burgeoning population growth: eighteen million children are added to the population every year, a rate that will result in India's mid-1993 population of approximately 902 million people doubling to 1.8 billion by about 2043. Rapid urbanization has also contributed to the problem. The Indian government's five-year plan for 1992-1997 reported:

> *There has been a marked acceleration in urbanisation over the past two decades. If the present trends continue, urbanpopulation may account for about one-third of the total population by the turn of the century.*

Urban population statistics for India reflect this observation. According to the United Nations Development Programme (UNDP), in 1960, 18 percent of India's population lived in cities. In 1992, this number had risen to 26 percent of the population. The UNDP estimates that by 2000, 29 percent of India's population will be urban-more than 261 million people. A major factor that contributes to rapid urbanization is the increased migration from rural areas to India's urban areas. Many of these migrants are landless agricultural laborers whose traditional occupations no longer exist or do not provide sufficient income, and who have come to the cities in search of employment.

In Bangalore, many are migrant construction workers who were promised work by agents and subcontractors for construction companies, but who were abandoned by the construction companies and their agents once the work was completed. In general, rural-to-urban migration can be explained by India's policy of development, which has favored urban, industrial development over rural development. While this policy did create greater industrialization and less reliance on agriculture as the engine of economic development, it did not alleviate rural poverty. According to the UNDP, 49 percent of India's rural population live at or below the poverty line. Some of these unemployed or underemployed people are forced to go to cities in search of economic opportunities. Cities provide a slightly better opportunity for these people. However, since the UNDP estimates that 38 percent of India's urban population is at or below the poverty line, this accounts for more than eighty-nine million people. A 1992 UNICEF study of street children in Bombay observed that the large-scale migration of families from rural to urban areas... has resulted in severe overcrowding, degrading work conditions, homelessness, deprivation of basic services and appalling living conditions in the city. Yet, to return to the village means starvation: to remain in the city means possible survival at least physically.

Within this population are children, who may become street children when they arrive in the cities. This process was described in a 1992 UNICEF study of street children in Calcutta:

> *To a great extent the issue of street children is closely associated with the process of fast urbanization that has been taking place in the major cities of India since the sixties... They [the children] come to the city with high expectations and full of hopes that they would easily get jobs there and be able to live comfortably with their families. But except for the fortunate ones the dream is shattered in the case of many. Finding it very hard to make both ends meet they are driven to a life of precarious survival. No place to live, no job to support their family with, they are forced to take to streets as their homes and live on the meagre earnings that they somehow manage by doing various odd jobs. The railway stations and their surroundings, under fly-overs [highway overpasses] and overbridges, and in unoccupied spaces they live in large clusters constructing tiny little shanties with bamboo poles and plastic sheets or torn cloths.*

Some of these children have been displaced as a result of development projects, like the Subarnarekha Irrigation Project which began in 1982 with a World Bank loan of $127 million. The goal of the project was to create irrigation for agriculture, industry, and cities, and hydroelectric power for the states of West Bengal, Orissa, and Bihar through the construction of two dams, two barrages, and seven canals. The World Bank estimated that 60,000 people would be displaced by the project, while NGOs estimated that the number of people displaced would be closer to 120,000. An example of this project's effect on children in the district of Palamu in Bihar was described by Jose Verghese, an advocate for the Supreme Court of India in 1991:

> *The project has involved displacement of large numbers of the population away from their means of livelihood. This development project, built with the aim of aiding the development of the area has had the opposite effect, it has impoverished large sectors of the local population and in particular children... Some of these children who have been displaced and whose families were impoverished have found their way on to the streets of New Delhi and other cities, others... have become... bonded labour[ers].*

Co-mingled with the migrant population and contributing to the phenomenon of street children is the local population of urban poor who were born in the cities, the temporary migrant families, children who travel to cities daily for work, and abandoned or orphaned children. All are subjected to the same economic and social problems that the poor throughout India face, including coping with significant increases in the cost of living. According to the World Bank, consumer prices increased 9 percent in 1990, 11.8 percent in 1992, 6.4 percent in 1993, and 10.5 percent in 1994, resulting in a 37.7 percent increase in consumer prices from 1990-1994. There has not been a corresponding increase in per capita income; in fact, per capita income has declined, from $340 in 1991 to $300 in 1996, according to UNDP figures.

As an increasing number of children face severe economic hardship, more and more children become child laborers in whatever occupations are available, including a practice that the Indian government described as, "decadent social practices like scavenging..." in the form of ragpicking, and increasingly, criminal activity.

According to NGOs, lawyers, and human rights activists working with street children, juvenile crime has been increasing, largely due to an increasing population of children and worsening economic conditions. The Swedish childrens' aid agency, Rädda Barnen, a member of a coalition of agencies affiliated with Save the Children, wrote in October 1995 that:

> *Limited data reveals that, in **1991, 29,591** juveniles were apprehended for various crimes. Most of them were charged with theft, burglary and riot. Of those, 20% were children aged between 7 and 12 and 64% were between 12 to 16. Over 60% were from families earning less than Rs. 500 [$14.29] a month. Girls formed 27% of juvenile offenders (an uncommonly high percentage). Very little information is available on what happens to these children. Legal representation is rare and there are few facilities existing for the detention of children separately from adults. Little is known about the effectiveness of any rehabilitation centres that may exist. Again, in India, juvenile crime rates are exploding.*

Very little information is available because very little information formally recorded and what information is available is not reliable. For example, the National Crime Records Bureau (NCRB) reported that in 1992 there were 1,102 juvenile arrests in India's five largest cities (Bangalore, Bombay, Calcutta, Delhi, Madras). The same year, the United Nations estimated that the population of children in these five cities was 8,919,474, which would mean there was one arrest for every 10,746 children. The figures show that juvenile crime was extremely low in these cities, but the figures are questionable. As author Srikanta Ghosh wrote in 1993:

> *In this country where normal crime statistics contain a large element of concealment and non-registration, it is not possible to present a correct picture of the situation.*

This fact is best illustrated by statistics on juvenile delinquency in Calcutta. The National Crime Records Bureau reported thirteen arrests of juveniles in 1992. In a city that has over ten million inhabitants and over 1.2 million children, including an estimated 100,000 street children, thirteen arrests is a remarkably low number. It is about one arrest for every 94,000 children and even if all of the arrested were street children, it would be one out of every 7,692 street children. What this indicates is that crime records do not accurately reflect the state of crime in India, and consequently, do not give proper indication of how many people are detained by the police or why people are detained by the police. It also contributes to an environment of impunity.

While the extent of juvenile crime is unknown, the police perception of street children as criminals is common and is a factor that contributes to police abuses against street children. A 1992 study on street children in Delhi reported:

> *Five police officials, one at Connaught Place and four at New Delhi railway station, were interviewed to find out their perception of these children and their experiences in dealing with them. The police invariably were quite critical about these children-excepting one officer who was quite sympathetic. According to the three police at the railway station and one at Connaught Place, these children are anti-social elements. They perceive them as thieves, rogues and drug addicts who have to be remanded in institutions and disciplined. They feel there might be only 2 to 3% who are "honest" and are at the station and street to earn a living.*

In the case of self-employed children working at railway stations, this perception is reinforced by provisions in the Child Labour (Prohibition and Regulation) Act, 1986 and the Juvenile Justice Act, 1986, which make it a criminal offense for children to be working. Once a child or anyone else is viewed as a criminal by the police, regardless of the validity of the perception, they are treated as such. This attitude was also reported by NGOs working with street children. An NGO representative in Bangalore told Human Rights Watch:

> *They [police] use street children as a scapegoat for all sorts of things. They are corrupt and cannot arrest the real criminals. Street children are always there, and they are viewed by the police and public as criminals or criminals-in-waiting.*

The view of children as criminals, a culture of policing that includes brutal treatment and other abuses, and an increasing population of street children have led to consistent abuses against children by the police, leading most observers to believe that the police pose the greatest threat to the welfare of street children. An NGO representative in Madras commented:

> *The most common and pervasive form of abuse street children experience is by the police. They force them to clean the stations, they beat them, they take money from them, and they torture them into confessing to crimes or to name who committed them.*

Another NGO representative with more than twenty-five years of experience with street children in Bombay told Human Rights Watch that the police were "the number one problem" street children face.

The combination of an increasing population of urban children driven to the streets in order to survive with a brutal police force that views street children as criminals has led to a situation in which detention, torture, and extortion have become the norm, practiced in an environment of almost complete impunity.

ILLEGAL DETENTION

A new procedure is being increasingly adopted by the police where a suspect is being picked up and detained for many days. No permission is sought from the court and no information is given to the relatives regarding the whereabouts of the detainee. Even if the detainee dies, the police do not own responsibility as there is no evidence to show that he died in police custody.

Although prohibited under Indian and international law, the illegal detention of street children is common in every part of India. Arbitrary detention is illegal under Articles 21 and 22 of India's constitution. Sections 50, 56, and 57 of the Code of Criminal Procedure mandate that no person can be detained in custody without knowing the grounds for arrest, and that a detainee must be presented before a magistrate within twenty-four hours of arrest. Section 160 of the code prohibits the detention of males under the age of fifteen or females of any age for the purposes of investigation or questioning by the police.

Article 9 of the International Covenant on Civil and Political Rights, and Article 37 of the U.N. Convention on the Rights of the Child prohibit arbitrary detention. India has ratified both. The United Nations Minimum Rules for the Administration of Juvenile Justice, called the "Beijing Rules" because they were drafted in Beijing, state that all juveniles arrested have the right to counsel, notification of charges and the right to have a parent or guardian present at the time of arrest. Both the "Beijing Rules" and the U.N. Rules for Juveniles Deprived of their Liberty state that the human rights of juveniles should be protected and respected while in custody. Moreover, India's Juvenile Justice Act prohibits the detention of juveniles in either police stations or jails.

Many observers have documented the tendency of police to arrest and detain children without good reason. A 1992 study sponsored by the Indian Ministry of Labour and UNICEF on the plight of street children in Bombay noted:

> *The most common complaint of street children without families was that they are rounded up and locked up by the police for two or three days merely on suspicion. This, they explained, was done to fill the "quota" which police are expected to do. Younger children are generally not caught; it is the older children the police have their eye on.*

An NGO representative and human rights activist in New Delhi had a similar comment:

> *For their reports and to make money, the police lock up a few children and majors [adults] everyday, only to release them later after having taken their money and/ or beaten them up. A few are also presented to the magistrate to show proof that the police are performing their "duties."*

The case of Anand, a thirteen-year-old ragpicker whom we interviewed on March 14, 1995, was typical. He was a pavement dweller who told us he lived with his mother, two brothers, and a sister "near a tree" in Triplicane, Madras. Because of their poverty, Anand had to work and spent much of his time on the street. He usually slept with other street children on the rail platform of Triplicane, a stop for the Madras local train. He earned about twenty rupees a day [$0.57]. He said he was ragpicking in January 1995 around 2:00 p.m. when two police officers came up to him. They told him they wanted him to pick up some garbage, so he went with them to the Zambazaar Police Station. Anand told Human Rights Watch:

> *When we were inside the station, the police started to beat me with their lathis (thick bamboo canes) and fists, calling me a thief and asking me to tell them where some stolen articles were. I said I had no idea what they were talking about. The beating continued for some twenty or thirty minutes. Then I was put in the cell in the station reserved for criminals and left there for about two hours. At around 4:00 p.m., the police let me go, one of the constables having first grabbed me by the shirt, slapped me, and told me to get out. No charges were filed, and no case was registered. It was the second time I've been detained without justification or explanation by the police.*

In some ways, Anand was lucky, because the detention was relatively brief, and he sustained no lasting injuries. Palini was not so fortunate. A thirteen-year-old child from Bangalore, Palini lives and works on the street selling tickets to popular films that he buys up and then sells at inflated prices, a practice known as selling "black" tickets. Sellers of black tickets give the police a cut, according to Palini, but at the end of the month, they do not have any money and so they cannot pay. He said that on September 30, 1995, when he was working near the Movieland Theater, the police came and took him to the Upparpet Police Station in Bangalore. There he was made to take off all his clothes except his underwear. An inspector and two uniformed police officers held his legs while the inspector hit Palini's legs and feet with a lathi. Palini told us:

> *He kept on asking me if I was selling tickets. There were about eleven other police in uniform and in plainclothes watching while they did this. They were yelling [in the local language, Kannada], "So you think you are a rowdy [a term for a hoodlum], your mother is a prostitute, you are the child of a prostitute!" They beat me*

> *for about half an hour. After this, they put me in the lock-up. There were around ten boys and three adults in there with me. They kept me in the cell until Monday. I think they kept me an extra day because my legs were so swollen. Before they presented me to the magistrate, they beat me again, the same way as before. Then they made me walk around and stretch my legs so that they would not look swollen. Then they presented me to the magistrate who fined me 300 rupees [$8.57]. I also had to pay two police officers forty rupees each because they allowed me to go to a shop owner to borrow money to pay the fine.*

Palini said new policemen beat ticket sellers and take all of their money. Police who have been around longer take their money and only beat the children if they do not pay up. The going rate is five rupees for every twenty-five rupee ticket. If the tickets cost more or if the film is popular, the police take more. Palini said he pays anywhere from fifty to 400 rupees a day in bribes to the police. Even though these acts are illegal, in reality, most children do not know that their rights have been violated and are intimidated by police, so they do not complain. NGO representatives and lawyers whom Human Rights Watch spoke to in Bangalore, Bombay, Delhi, and Madras said that even if children wanted to complain, magistrates, specifically in the remand and bail phases of dealing with an accused, do not spend enough time on any one case to provide the accused with a forum for complaint. The magistrate also relies on the First Information Report (FIR) to decide the status of the accused. The FIR is the first description of the alleged crime. Because is written at the discretion of police and has no input from the accused, the police can easily use it to frame false charges. This is illustrated in a 1993 study of Bombay's criminal justice courts:

> *The usual processing of the remand or first appearance of the accused was that an interpreter rapidly yelled the names of the accused and the police constable on duty seldom allowed the accused to remain before the magistrate for more than a few seconds. Often, they were pulled back even before they heard the next date*

> *of appearance. Consequently, they were forced to depend upon the policemen for this vital information. The magistrates, on their part, either briefly looked at the accused or continued with the court files. Most of the accused reported that "they did not get attention from the magistrate. Without making any enquiry or looking at them, remands were extended; the understanding of the accused was that the clerk calls names and accordingly they have to respond. The submission of the police officer was relied upon and as a matter of routine remands were granted mechanically." However, if the accused were produced in the court accompanied by an advocate, remand would not be extended in such a manner.*

This process holds true for both adults and children and was described to Human Rights Watch in interviews with social workers, human rights activists, and lawyers throughout India.

Magistrates also fail to inform children of their rights or to check on the legality of police action. Moreover, magistrates routinely neglect to inform the accused of the charges against them. The Bombay study noted:

> *After the accused are produced before the magistrate, the magistrate by statute, must inform the accused that they have a right to remain silent, that their testimony can be held against them, and they can have a reasonable amount of time to engage an advocate. Finally, if an accused person cannot afford private counsel, (s)he has a right to court appointed counsel... In the magisterial courts of Bombay, it was observed that in all cases, the magistrates did not apprise the accused of his/her rights. In a majority of cases (95 percent) the accused were not even informed of the charges under which the police had produced them before the court. What is more, in nearly three-fourths (72 percent) of the cases no time was given to hear accused person's point of view.*

The lack of adequate judicial oversight and the magistrate's reliance on the FIR and police accounts have contributed to an environment that allows police to illegally detain, beat, and extort money from street children without fear of scrutiny by the judiciary. Mohan's experience is illustrative in this respect; it was provided, in writing, to Human Rights Watch on December 12, 1995, by a lawyer in Bombay who represented him.

Mohan, who is mentally retarded, was working as a mason in Bombay at the age of fifteen when he was arrested on January 2, 1991 at approximately 10:00 p.m. According to his statement he was walking home after buying cigarettes when a constable named Kadam offered him a ride in an autorickshaw. When Mohan refused, Kadam hit him with his belt and took him to the Trombay Police Station. At the station Mohan was again beaten by Kadam and several other policemen and then accused of allegedly stabbing another person. The next morning, after being fingerprinted, Mohan was taken to the metropolitan magistrate at Kurla. Although he told the magistrate about his treatment by the police, the magistrate refused to release him and remanded him to judicial custody at the Bombay Central Prison. According to Mohan, the warden beat him every night simply because he was mentally retarded.

Mohan's family was never notified of his incarceration. After one and a half months of searching, they found him at the Bombay Central Prison. After obtaining bail of 550 rupees ($15.71), Mohan was released. Mohan was arrested again several months later, during the Ganapati festival, because he was part of a crowd in which some boys were fighting. He was detained at the Deonar Police Station for ten days as a result of this incident. He later left to work in Delhi but was arrested on November 3, 1993, because he did not appear in court in relation to the Ganapati arrest. He was eventually acquitted of all charges but only after being imprisoned from November 3, 1993, to March 12, 1994.

The Juvenile Justice Act

The Juvenile Justice Act, 1986, was enacted in an attempt to address the plight of children within the justice system. It was based on the United Nations Standard Minimum Rules for the Administration of Juvenile Justice (the Beijing Rules). Generally, this law, like constitutional rights and other legislation intended to protect children's rights, is ignored.

The Juvenile Justice Act prohibits the detention of juveniles in police station or jails for periods longer than twenty-four hours. It also requires the registration of "neglected" and "delinquent juveniles" and requires that juveniles be sent back to their parents or guardians or to a remand home immediately following either their identification as a "neglected juvenile" or their arrest as a "delinquent juvenile." But, the act also makes the police responsible for identifying neglected juveniles and arresting delinquent juveniles. The police actively abuse this authority, resulting in a pattern of arbitrary arrest, detention, extortion, and beatings of street children, and a practice known as the "round-up," in which children are detained in large groups and either sent to remand homes or disciplined in the police station. There are several reasons for the round-up.

The act views children working in railway stations as "delinquent juveniles;" such children are frequently victims of the round-up. In other cases, juvenile boards, the authority designated by the act to handle cases of neglected children and send them to the remand homes, pressure the police to fill vacant remand homes. NGO representatives and lawyers that Human Rights Watch spoke to said that because the shelters were ostensibly designed to care for both neglected and delinquent juveniles, officials fear that an empty home might invite criticism that the juvenile boards, the courts, and the police were not doing their duty. The round-up is also used as an expedient method of detaining possible suspects. Because police generally view street children as criminals, a round-up is an easy way to catch and interrogate them. The 1992 UNICEF study of street children in Bombay described the practice:

> *When some property (e.g. a bag) belonging to the public is lost/stolen at the station, these children are rounded up and some even framed. To prove that they are not guilty, the children have to do their best to find the culprit and save their skin.*

Social workers, NGOs, human rights activists, and lawyers throughout India have documented such arbitrary arrests of street children. The following series of incidents that occurred at the Bangalore Railway Station during 1995-96 is illustrative of the pattern:

On June 29, 1995, forty boys aged between eight and fifteen were taken to the police lock-up by the RPF because government officials had complained about the security risks passengers at the train station faced from street children asking to carry their luggage. They also complained about the station being dirty. Consequently, the boys were beaten with lathis, verbally abused, and then warned not to be seen around the railway station's premises ever again. The police also demanded a payment of twenty-five rupees ($0.71) each as a bribe.

On October 8, 1995, thirty-two boys aged eight to fifteen were apprehended by the RPF for being a nuisance around the station and begging passengers to carry their luggage. The RPF forced them to clean the ten railway platforms, the toilets, and the playground. Then the boys were stripped of all their clothes except underwear and put in the lock-up for three days. After three days, they were sent to remand homes because the júvenile board notified police that the homes were vacant and needed to be occupied.

On February 1, 1996, two foreign tourists were robbed of a camera and $ 2,000 in the bus stand and railway station area. Thirty to forty boys, aged twelve to seventeen, were apprehended, beaten, and kept in the lock-up for four days. They were released after being photographed holding a slate on which their names, crime numbers, and the alleged offenses were recorded. The NGO working with street children filed a complaint with the police because the children were unlawfully arrested and offenses were recorded against them without any proof. The way the act has been implemented led a Bangalore-based NGO to make this comment:

> *The Juvenile Justice Act, 1986, introduces itself as one meant "to provide for the care, protection, treatment, development and rehabilitation of neglected or delinquent juveniles and for the adjudication of certain matters relating to, and disposition of, delinquent juveniles." This well-meaning statement, in reality, reads, "Letting a child know in no uncertain terms that he is a criminal, therefore cannot live with his parents but with other little criminals, must work while other children play, is 'asking for it' if sexually-molested or*

> *raped, is liable to be rounded up fiercely by the police on the slightest murmur of a crime taking place in any locality where he may be, is watched over by people who hate their jobs and couldn't be bothered about probing the child's mind to ensure that he never has to come back there again."*

Observation, Remand, Special, and Juvenile Homes

From police custody, the children may be sent before a juvenile board, or a juvenile court, headed by a magistrate with jurisdiction over juveniles who have been arrested on a criminal charge. Both the court and the juvenile board have the authority to send children to institutions known variously as observation, remand, special, or juvenile homes. Thus, regardless of their status as juvenile offenders, abandoned or orphaned children, or children awaiting trial, all children are remanded to the same institutions. This situation was described by the additional commissioner of the Delhi police (ACP), Amod Kanth, who also runs a shelter for street children in Delhi:

> *Rather than providing custodial care like parents provide, juvenile homes have degenerated into jail-like custodial centres. The JJ Board [Juvenile Justice Board], despite its authority, has remained a mute spectator to the pitiable conditions of the homes. The Juvenile Justice Act strongly advocates that children should not be kept in lock-ups as juvenile justice is distinguished from criminal justice. Most children arrested are non-offenders but the two categories-neglected children and juvenile delinquents are wrongly clubbed together.*

The arbitrary nature of detention in observation homes has been documented in studies on street children. The joint reports on street children by the government of India's Ministry of Labour and UNICEF list some of the reasons children had been sent to remand homes:

In Bangalore, the bulk (81.5 percent) of children were sent to remand homes on charges of theft, the second largest group were sent on "doubt" (11.3 percent). This means that 11.3 percent of children were sent to remand homes without having been informed of the reasons. The Bombay study reported that the majority of children (74.6 percent) were sent to remand homes on charges of vagrancy or suspicion. In other words, they were arrested because the police considered them vagrants or suspected they might commit crimes or may have committed a crime. But these children were never formally charged with any offense. The Madras study found that 87.2 percent of children were sent to remand homes on "petty cases" or other charges not including drug peddling, loitering, theft, or robbery. The study commented:

> *This analysis would not be complete without a reference to delinquency. The cross tabulation reveals that 109 boys and only one girl of the total sample of 2,000 had been remanded to a juvenile house of correction, a very small percentage indeed. But out of this small number, the cross tabulation reveals that seven of these children are between the ages of six and ten years. A shocking revelation about our penal system that such small children should be remanded at all!*

The homes function as virtual prisons. Nationally, the capacity of the homes is estimated at 350,000. According to lawyers and NGO representatives working with children, the homes are poorly maintained, inadequately staffed, and are not rehabilitative. In addition to the appalling conditions, NGO representatives, lawyers, and children themselves consistently alleged physical abuse and sexual abuse. A lawyer working with children in the remand homes told Human Rights Watch:

> *The situation in remand homes is just as bad as what happens in the police station. The masters and older boys beat and molest the younger boys, there is rampant bribe taking. The conditions are bad.*

The case of Habib, a twelve-year-old unlicensed porter at the Bangalore Central Railway Station exemplifies the treatment children are subject to in the remand homes. He told Human Rights Watch about an incident that occurred in August 1995. He was walking to a shelter for street children to watch a movie on the shelter's VCR when a group of "crime police" affiliated with the Railway Protection Force (RPF) of the Bangalore Central Railway Station picked him up in a jeep. He was detained as part of a round-up. Habib told us:

They took me to the RPF lock-up where there were around forty other children like me. The police checked all of us for money and took it all. Then they started to beat us with lathis. Two police hit me on my feet, knees, and hands. They called me foul words and insulted me. I was beaten for ten minutes, then they beat others. They were just beating us. After they beat us, they sent all the boys under sixteen to the observation home. The older boys were taken to clean the station.

At the observation home, I was stripped and a guard with a crippled hand was there. He told us to call him "Daddy." He made us face a pool of water, then he told us to look at all the pictures of Gandhi, Nehru, etc. on the wall. While we were doing that, he would walk behind us and kick us into the pool of cold water to make us clean. Later he would just make us stand while he kicked us and we could not move. When "Daddy" was tired of beating us he gave the younger boys to the older boys-they get the boys of their choice. The older boys are called monitors and they beat and molest the younger boys. I was in the remand home for about three months and then let go. The treatment in the observation home Habib described is similar to the treatment Ram reported he experienced in an observation home in Bombay. The account that follows is drawn from his statement, provided by a lawyer representing him whom Human Rights Watch spoke on December 12, 1995, is summarized below:

Ram is from Uttar Pradesh and left home when he was around seven years old. In 1991, he was working as a ragpicker near Kalyan Bus Depot, collecting scrap iron and steel and selling it. He and his associates, Bansilal and Rajesh, both aged twelve years, were caught one morning at around 10:00 a.m. and taken to Kalyan Bus Depot by the police constables. The constables beat them and asked them where they had sold the scrap. After the boys told them, they were taken to the police station where they remained for three hours. They were made to stand with their bodies bent forward while they were repeatedly asked their age. When it was confirmed that they were "juveniles," they were taken to the remand home in Bhiwandi.

At the remand home, Ram was subjected to constant beating for one month. This was done by the older inmates at the instigation of the house master. The house master, in order to elicit total obedience from the new boys, hit them on the slightest provocation. He hit boys with a belt, hockey stick, cricket bat, or any other instrument; if the boy was injured, the master would claim that he had fallen down. After a month, Ram was elevated to the status of an "older boy" and told to hit the new entrants. Refusal to beat the boys led to torture: the house master would place a weight on the recalcitrant boy's head, make another boy sit on each thigh, and beat the boy with a cane. Seeing other boys go through it, Ram quietly complied with the house master's orders. Boys who had visitors were targets and their gifts were taken away. One night at 2:00 a.m., Ram along with a dozen other boys was called by the house master who hit them, opened the door and told them they could escape. But he warned them that if they were caught, then he would break their bones. None of the boys left. Ram's case was brought before the juvenile magistrate. After nine months, he was charged with theft, admitted his guilt, and was released with help from an NGO working with street children.

Children in remand homes have died as a result of severe beatings and other forms of torture. On March 6, 1996, fourteen officials, including six caretakers, two welfare officers, three cooks, and a chowkidar (security guard), of the Kasturba Niketan remand home in the Lajpat Nagar area of New Delhi were suspended in connection with the death of an eleven-year old boy, Rohit, who was allegedly beaten to death by an eighteen-year old boy, Dabloo. Rohit had been sent to the remand home after having been arrested for loitering. Apparently he had tried to escape from the home on March 2, 1996 and as punishment, a caretaker had ordered Dabloo to beat him. The Times of India reported that the caretaker, Subash, had been arrested on March 4, 1996 because he had told Dabloo to "teach Rohit a lesson."

The Statesman, a Calcutta-based national daily, reported that Dabloo had forcibly taken Rohit, rubbed oil on his body, forced him to bathe, and then hung him upside down from a wooden beam on the ceiling. Then Dabloo beat Rohit on his heels, back, and stomach. Later that evening, Dabloo beat Rohit again. On the morning of March 4, Rohit did not respond to calls of other children in the home and when the caretakers found him, he was dead. Children in the home said that despite Rohit's repeated cries for help none of the three caretakers on duty tried to investigate the source of the screams. This allegation was corroborated by the officer-in-charge of the Lajpat Nagar police station, Vijay Singh Chauhan, who said, "Despite being on duty, not one of them [the fourteen remand home personnel] informed a senior official about the thrashing."

According to the post-mortem report, the body revealed several injury marks which could only have been inflicted over a prolonged period of time. The report also revealed cigarette burns on Rohit's genitals and observed signs of sexual abuse "which casts a shadow on the condition of other children in the Home." The Statesman also reported that: Residents of the area had also alleged that they would hear frequent screaming from the children's home and were convinced that the children were subjected to torture on more than one occasion.

On July 30, 1996, fourteen-year-old Hira reported to the Times of India that after he had been found on the streets by police, he had been detained in the Lajpat Nagar Remand Home for five years. Originally from Madhya Pradesh, the boy left home at the age of nine on an "impulse" which led him to Delhi. The police rounded him up on the street and he was sent to the Lajpat Nagar Remand Home. His parents were never notified of his detention and said, "We searched for our first-born for many months after he was missing. We thought he was dead." Hira alleged that while in the home, he had been subjected to constant torture by Dabloo, who was arrested for killing Rohit. Hira recounted one incident of being beaten because he forgot to clean a teacher's room:

> *I was asked to strip down to the waist, made to lie on the floor and my body was oiled. Then I was beaten with a stick until I fell unconscious.*

On May 8, 1996, one hundred juveniles detained in the Rajkiya Kishore Graha juvenile home escaped, claiming that "...food shortage and atrocities had forced them to flee." The district magistrate, Ashok Kumar, concurred with these claims:

The inmates were indeed living in sub-human conditions at the juvenile home. Severe beatings and denial of food by the home officials had driven the boys to desperation and forced them to flee. The conditions in the home led one boy to say that, "It is better to live a life on the streets than lead a hellish life here." There is some statistical evidence of conditions in the remand homes nationally. A number of the joint UNICEF and Ministry of Labour studies which interviewed street children who had been in the homes found that the majority of children reported that their treatment by staff at the homes and the provision of basic necessities in the homes was "bad," as Table 1 illustrates:

Table 1

Conditions In Remand Homes			
City	Total Number of Children Who Had Been Institutionalized	Percent of Children Who Reported Treatment by Staff as "Bad"	Percent of Children Who Reported That the Provision of Basic Necessities was "Bad"
Bangalore	48	75.0 (36)	91.7 (44)
Bombay	126	75.4 (95)	53.2 (67)
Madras	110	83.6 (92)	71.2 (79)
TOTAL	**284**	**Average: 78.5 (223)**	**Average: 66.9 (190)**

On July 28, 1996, the National Human Rights Commission announced that it would begin to investigate the conditions in juvenile homes in several Indian states. Unfortunately, this investigation is likely to be subject to the same limitations to which all of the commission's investigations are subject.

TORTURE

The criminal justice system in our country should be reviewed for making it more purposeful and effective. The criminal is happy with the court proceedings, with the law of the land, with the punishments imposed by the courts and with the easy life and comforts in the jails and is unhappy only with the police investigation and their preventative measures involving torture and harassment. It is therefore reasonable to believe that a certain complacence arising from authority derived from law motivates some policemen to resort to violence against those held in their custody, lawful or otherwise. Torture, usually in the form of severe beatings with fists, lathis, or other instruments, and kicking is a common feature of police treatment of street children. Beatings themselves are used extensively as a means of investigation, punishment, and retribution. As an NGO representative in Madras told us:

> *Regardless of the situation the police beat the children. I have seen broken bones, broken teeth, bruises, etc... The older a child is, the more horrible the treatment. They will tie boys down in a spread-eagled position and beat them, use knives or needles, they will hang them up by the arms and beat them brutally.*

The brutality of police in the course of investigating crime, especially in investigations of crimes against property, and as a form of retribution or punishment are acknowledged characteristics of police behavior. A senior state police officer, Inspector-General I. Ravi Arumugam, himself described this behavior in a paper he presented in 1994. An excerpt of his extraordinary statement, including the two charts which he used to describe illegal detention, torture and punishment, follows:

> *The police short-cut is brutality and it has become a way of life. In a house breaking case, the process of making enquiries from various people, from the Modus Operandi Bureau and from the various fences of stolen property takes time: for the normal police officer it is faster to catch the servant in the house, hammer him and if it works and, at his instance, some stolen property is recovered well and good, otherwise tough luck for the complainant; the case goes undetected. Of course, in India, the most superior short-cut is not to register the burglary at all; harass any one who comes to the police station so that an ordinary citizen would think several times before coming to report an offense. Brutality works even better in handling a law and order situation. And, sadly enough, under pressure it seems to be the natural response of police, regardless of country. Yet the desired change in police behaviour is not an impossible*

undertaking. The general awakening of society against police brutality is a good sign.

Inspector Arumugam then provided these charts to illustrate his point:

Table 4.1: This table was presented by Inspector-General Arumugam to illustrate the normal procedure for investigation compared to the "short-cut" investigations which he said occurred in India.

SHORT CUT INVESTIGATION	NORMAL INVESTIGATION
Offence Reported	Offence Reported
1. Visit to spot	1. Visit to spot
2. People including complainant questioned	2. People including complainant questioned
3. If available, scientific evidence collected	3. If available, scientific evidence collected
4. Await result	4. Await result
5. Suspect(s) identified	5. Suspect(s) identified
6. Suspect put through Third Degree `Confesses'	6. Suspects questioned
7. Recovery of property or weapon of offence made at instance of suspect	7. Alibi statement of suspect is verified by movements
8. Case put up in Court	8. Traveling to places for verification
	9. Questioning people regarding suspect's whereabouts
	10. Case built up
	11. Suspect(s) confronted with evidence collected against him
	12. Pressure of evidence against suspect mounted
	13. If stolen property or weapon of offence made at the instance of suspect
	14. Fences questioned
	15. Suspect confronted
	16. Recovery of property or weapon of offence made at the instance of suspect
	17. Case put up in court
Brutality: 8 Steps	Legality: 17 Steps

Table 4.2: This table was presented by Inspector-General Arumugam as an example of how the police actually deal with a "Goonda" (A term for a habitual criminal).

SHORT-CUT: ACTION AGAINST A GOONDA		
SHORT-CUT	SHORT-CUT #2	NORMAL LAW
1. The Goonda is caught and hammered	1. Reports of cognizable offences registered against the Goonda, usually last three years collected	1. Complaints recorded
	2. Non-cognizable reports also compiled	2. Goonda watched: his activities and his associates
	3. Goonda's activities kept under observation	3. Report filed in Magistrate's court for action under Section 110 Code of Criminal Procedure
	4. Details of preventive action taken already compiled	4. Interim order
	5. Goonda file examined in S.P. [Superintendent of Police] office	5. Witness examined
	6. District Magistrate moved, warrant issued by District Magistrate	6. Adjournments
	7. Goonda arrested	7. Defense evidence concluded
	8. District Magistrate reports to Government within 10 days	8. Goonda bound over for good behaviour for 6 months
If he misbehaves, he is beaten up again	9. State Government confirms District Magistrate's detention order	9. Again misbehaves
	10. High Court confirms detention order	10. Report filed in court
	11. Goonda in detention	11. Court may call witnesses
	For externment, District Magistrate examines witnesses of prosecution and defense	12. Court orders forfeiture of bonds
		13. Notice to sureties issued
		14. Await reply
		15. Order issued to attach property
		16. Auction and realization of amount
		17. Goonda free
Brutality: 1 or 2 steps	Preventative Detention Act or National Security Act. Externment: 11 steps This is also a short cut	Normal Law: 17 steps Goonda free

ABUSES ASSOCIATED WITH THE INVESTIGATION OF CRIME

During the course of crime investigations, expedience is not the only reason police resort to brutality. Section 25 of the Indian Evidence Act states that confessions made to a police officer while in custody are inadmissible. The provision is intended to prevent police from torturing suspects to gain confessions. But Section 27 of the Indian Evidence Act allows evidence obtained through confessions into court through a back door. For example, if a suspected thief is tortured into telling the police the whereabouts of stolen property or other facts not amounting to a confession, the police can then seize the stolen property or investigate the other facts and use this evidence against the accused. The justification of torture to obtain admissible evidence under Section 27 of the Indian Evidence Act is well known and acknowledged by senior police officers, as Inspector General I. Ravi Arumugam observed in his 1994 paper:

> *In [the] Indian Evidence Act, section 25 says that, "No confession made to a police officer shall be proved as against a person accused of any offence." This clearly shows... how a policeman is regarded in our country. Until this suspicious concept is removed from the law book, the police may harp on getting some evidence for the "hard-nut to crack criminals" under section 27 IEA, they are forced to use violence to extract information in a case.*

However, instead of arguing that torture should be eliminated from investigations or that Section 27 should be amended or removed from the Indian Evidence Act because it leads to torture, Inspector-General Arumugam argues that Section 25 should be eliminated, thereby removing a suspect's only legal protection from torture when evidence is being gathered by police.

The police routinely torture children in order to obtain both evidence and confessions, as the case of Shantanu illustrates.

Shantanu, along with a friend, committed a robbery at a wedding in Bombay on December 31, 1992. Eight days later, on January 8, 1993, two plainclothes police officers, Sheikh Sahab and Arun Hawaldar, came to Shantanu's house at about 10:00 a.m. and took him to the D.N. Nagar Police Station in Bombay. The following is the account Shantanu gave of his case:

> *At the station Shantanu was taken to a "separate enquiry room" where he was asked to put his hands on a table, palms up, and was then beaten with a police baton on the hands. After about an hour, the person who filed the complaint came to the station and identified Shantanu as the robber. Once identified, Shantanu was taken back to the enquiry room where the police hung him from the ceiling and proceeded to beat him for about forty-five minutes with police batons on the shoulders, back, and thighs. Following this, he was forced to lie on a block of ice while his legs were held in place by police. The police hit him whenever he tried to move. Then he was taken outside and made to lie in the sun for two hours while police asked him where the stolen property was kept. When he said that he did not know where the property was, the police beat him.*

Two days later, while Shantanu was still in custody, the police brought his parents to the station and threatened to beat his parents if he did not confess to the robbery. He confessed, the stolen property was recovered, and the police released his parents. The police then beat him and told him to confess to any crimes he had committed in the past. He was kept in the police station for ten more days. During that time, Sheikh Sahab would take Shantanu to the beach and ask him to escape so that he could shoot him. Shantanu claimed that Sahab tortured him because Shantanu had once fought with Sahab's brother.

On January 18, 1993, Shantanu was produced before the 10th Metropolitan Magistrates Court at Andheri in Bombay. The police falsely recorded his age as nineteen, even though he was fifteen. The police brought him before the court with his face covered and he could not hear the court proceedings. Shantanu reported that he had been tortured so badly that he could not stand, and two policemen had to hold him up during the proceedings. Despite this, he was remanded to police custody for eight days, during which the police beat him for five days. Then he was sent to the Bombay Central Prison.

The inspector-general of the prison was not convinced that Shantanu was an adult and asked the magistrate to provide age verification. Upon seeing his birth certificate, the inspector-general sent him to an observation home where he was subjected to frequent beatings by the house master. One day before his release, Shantanu struck the house master, which led to his remand being extended by one month.

Upon his release, when Shantanu was presented before the juvenile court, the magistrate asked if he had been mistreated by police. Shantanu stated that he had and as a result Sheikh Sahab was suspended and Shantanu's case was dismissed. Shantanu spent the next twenty days in the hospital as a result of the torture he received in police custody and in the observation home.

Police also torture possible witnesses, accomplices, or people who were near a crime scene into revealing the identity and location of the perpetrator. Although it is illegal under Section 160 of the Code of Criminal Procedure to detain males under the age of fifteen and females of any age who are not suspects, this tactic is extremely common. On January 11, 1995, between 2:00 and 3:00 a.m., six boys, aged twelve to fourteen, who had been sleeping at the Triplicane Railway Platform in Madras were detained by two plainclothes police officers. These police officers are known as "crime police"; they are plainclothes officers in charge of investigating theft and robbery.

The boys told Human Rights Watch that the police officers woke the boys up and took them in a jeep to the D-1 Police Station in Triplicane, Madras. When they arrived at the police station, the boys were placed in the station's holding cell or "crime cell." There were three older boys (possibly seventeen or older) in the cell with them. A total of nine people were in the twelve-by-fifteen-foot cell, which had no toilet. Rajiv told us that the police threatened to put him in the "minor jail" (an observation home) if he did not confess. Vikram told us that when he woke up and saw the police with lathis, he feared he was going to be beaten.

After about three hours, at approximately 6:00-6:30 a.m., three plainclothes officers entered the cell and brought a table with them. They forced all nine detainees to place their hands, palms down, on the table and proceeded to beat the boys' hands with lathis. Then they made the boys turn their hands over and proceeded to beat their palms.

The boys told Human Rights Watch that the beatings continued for approximately thirty to forty-five minutes. The police then stopped and told the boys that some auto parts, a gas cooking stove, and 10,000 rupees had been reported stolen from a lawyer's house which was near the Triplicane railway platform. They told the boys to confess or to tell them who committed the theft. According to Vikram, the police said, "Only if we beat you will you tell us the truth. If you do not tell the truth, we will beat you more." Then the police made four of the boys sit down "ladam" style, a position in which a boy sits on the ground with his hands behind his back and his legs straight out in front. The police then beat the four boys with lathis on their legs, feet, and soles of their feet. The other five boys, who were made to sit in a corner of the cell and watch, were periodically beaten with fists and lathis.

Vikram told Human Rights Watch:

> *They made me and some others sit down ladam. Then they said: "You better tell the truth in five minutes or we will beat you more." Then they just started to beat my feet and legs with lathis. I kept telling them that I was in a Red Cross program learning horticulture training. I kept telling them that I didn't know anything, but they kept on yelling at us and beating us.*

Suresh told us:

> *I told them that I was a ragpicker and didn't do such things. I told them to call the NGO and they [the police] would see that I was telling the truth. But they just kept beating us. Even when we said we didn't know anything, they just beat us.*

The beatings continued until approximately 8:30 a.m., when mothers of the boys began to arrive at the police station. Neighbors had apparently told the boys' mothers that they were at the police station. The mothers came individually and were allowed to feed the boys. Vikram asked his mother to contact the NGO he was affiliated with in order to help secure his release.

At about 10:30 a.m., the police told the mothers to leave. The boys told Human Rights Watch that police then proceeded to beat the children with their fists and lathis. They continued to tell them to confess and threatened them with more torture. Rajiv told Human Rights Watch:

> *When my mom left, they came back in [the cell] and told us to "Tell the truth." They yelled at us and called us filthy things and beat us. One policeman with a bald head and a short lathi screamed and beat us very hard.*

Vikram added:

> *They kept beating us and told us to confess. They called us "fucker" and other filthy things. Another policeman told them, "What is this, you shouldn't hit such small boys." This made them stop, but when he left, they beat us even harder.*

According to the boys, this treatment continued until approximately 12:30 p.m. The police then stopped and left the boys in the cell. No case had been registered. At approximately 3:30 p.m., an NGO representative arrived and demanded that the boys be released. He had been informed of the boys' whereabout by some of the boys' mothers.

The boys were released at approximately 6:00 p.m. All the boys were fingerprinted, their names and addresses were recorded, and the reason they were taken into custody was recorded. No charges were filed. Vikram told us that it was very difficult to walk because of the pain in his legs, so he and the other boys had to hold each other and walk slowly, but he was "glad to leave the station."

The NGO representative who saw these boys at the police station told Human Rights Watch:

> *Whatever the police want from the children, you can always guarantee they will beat them. For our boys, they weren't beaten that badly.*

The children said that they were kept in police custody for approximately fifteen to sixteen hours in total, of which they reported that they spent approximately four-and-a-half hours being beaten.

Human Rights Watch was told by several NGO representatives and lawyers that sometimes the police are aware that their methods are illegal and as a result torture children in ways that are less conspicuous. An NGO representative in Bangalore explained:

> *The types of injuries seen are those associated with severe beatings. The police are careful not to go too far and attract public attention. They won't beat the head or face because then the magistrate might be suspicious, or the public. Some children are chained for days at a time.*

Sanjiv's experience is indicative of this. He was seventeen at the time of this incident. We interviewed a lawyer working on his case on December 12, 1995, who provided us with Sanjiv's statement:

> *Sanjiv dropped out of school after the fourth grade and was living in Matunga, Bombay with his parents. One of his friends, Yusuf, was involved in thefts and would frequently give stolen items to Sanjiv for safe-keeping until Yusuf claimed them. Sanjiv's parents were not happy with his activities, so Sanjiv slept on the streets, outside his house.*

On March 21, 1991, four police officers from the Matunga Police Station had come to his neighborhood inquiring about a theft. Several boys in the area told the police that Sanjiv might be involved in the crime and told them where Sanjiv lived. At approximately 2:30 a.m. on March 22, 1991, Sanjiv and two of his acquaintances, Kanhaiye and Vijay, nineteen and seventeen respectively, were taken to the Matunga Police Station. The police made Sanjiv lie on his stomach on a bench and tied him down. Then they beat him on his feet and back while the police told him to give them the whereabouts of Yusuf, who was wanted in connection with a theft. Sanjiv refused to reveal Yusuf's whereabouts, but Kanhaiye and Vijay revealed the whereabouts of a hut that contained the stolen property, and the police took Sanjiv there. The police, along with Sanjiv, then went to Yusuf's house in Chembur, Bombay. Yusuf was not there, but his brother was, so the police beat Yusuf's brother and told him to bring Yusuf. His brother promised to send Yusuf to the police the next day.

The next morning, Sanjiv was produced before the metropolitan magistrate at Bhoiwada in the Dadar area of Bombay. The magistrate remanded him to fourteen days of police custody. The first two days, Sanjiv reported that he was not tortured, but following this, the torture began. He was made to stand with his hands tied to two stationary poles while police hit him with a wooden pole all over his body, including his face. Then his legs were tied and placed in a tire and he was beaten on the legs. After the beating, the police made him "exercise his legs" so that there would be no signs of torture.

Sanjiv was implicated in thirteen cases and remanded for two-and-a-half months to police custody, during which he was again badly beaten. He was then sent to Bombay Central Prison where he reported mistreatment at the hands of prison guards and inmates. While in prison, he came in contact with an NGO and now works for the same NGO.

The torture of children as a part of investigating crime is extremely common, as the following cases from Bangalore, Madras and New Delhi illustrate.

Kalasipalyam Police Station-Bangalore, July 7, 1995: Satish, sixteen, and Ayappa, twenty, were taken into custody by the Kalasipalyam Police Station for selling peanuts and cigarettes near a shop. This shop was robbed the next day, and the two boys were taken in for questioning. The boys pleaded that they knew nothing, but reported that the police beat them. After five days, an NGO secured their release. No charges were filed.

K-3 Police Station, Madras-September 1995: Shiva was sixteen and he had been on the street since 1992. He comes from the outskirts of Madras. He came to the street because he had no father, his mother was a drug-addict, and his twelve-year-old sister became pregnant. He decided to work as a ragpicker to help his sister and earns twenty to thirty rupees a day ($0.57 to $0.86).

He told Human Rights Watch that he was picked up by the police in September 1995 because they wanted information on a friend. He was taken to the K-3 police station and questioned about the whereabouts of his friend. The younger police officer started to beat him with a lathi, yelled at him, and asked him where his friend was. When he said he did not know and that he was an "NGO kid," an older officer said, "Do not beat NGO kids," and the younger officer stopped.

After this they searched his rag-bag. They found plastic scraps, which they said may have been from stolen goods and kept him at the station overnight. They did not beat him any more.

Shiva said this about the police:

> *Some are very good and they say don't sleep in the road, be careful. Some are very bad and they beat us brutally and take the money from our pockets.*

Vyalikaval Police Station-Bangalore, September 9, 1995: Murugan, aged thirteen, was apprehended by police from the Vyalikaval Police Station on September 9, 1995, at 6:00 a.m. on suspicion of stealing 4,000 rupees from the house where he worked as a car cleaner. The money had been lost one week earlier and the owner's wife had accused him of taking the money. Murugan had been waiting to collect his salary for the past seven months so that he could return home. A constable at the police station informed the NGO representative, who managed to get Murugan released, obtained his back pay for one-and-a-half years and sent him home to his family. Before being released, Murugan was again beaten by the police and given no food for the entire day.

Railway Protection Force Police Station-New Delhi Central Railway Station, New Delhi, December 1995: Girish was fourteen. He worked as an unlicensed porter at the New Delhi

Railway Station. He was taken by the Railway Protection Force (RPF) to the RPF police station in late November-early December 1995. Girish told Human Rights Watch:

> *I was sleeping in the parking lot when the police came. They asked me who stole 10,000 rupees from a passenger. They said the passenger had left his suitcase at the station. I said I didn't do it. Then they asked me to name who did, but I didn't know anything. They took me to the station and two police started to beat me all over with lathis. They kept on saying, "Name the person," and beating me. I kept on telling them I didn't know anything, but they just beat me. They did this for about an hour and then they let me go. They didn't file any charges.*

Other Situations in which Torture is Used

The torture of children in the course of investigations was only one situation where children are tortured. In some instances, the police detained and beat children because they claimed it was a method of crime prevention. Mohammed's experience was indicative of this. We interviewed him in Bangalore on January 12, 1996. He told us that when he was a luggage porter at the bus stand, he was picked up by the police in January 1995 and taken to the Upparpet Police Station in Bangalore. Mohammed told Human Rights Watch that he was sitting on a railing at the bus stand with about nine to fourteen other children when eight or nine police officers came and rounded them up; when they asked where the police were taking them, the police beat them with lathis.

They were all taken to Upparpet Police Station where they were forced to move confiscated items, such as weapons and drugs, to a storage room. They were not beaten, and were released when the work was done.

Two days later Mohammed was sleeping at the bus stand. Around midnight he and two others were picked up by about eight uniformed police officers and taken to the police kiosk at the bus station. No reason was given. Mohammed told Human Rights Watch that he was then made to sit, holding his ears with his hands through his legs-the "murga" or cock-position, and that policemen beat him for an hour with lathis on the soles of his feet and knees, saying: "If we don't beat you, you will commit crimes." Afterwards, they released him without charges.

Approximately eight months later, Raju was subjected to similar treatment at the Upparpet Police Station. He was apprehended by the police on August 18, 1995. The NGO representative who helped secure his release wrote this about the incident:

> *Raju from the Bus Stand was apprehended by Upparpet Police Station for loitering in the area. [He was] kept in [the] lock-up, beaten, and abused in bad language, so as to prevent him from committing any crime. This is the reason given by the police regarding Raju who is a high school student, earning his livelihood by cleaning private buses, vans, and cars.*

> *"Preventative torture" is one symptom of the overall lawlessness of the police; another is the use of torture and beatings as a form of pre-judicial or extrajudicial punishment. The Andhra Pradesh Civil Liberties Committee, a human rights organization, described this aspect of policing in a 1995 report on custodial deaths in Andhra Pradesh:*

> *The habit of "teaching lessons" on somebody else's behalf by the unlawful use of force is an aspect of a more general habit that the police have cultivated. This is the habit of acting as judge and executioner rather than as merely the police. This attitude has been allowed to develop, and has been implicitly sanctioned and encouraged by the political establishment. Whatever the niceties of the penal jurisprudence developed by civilised thought, in India it is in the police lock-up that the investigation, trial and punishment of crimes takes place. Often, the three take place simultaneously or even in reversed order. The punishment starts before the investigation begins, and it is in the course of dealing out the punishment that the investigation is completed and the judgement delivered, including a possible verdict*

of not guilty. And the norm of punishment is preventive and retributive, not reformative.

This behavior was also acknowledged by a senior police officer who said that, "A strong sense of professional duty and little faith in the judicial system has sometimes led the police to take justice in their own hands and to do away with as many common criminals as possible." Police punish children as a means of discipline and as a form of retribution. In general, the tendency of the police is to resort to beatings and torture, and the reasons for the violence are often arbitrary or incidental.

The case of Bhaskar is an example of how little provocation is necessary for the police to retaliate against street children. Bhaskar was selling illegal movie tickets in Bangalore on July 2, 1995. He was beaten by the crime police affiliated with the Upparpet Police Station, apparently to punish him for having previously mocked the police and having run away from them. The NGO representative who helped to secure his release from custody wrote:

Bhaskar, aged fifteen, was badly beaten by the crime police at Upparpet Police Station for making faces at the police on a previous occasion while running away after selling cinema tickets in black [scalping tickets]. He was released the next day with a warning.

Sharad, a fifteen-year-old ragpicker was caught in the act of stealing milk cartons in January 1995. The police of the V-1, Villevakkam Police Station in Madras, apprehended, beat, and released him. Sharad told us:

I took some milk cartons from a house and the police caught me and took me to the police station. When I got there the police officer started beating me with a lathi all over my body. He kept on saying: "Don't do this again." He never used abusive words. He beat me for ten minutes, then made me sit in the station. I was caught in the morning and they let me go in the evening. When I was there, I saw about five other boys sitting in the cell. The police made them remove all of their clothes, except their underwear, and started to beat them with lathis. I don't know why.

In the bus terminals and train stations of India's cities, police routinely beat street children as a result of a reported theft or other crimes. A study on street children in Delhi observed:

> *The other major problem faced by street children is that they are often nabbed by police for crimes they have not committed. For example, a lady passenger's necklace was stolen for which all the boys at the station were rounded up and put in the lock-up for two weeks. They are mercilessly thrashed and sometimes put in lock-ups under charges of vagrancy, gambling or street brawls or sent to remand homes.*

The previous description, published in 1992, accurately describes what happened to fourteen-year-old Ramesh in the Police Chouki at Delhi's Interstate Bus Terminus (ISBT), in June 1995. He has been on the street since 1991 when his father was seriously injured in a bus accident. He left home to work and help support his father and at the time Human Rights Watch interviewed him, earned about ten to twenty rupees a day ($0.26 to $0.57) as an unlicensed porter at the bus station. The Police Chouki is a small station within the station's premises and is under the control of the Kashmiri Gate Police Station. Ramesh told Human Rights Watch:

> *A stranger came to the ISBT and had his luggage stolen. Around 10:00 in the morning, the police picked me up because I am an unlicensed porter and took me to the chouki [police station at the station]. They told me to bend over and grab my hands behind my calves and hold my ears, in the "murga" (cock) position. The police told me to stay in that position until the officer in charge came. I waited, then the officer came and started beating me with a lathi. He made me stay in that position while he beat me. He called me the son of a prostitute, thief, and other things. I had to stay like this for two or three hours while he beat me. After that they told me I could move, but I couldn't stand because of the position I was in.*

The police then told him to stay in a corner of the police station. While in the corner, four or five policemen beat and verbally abused him. Ramesh told us that, "Some police are humane and will give you food and let you go to the toilet, but not that day." The police then recorded Ramesh's name and address, then made him sign a blank piece of paper, but Ramesh was not sure what it was. He was released sometime between 6:00 and 7:00 p.m. Ramesh said that he had been detained by the police on at least five occasions and whenever a theft occurs, the police will apprehend children and beat them. Ramesh said:

> *If they arrest us, we should not be beaten like this. They should be human. We aren't thieves, we are just working to live.*

As the previous cases illustrate, children are routinely beaten by the police for a variety of reasons. Ramesh was one of several children who told Human Rights Watch that they had been subjected to beatings by the police on multiple occasions and for different reasons. The experiences of Manik and Surinder are similar.

Beginning in 1992 at the age of fifteen, Manik was harassed and beaten by police several times. His story was provided by a lawyer working on his case.

Manik has studied up to the eighth standard (eighth grade) and lived with his father, stepmother and younger stepbrother. Manik had friends involved in petty thefts and when he was fifteen years old, he committed a petty theft along with his friends. He was arrested by the watchman of the building, who was a witness, and taken to Kherwadi Police Station. There Manik was stripped of his clothes, a rod was passed through his armpits and he was beaten by a wooden bat on his hand and on his head.

The beatings continued from 7:00 a.m. until 6:00p.m. He was not given anything to eat. After he confessed to the offense, he was then taken to the observation home at Umerkhadi where he underwent a medical check up and was treated for the bruises on his back. He was then taken to Nagpada Police Hospital for age verification. After he was produced before the juvenile court magistrate, his father furnished bail and Manik was released.

Although Manik severed his relations with his friends, the police often arrested him because they suspected him of criminal activity. The police on three occasions registered false cases of theft against him and later released him. On some occasions, they would arrest Manik while he was asleep at night and beat him up.

In December 1992, Manik and a friend, Bhanwar Singh, were stopped in their car by police from the Azad Maidan Police Station at about 1:00 a.m. When Bhanwar Singh was unable to produce a license and car papers, they were taken to the Azad Maiden Police Station. The police forced Manik to lie on a bench and beat him until they broke his leg. He was repeatedly questioned on his involvement in the theft of the car. His legs were swollen and he could not stand. He was produced before the Metropolitan Magistrates Court at Esplanade next day. The police threatened to break his other leg if he told the magistrate how his leg had been broken. When Magistrate J. Basu asked him why he could not stand, Manik first lied, saying he had fallen. But when the magistrate repeated the question, Manik told the truth and asked to be given judicial custody. The magistrate asked him if he wanted to prosecute the police. Manik declined. He was then remanded to judicial custody for one day and directed to be sent to the hospital for medical treatment.

He was taken to Bombay Central Prison, which was overcrowded with prisoners arrested during an outbreak of communal violence that had occurred at that time. Two days later he was taken to the hospital and given an injection, but the pain did not ease. On the orders of the magistrate, he was given a medical examination, but although he told the doctor what had happened to him, and despite the fact that he could not even walk, the doctor reported him to be fit.

Manik was named as the main accused in the case. He was initially remanded to fourteen days custody, then further remanded to an additional fourteen days, and was then granted bail. Although he claimed he had been falsely implicated, on the advice of the magistrate he pleaded guilty and was released on probation in January 1993. A social worker who had been sent by the magistrate visited Manik at home and got him a job as a lawyer's clerk.

Two months after Manik's release, policemen from Azad Maidan Police Station came to his house at 2:30 p.m. and took him to Azad Maidan Police Station in their jeep, allegedly for work. In the jeep, they threatened Manik that they would get even with him. He was taken to the lock-up and his hands and feet were tied. The inspector who examined Manik's record saw a letter to the police station written by the social worker asking for Manik not to be arrested.

The inspector questioned Manik about the social worker's organization. Manik showed him the identity card he had received from the NGO. After the questioning, Manik was untied and in the morning he was released. He immediately contacted the social worker who went to the police station and was informed that Manik had been called in for a routine inquiry. At the time Human Rights Watch reviewed his case, Manik was training with the NGO.

Surinder was fifteen when we met him. He dropped out of school after the fifth standard (fifth grade) and came to Delhi from Bihar in 1994 to find work. He worked as an unlicensed porter at the Interstate Bus Terminus and earns between thirty and fifty rupees ($0.86-$1.43) per day. We interviewed him at the bus station on January 1, 1996, when he recounted three incidents involving the police from the Police Chowki there.

In August 1995, he was carrying the luggage of a passenger. When he asked for ten rupees ($0.29) as payment, the passenger refused and would only give him five rupees. They began to argue and push each other, so the passenger called the police. Two police officers started to beat Surinder and took him to the police station. There, they beat him with lathis on his hands and arms while they accused him of being a thief. He reported that other police watched this, but nobody intervened on his behalf. After the beating ended, the police told him to leave the bus station and released him.

On December 29, 1995, as he was watching a card game at the bus station, two police officers started to beat the card players and spectators with lathis and accused them of gambling.

The police took Surinder to the police lock-up, which held two other detainees. Surinder told Human Rights Watch:

> *There were three police in the station and they told us, "If you do not pay money, we will chargesheet you and send you to jail." We only had one hundred rupees [$2.86] between us, but we gave it to them. They didn't think this was enough so they started to beat us with lathis. Then I guess they realized this was all we had so they took the money and let us go without filing charges. Some police will take money and release you, some police will take money and keep you in the lock-up or send you to jail. The police are very, very bad.*

Two days later, on December 31, 1995, as Surinder was again watching a card game, a policeman came and beat him on the arms and hands and with a lathi and told him to go away and to stop watching people gamble.

EXTORTION

In reality cynicism protects a policeman from any feeling of revulsion against either corruption or brutality. He starts ensuring that he would not be cheated out of the prize.

Corruption, in the form of extortion, reinforces the use of custodial violence. With street children, extortion by police is an integral part of the processes that perpetuate illegal detention and custodial violence. The police prey on street children for money. When children are arrested, they or their guardians are asked to pay money in order to get them released. This is true whether the charges are fabricated or real. The police threaten the families and children by telling them that their children will be beaten, kept in custody, or sent to jail if they do not pay. In one case reported to Human Rights Watch, the police told children and their families that failure to pay would lead to the deaths of their children.

In detention, it is standard operating procedure for the police to take whatever money is in the child's possession.

Children working on the street as ragpickers, porters, shop vendors, or shoe shiners have all reported the payment of hafta (protection or kickback money) to the police. Failure or inability to pay usually results in a child's being beaten, detained, or arrested by police. In some cases, payment is no guarantee against further extortion.

The link between torture and corruption has been described by former deputy inspector, and former director of the National Police Commission, Shailendra Mishra:

> *With a policeman, the reputation for expert brutality fetches more money than actual brutality, but, of course, the reputation has to have a solid foundation. Once a policeman acquires a reputation for expert third degree he makes enormous quantities of money in daily crime work by simply withholding customary brutality.*

As with the case of torture in general, extortion and brutality are not limited to the investigation of crimes, but certain types of investigation, specifically crimes against property, are notorious for their promotion of corruption, as the Andhra Pradesh Civil Liberties Committee noted:

> *Investigating theft cases is a lucrative business for the police. The one who has lost property will pay, the one into whose hands the stolen property has passed will pay, and even the one who is falsely accused of stealing or receiving stolen property will pay, provided that all the violence that the police are capable of is brought to bear on the matter. And that is why theft charges turn up so frequently in the list of custodial killings. We emphasize this point because in all the discussion that usually takes place on the causes and reasons for custodial violence, the factor of corruption is downplayed, though it is a very important factor. The police routinely extort money from people they lock up, not only on theft charges but any charge or even no charge at all.*

The amount of money paid to police largely depends on the child's (or his family's) ability to pay and the discretion of police. In Madras, Delhi, and Bangalore, social workers and children told Human Rights Watch that unlicensed porters have to pay approximately 50 percent of their earnings to the police as a form of protection money. A social worker in

Bangalore stated that policemen extort amounts ranging from fifty to eight thousand rupees ($1.43 to $229) from a detainee or their family. According to the People's Union for Civil Liberties (PUCL) report on the death of Satish Kumar, the thirteen-year-old boy who died after being held in police custody, the police asked parents of one detainee to pay a bribe of 20,000 rupees ($571). The range Human Rights Watch encountered was from ten to 2,500 rupees ($0.29 to $71). A 1993 study on the justice system in Bombay found that the average non-legal expenditure incurred at a police station was 557 rupees ($15.90), with a minimum payment of ten rupees ($0.29) and a maximum payment of five thousand rupees ($143).

The fact that police extort money from street children is well known. In the Third Report of the National Police Commission, published in 1980, the commission reported several situations where extortion by police is common, including:

* Extorting money by threatening persons, particularly the ill-informed and weaker sections of society, with conduct of searches, arrests and prosecution in court on some charge or the other.
* Fabricating false evidence during investigation of cases and implicating innocent persons or leaving out the guilty persons on mala fide considerations.
* Extortion of periodic payments as hafta from shopkeepers, platform vendors, brothel keepers, promoters of gambling dens, and others.

Abuses and Extortion Associated with Investigation of Crime

Every child Human Rights Watch interviewed who alleged extortion while in custody in conjunction with a crime investigation had been detained on charges of theft or suspicion of theft, as the following cases illustrate.

Firos is a seventeen-year-old ragpicker who lives near the Valluvar Kottam in Nungambakkam, Madras. In an interview with Human Rights Watch he said that he earned about thirty rupees a day ($0.86). He had a brother and an uncle, but because they live in a hut in a slum, he spent most of his time on the street. At the time of our interview, he was taking part in a non-formal education program run by an NGO two hours a day.

Firos told Human Rights Watch that on Sunday, February 5, 1995, he was near the Valluvar Kottam when a woman and three men accused him of stealing some auto parts and a sari. He told Human Rights Watch:

> *I said I didn't do these things. They told me to come to their house and talk, but I was afraid that they would beat me if I went to their house. I told them to come to the NGO and we could talk there, but they wouldn't come. They started to beat me on the street. Even the woman beat me. They took me to the [Nungambakkam] police station and the woman told the police that I had stolen these things and that I should be put in jail.*

The police took Firos and his four accusers left. Two uniformed police officers took him to a fifteen by fifteen foot storage room within the police station, adjacent to the jail cell. Firos described it has having a desk, bench, a single bulb, no windows, and some iron rods. Firos said that after bringing him to this room, the two police officers began to beat him with lathis and told him to confess to stealing. He said that when he fell as a result of the blows, the officers kicked him.

They took me in the room and started hitting me with lathis. They hit me on the arms, shoulders, hip, legs, knees. I fell down because they were hitting me so hard. When I fell they started kicking me with their boots. They kept saying: "You better tell us you stole these things or we will beat you more." They were yelling and kicking and beating me and calling me "fucker" and "thief."

Firos told us that this continued for approximately thirty minutes. Then the officers manacled one of his legs to the bench in the storage room. He was forced to crouch next to the bench as a result of being manacled. This put him between the bench and a wall. With the exception of being taken to the toilet once a day, he was forced to remain in this position until he was released, three days later.

Later Sunday evening, another uniformed police officer came into the room. A second police officer came in later and told him to confess to stealing and then hit him with his fists while continuously telling him to "tell the truth." Firos said that there was no room because he was still manacled to the bench, and every time the policeman hit him, his head would hit the wall. Firos said that his head "was paining and everything hurt a lot."

Firos was left alone all night. He said he slept a bit, but was not given any food. The following morning, two uniformed police officers that Firos did not recognize came in the room.

Firos described what happened:

> *Two new police came in and they told me: "You better admit to stealing or tell us who did." They were hitting and kicking me and my head was hitting the wall. I told them I took a clutch wire from some vehicle on the street and that maybe M., V., and S. took those other things. I told them because I wanted them to stop beating me. They stopped beating me and asked for my address. I gave them my uncle's and then they left.*

Firos remained manacled to the bench. Later that afternoon, Firos said his brother and uncle were brought by the police to the station. Firos said that his brother fed him, and that the police told his brother that he had admitted to stealing a "clutch wire" and that his brother should come back to the station the next evening. According to Firos, this was the first time in two days that he had eaten any food or seen anybody other than the police. He said he was left alone except when being beaten and questioned by the police.

The next evening, the NGO representative and Firos' brother came to the station to get Firos released. The police told them that since Firos had confessed, they would have to pay the police for his release. The NGO representative told Human Rights Watch:

> *The police told us: "He has said he stole auto parts and he has named other boys. You better pay us, otherwise we will keep him and file charges!" I refused to pay, but*

Firos' brother was scared and went to his uncle's to get money. The next day his brother paid the police about 2,500 rupees [$71.40] and they let Firos go without filing charges.

Narayana is fourteen. He came from Nepal about two years ago because his friends told him that Delhi is a very good place where one could earn money and he had a "dream to make money in Delhi." He is a fifth standard (fifth grade) drop out. When we spoke to him on January 1, 1996, he told us that he was working as a valet at the Interstate Bus Terminus in Delhi on November 27, 1995 when a customer refused to pay a three rupee ($0.09) storage fee and tried to leave on his scooter without paying. The argument escalated into a fight. The customer beat Narayana and then called the police. A policeman was watching and took Narayana to the terminal's police chowki. Narayana told us:

At the station I was made to stay in the murga position and three officers beat me with their lathis. They beat me like this for two hours. The police demanded money. They told me: "You're in no position to bargain, you beat that customer." They finally let me go when my boss paid them 300 rupees. I don't work there anymore.

Abuses Associated with the Payment of Protection Money

The other way extortion is committed is through the payment of hafta-protection money. Children are either beaten on the street or brought to the police station and beaten; they are told that they must pay the police otherwise they will face beatings. Hafta is also required when children are involved in illegal activities.

Children who sell "black" movie tickets told Human Rights Watch that they had to pay about 25 to 50 percent of their earnings to the police, otherwise they would be beaten, arrested, or both. At railway stations, children pay hafta in order to get around the minimum age requirements for obtaining a porter's license and to avoid being arrested under laws which make it a criminal offense for a child to work in railway stations.

Many children who work in railway stations are migrants from other parts of the country and railway stations are their first entrance into a city. Faced with a new and unknown environment, no shelter, and no means of income, children stay in and around the railway station because it is covered shelter, it is perceived as "safe," there are other children there, and they can immediately began earning money as self-employed, unskilled laborers, like railway porters. In this respect, the railway station, especially for unaccompanied migrant or abandoned children, represents an area where they can immediately begin to meet their survival needs.

The problem for children is that any work involving the "transport of passengers, goods, or mails," working as a food vendor, clearing ash-pits or cinder picking, and any work which "is done in close proximity [to] or between the railway lines" represent some of the occupations explicitly prohibited under the Child Labour (Prohibition and Regulation) Act, 1986. Because most of these children are self-employed, this prohibition allows police to arrest children in accordance with the "delinquent juvenile" provisions of the Juvenile Justice Act, 1986, which defines offense as "any offence punishable under any law for the time being in force."

For older children, the situation is not much better. According to every NGO representative and lawyer who works with street children at railway stations that Human Rights Watch spoke to throughout India, the minimum age to obtain a railway porter's license is eighteen, thereby prohibiting any child from legally working as a porter. Those children who are too old to fall under the Juvenile Justice Act, can still be viewed as criminals because they are unlicensed.

By using threats of prosecution and beatings in exchange for hafta, the police have created a profit-making enterprise out of the increasing population of street children who come to railway stations in need of shelter and work to survive. In this way, the police exercise almost complete control over children who work at railway stations. But even when hafta is paid by children, it does not ensure protection from the police, as a 1992 study on street children in Delhi observed:

Street children who are self-employed such as porters, vendors and shoe blacks spoke of harassment from police and municipal authorities because they do not have licences to work. By paying the officials the children get some respite from their harassment. While talking to Habib, a 15-year-old coolie, about police harassment, he mentioned small children usually pay the bribe out of fear. He does not any more give hafta (a bribe given every week) to the police as it did not guarantee trouble free work at the station.

NGO representatives and lawyers working with street children interviewed by Human Rights Watch corroborated this account. The following cases describe a series of incidents involving unlicensed porters and the abuses they experienced associated with hafta payments to the police affiliated with the Railway Protection Force (RPF) police station at the New Delhi Central Railway Station.

Human Rights Watch interviewed fifteen-year-old Rakesh on January 1, 1996. Originally from Calcutta, where he had lived on the street, Rakesh had gone first to Bombay and then to Delhi where he has been working as a porter at the New Delhi Railway Station since 1993. He had never been to school. In June 1995, at about 2:30 a.m., he was sleeping on one of the New Delhi Central Railway Station platforms when eight policemen from the Railway Protection Force (RPF) woke him, along with three other boys and began to beat them with lathis. Then they took them to the RPF police station.

At the station, Rakesh was made to lie on his back with his arms outstretched. A policeman stood on each of his hands, then his legs were tied and placed in the air. He said that this happened to all four boys. Another policeman started to beat their legs and feet with lathis while the police called them thieves and sons of prostitutes. He said that he was beaten for a long time and so badly that his legs and feet bled.

The next morning the police sent the other children to observation homes, but they did not send Rakesh because they had injured him so badly they did not want a magistrate to see him. Instead they called two strangers who carried him back to the street. He was not charged with any offense. After he was left outside the railway station a friend took him to a nearby health van where he had his injuries treated. He said that he had to walk with a cane for eight weeks because of the injuries he sustained. Rakesh told us:

> *If you work as a porter, the police beat you. On the same day I was beaten, someone stole 24,000 rupees from a suitcase. The police caught the thief and took 23,000 rupees for themselves and gave 1,000 rupees to the thief and then let him go. Then they beat us. If this happens regularly, then maybe we should stop working and start stealing so we can pay the police more and lead a better life. What can we do? In this condition people can do anything to fill the policeman's stomach and lead a good life.*

Sabir is fourteen. At the time Human Rights Watch interviewed him, he worked as an unlicensed porter at the New Delhi Central Railway Station. Sabir told Human Rights Watch that on November 16, 1995, he was detained by the RPF.

Some friends and I were sitting on the platform. Somebody set fire to some rags on the platform. The police came and started to beat us with lathis, then they took us to the lock-up and made us sit murga position and beat us with lathis. They took all of our money; I had fifty rupees [$1.43]. The police told us, "If you pay regular, we will not beat you, otherwise we will always beat you." We were kept in the lock-up around fifteen hours. They didn't give us any food. To get food, you have to pay them. We were let go without being charged. The police are useless.

Susai, a fourteen-year-old unlicensed railway porter at the New Delhi Railway Station, earned about fifteen to twenty-five rupees ($0.43 to $0.71) a day. Susai told Human Rights Watch about an incident at the RPF police station on December 1, 1995:

> *At around 9:00 p.m., I was waiting with some others for a train. Five policemen came and began to beat us with lathis. The police arrested me and three of my friends. They took us to the police station and beat us.*

They said, "If you clean the station, we will release you." So we cleaned the station. When we were done, they put us in the jail. This was late in the night. In the lock-up, the police beat us with their fists and lathis. They would say, "Don't sleep, this isn't your father's house," and beat us. They said: "If you pay us fifty rupees each [$1.43], we will leave you alone." We did not have the money, so they kept us in the jail and beat us.

The next morning, Susai told us that they were taken to the RPF Magistrate. He asked them what they did wrong and when they told him that they didn't do anything, he released them.

Abuses involving extortion are, in large part, a result of an environment which has tolerated abuses in the normal functioning of police. In the absence of accountability for custodial violence, the police have evolved and refined the tactics of illegal detention and custodial violence to propagate a profit-making enterprise. Thus, remedies that seek to improve the investigative skills of the police as a way to reduce torture overlook one of the principal reasons for torture: In many cases, detention, ill-treatment, and torture have nothing to do with the investigation of a crime, they simply represent a way for the police to make money.

NGO INITIATIVES TO ADDRESS

Police Abuse of Street Children

They [children] are kept in detention at the station for a few hours [or] up to six months (one case). Generally it lasts for a few days. No advocate or social worker is present. I only go if another boy or a family member informs me, otherwise I have no way of knowing. The police do not inform anyone.

Police abuse of street children is so common that it has forced NGOs to monitor the police to ensure that they do not break the law. NGOs working with street children have addressed the problem in several ways. The most common strategy, adopted throughout India, is for NGOs to directly intervene at police stations when children are reported to be in custody.

The following accounts describe a series of interventions by an NGO in Bangalore. They are from written accounts by the NGO representative who is responsible for going to the police stations when children are detained.

Goripalya Police Station-June 11, 1995

Raju and Anand, aged twelve, and Yusuf, aged thirteen were taken to Goripalya Police Station for interrogation about a theft of 550 kilograms of iron from a nearby construction site. A security guard at the site had allowed the boys to sleep in the basement in return for some odd jobs the boys had performed. The police lured the boys to the station to speak to their sub-inspector; there they were stripped of their clothes, beaten on the knees and soles of their feet and knuckles. After the NGO's intervention, they were released after three and a half days.

Kengerigate Police Station-July 7, 1995

Krishna, Anand, and Faisal aged fifteen, fifteen, and sixteen, were apprehended by police from the Kengerigate Police Station and accused of the theft of three plastic pots. They were beaten at the spot of arrest and again at the policestation. They were asked to bring three brass pots and three thousand rupees ($85.71) if they did not want to go to jail. One of them was kept in lock-up, while the other two were sent to bring the money and pots. The two boys went to the NGO. After the NGO called the concerned officials and then met with the crime sub-inspector, the other boy was released after two days.

Vyalikaval Police Station-July 15, 1995

Babu and Krishna, aged twelve and fourteen, were in Vyalikaval Police Station for nine days. The NGO discovered their whereabouts, but over the phone, the police denied any knowledge of the boys. When the NGO representative went to the station, she saw the boys; the older boy had been sick with a fever for the previous two days. After she wrote a letter to the commissioner and the concerned officer, the police released both of the boys the same day; Krishna was sent to the government hospital with a police escort.

Railway Protection Force Police Station-July 26, 1995

Anil, aged eleven, was apprehended by the railway police for being in possession of a bag with about fifty gold bars. He told the police that he had been carrying the luggage for a passenger who had disembarked from the train (Rajabhadi Express) and that the man had taken his other bag and suitcase to an auto-rickshaw and had never returned. Anil was beaten and suffered a one-inch cut on his forehead before the NGO was able get him released from police custody.

Railway Protection Force Police Station-October 26, 1995

Four boys were very badly beaten by the Railway Protection Force (RPF), two had their arms fractured, one had his lips torn and lost two teeth. The NGO representative wrote to the railway commandant who ordered an inquiry and then the NGO pressured the officials to suspend the policemen who were responsible. The medical expenses were partly covered by the RPF.

Kalasipalyam Police Station-December 12, 1995

John, aged fourteen, was apprehended and taken to Kalasipalyam Police Station for interrogation about the murder of a woman in the market where he had been selling vegetables the previous day. The crime police beat him with the lathi on his inner calves. The NGO representative, after three days of repeatedly going to the police station and calling senior police officers, was able to obtain his release.

Another common strategy to address the problem of street children and police is issuing identification cards to children in contact with the NGOs so that if a child is detained by the police, the child can show the I.D. card to the police who can then notify the NGO that the child is in custody. The cards are also a way of alerting the police that the children are affiliated with NGOs, so the police then understand that if the child is illegally detained or mistreated an organization will know about it. NGOs have tried to get police to officially recognize the system of I.D. cards, but as of September 1996, no police force has officially agreed to do so, limiting the effectiveness of the strategy. Also, children frequently lose the cards. An NGO representative in Madras reported:

> We have introduced the I.D. card system, but the I.D. card system doesn't work because every individual police officer may not know about it and may not respect it. Children may not use it.

Some NGO representatives carry I.D. cards that have been signed by a high-ranking police officer. The card is used to gain access to police stations when NGOs learn that children are being detained, and is supposed to allow the NGO representative easier access to police stations and children. In some cases the I.D. card identifies the NGO representatives as the guardians of the street children. While some senior police officers have agreed to sign the I.D. cards, police stations frequently do not recognize them, often claiming that they do not believe the signature of the police officer is real.

Even when NGO representatives gain access to the police station, such interventions may not work. NGO representatives told Human Rights Watch that the police have denied that children are in their custody. Moreover, NGO representatives said that they have been denied access to children, verbally abused, asked to pay bribes for the children's release; and in one case, the NGO representative was detained and beaten along with the children. The following three incidents illustrate police responses to NGO representatives.

Magadi Road Police Station-Bangalore, September 1995

The social worker involved in this incident was given a "special police officer" designation by the Additional Commissioner of Police (ACP), granting her the powers of a circle inspector (a police officer who has jurisdiction over several police stations), who outranks any police officer at a police station.

The social worker told Human Rights Watch:

> *One night a few months ago, we had heard some boys were in the station near Magadi Road. I went there with another lady in the program to the police station but the officer would not let us in. When I showed the officer*

> *my Special Police card, he said: "You think because you are some VIP that you can come in here, but I don't care." I told him that I was no VIP, that the ACP had given me this designation because I worked with street children, and that he should let me see the kids. He took our I.D. cards, looked at them and threw them on the street.*

The NGO representatives told the police officer that it was their right to see the children, but the officer refused and verbally abused them, calling them names like "prostitute." The NGO representative told us that after this:

> *I said, "If you do not let us see the children I will scream `rape' and yell as loud as I can. Then there will really be problems." Then he let us see the children. Afterwards, I calmly went to the street, picked up the I.D. cards, and left. I was shaking because I was so scared. The woman with me was terrified. I don't think she will do that again.*

Kengerigate Police Station-Bangalore, November 4, 1995

The same NGO representative in Bangalore learned that six boys aged fifteen to sixteen were apprehended and taken to Kengerigate Police Station, for no apparent reason. One of them was released in order to go to the NGO and bring 200 rupees ($5.71) each for their release. The NGO representative called the deputy commissioner of police to complain about the matter but then took the money to the station. There were no police available, so she went back after some time and a constable took the money. She asked him to provide a receipt as a record of the payment. Instead, the officer gave back the money and filed charges against the boys. The boys were beaten and then brought to the court to pay a fine of 120 rupees ($3.42) each.

New Delhi Central Railway Station-New Delhi, November 16, 1995

Krishna Kumar Tripati is a social worker for an NGO that works with street children. He had previously been a human rights activist for the People's Union for Civil Liberties (PUCL) in Delhi, and before that was an activist for the PUCL in Bihar.

Tripati told Human Rights Watch that on November 16, 1995, he learned that the police at the New Delhi Central Railway Station were beating street children and went to intervene.

When he went to platform number ten at the station he saw uniformed and plainclothes police officers beating children. Tripati went to the senior station manager, Mishree Lal, who had ordered and was supervising the beatings and asked him why they were beating the children. Lal had Tripati's platform ticket (a ticket needed for a non-passenger to be on a train platform) torn up and ordered police to take Tripati, along with some children to the police station. Tripati was beaten by the police on the way to the police station, in a train conductor's office, and in the police station. He was detained in the police station's lock-up overnight where Tripati alleged that police beat children throughout the evening. Tripati was forced into a cell that was fouled with excrement.

Before he was presented to a magistrate, the police told him to plead guilty to the charges that the police were framing against him, namely being on a railway platform without a ticket and interfering with police function (not allowing police to beat children), otherwise he would be subjected to more beatings. Tripati told the magistrate about his treatment and the magistrate fined him 753 rupees ($21.50) and released him. Even though Tripati alleged misconduct by the police and the incident was publicized in the Times of India, a Bombay-based national daily, no investigation was launched into the conduct of police. A complaint was also made to the National Human Rights Commission. A full account of this incident is provided in Appendix V.

A longer-term approach to curb police abuses against street children began in 1994 when UNICEF, the Indian government's Ministry of Home and Welfare, and a Bangalore-based NGO working with street children initiated a "Police Training Curriculum." The curriculum is designed to sensitize police to the special problems that street children face and educate police about the provisions andimplementation of the Juvenile Justice Act. UNICEF eventually expects this curriculum to be implemented at the national level, but as of September 1996, the preliminary training curriculum had just been submitted to UNICEF, and a program for implementation had not yet been finalized.

A pilot project was carried out by the NGO in Bangalore from 1994 through 1995. NGO representatives reported that during the training of the Bangalore police there were improvements in the way police treat street children, but noted that police abuses were still common. For example, from June 1994 to May 1995, the same period in which the NGO was implementing the police training curriculum, the NGO recorded 154 interventions at police stations, involving 198 children kept in police lock-ups. According to the NGO representative in charge of interventions, this was a rate of about one intervention every two days. The most common reasons for detention reported by the NGO were theft, "false cases filed by police and public," and harassment by the RPF.

The main difficulties the NGO has reported is that they do not have the resources to train every police officer in the city and that while greater sensitization to the rights of children and the Juvenile Justice Act may reduce abuses resulting from a police officer's ignorance of the law or human rights standards, they have no effect on police who do not care or who commit abuses to further other illegal activities such as extortion or bringing false charges. Nevertheless, NGO representatives did feel the curriculum was a positive step and should be pursued nationally.

Because some laws which prohibit child labor effectively criminalize specific groups of self-employed children, thus making them more vulnerable to the lawlessness of the police, many NGOs have sought to organize street children into trade unions. A number of NGOs have called for the amendment of the Trade Union Act to allow children to form trade unions as a means to provide them with a legal basis to protect their physical integrity and means of survival. NGOs in Bangalore and Delhi have attempted to form informal unions of street children. As a result of this experience, many NGOs working with street children are opposed to blanket prohibitions on child labor, arguing that such approaches do not take into consideration the repercussions of such laws on child laborers and the circumstances that force children to work.

NGO interventions and I.D. cards, while having a positive effect on reducing abuses against street children, suffer from several drawbacks, namely that they are not guarantees that police will stop mistreating children and that there are not enough NGO personnel to monitor every child to ensure that they do not face abuses by police. Most importantly, these initiatives, along with the police training curriculum, only allow for voluntary participation by police and do not mandate their cooperation, nor do they make police institutionally accountable for abuses. For these reasons, none of these efforts can be considered strong enough to actually eliminate or prevent police abuses against street children, and are no substitute for institutional and statutory measures aimed at stopping abuses and eliminating impunity.

CUSTODIAL DEATHS, IMPUNITY, AND THE NEED FOR REFORMS

I remember a case when I was DIG [Deputy Inspector General Police] CID [Crime Investigation Department] in Orissa of an Inspector of Orissa Police posted in Karaput district who brutally kicked to death in the police station a bright school boy when the latter at the time of interrogation had the temerity to ask him that under which section of the law he had the authority to misbehave or use third-degree methods during the investigation of a case. The Inspector's blood was up. He gave two hard kicks with his boots on the chest of the boy and two in the genitals. The poor boy gave a loud shriek and breathed his last. The Inspector now tried with the help of the police station staff to show it was a case of suicide by hanging the body from a nearby electric pole. The investigation done by the CID team sent from State Police Headquarters unraveled the truth. The Inspector was prosecuted u/s [under section] 302 IPC [Indian Penal Code] for murder. But the Sessions Judge in a mood of clemency exonerated the officer of the charge of murder and convicted him under section 323 IPC for causing hurt. But nemesis overtook him. He lost his life in a road accident. Custodial violence occurs because successive state and national governments have failed to implement any institutional reforms, such as the recommendations of the National Police Commission, to prohibit or prevent these abuses. Custodial abuse of street children is only part of the larger problem of custodial violence; the impunity enjoyed by police who torture and kill street children is shared by their counterparts in the security forces throughout India. This impunity occurs on three levels: the first is the impunity derived from the failure to register and acknowledge detentions, the second is a failure by authorities to investigate custodial crimes, and the third is a failure by authorities to prosecute custodial crimes.

Custodial deaths are consequences of the most extreme form of custodial violence. In its 1994-95 Annual Report, the National Human Rights Commission observed that torture was the predominant reason for custodial deaths when it recommended that India ratify the 1984 United Nations Convention on Torture and Other Forms of Cruel, Inhuman or Degrading Treatment or Punishment:

> *The Commission believes that a further, major step is required to proclaim the impermissibility, in our country, of custodial deaths, rape, torture, and other forms of cruel, inhuman and degrading treatment or punishment. Accordingly... the Chairperson recommended that in this 125th year of the birth of Mahatma Gandhi, the Republic could best pay tribute to the values he embodied by acceding to the 1984 Convention against Torture and Other Forms of Cruel, Inhuman and Degrading Treatment or Punishment... Referring to the prevalence of third-degree methods as a reason for custodial death, he asserted it was wrong to believe that investigations could not be successfully handled without recourse to such methods. Noting that a permissive approach towards the use of third-degree methods led to the violation of the fundamental rights of citizens, the Chairperson urged again that the use of third-degree methods and torture in investigation should be banned and eliminated.*

An NGO representative in Madras was more blunt about the reasons for impunity:

> *The lack of serious concern and political will to prevent custodial violence on the part of the state is one of the primary reasons for the increasing incidence of such crimes. As a general rule, even when a commission for Inquiry into such illegalities is ordered [this occurs] only when compelled by strong public and political reaction. The state ordering an independent inquiry suo moto, is rare... The indifferent attitude of higher echelons of Government to serious lapses on the part of police personnel at lower levels amounts to abetting illegality and emboldening the latter to continue indulging such atrocities. In such a "permissive" atmosphere, it is hardly surprising that the police feel no sense of accountability to the public for its misdeeds.*

In the case of custodial abuses, state governments, if the officers involved were state police, are responsible for initiating an investigation into the incident as if it were a criminal offence. Generally, the state orders an investigation only after media coverage or public protests. But even when an investigation is ordered, it is done by the police themselves, in some cases, by members of the same department or station in which the alleged abuse occurred, which is a major obstacle to adequate investigations and subsequent prosecutions or convictions, an issue discussed further below. Another obstacle is that medical examiners in India are employees of the police and are known as "police surgeons" who are subject to the same institutional pressures and biases as investigating officers. Consequently, investigations may not be reliable, and if the case proceeds to a judicial magistrate, the evidence may not be thorough or accurate enough to warrant a conviction; or as one former police surgeon told us, "Some police surgeons are `real' police surgeons, they do whatever the police tell them."

In a case in point, police initially said that thirteen-year-old Satish Kumar, who died in police custody on June 11, 1994, was never in custody. A report in the New Delhi-based Indian Express and the protests of the local community prompted the

People's Union for Civil Liberties in Tamil Nadu (PUCL-TN), a prominent Indian human rights organization, and the Campaign against Child Labour (CACL), an organization working to eliminate child labor, to conduct a fact-finding investigation into his death.

According to their report, Satish Kumar was employed by a tailor, Vijay Kumar, in his shop in the Mylapore area of Madras. On June 8, 1994, Satish skipped work to go to a movie. On his way home, the staff of an electronics shop called Trillions and Trillions caught Satish and accused him of stealing. Babu, a friend of Satish's brother Senthil, told the fact-finding team:

> *A small boy came and told me that Senthil's brother had been caught by the shop staff of Trillions and Trillions. I immediately went there. Satish Kumar was tied up and kept in a corner of the shop near the cash counter. I asked the shop person what had happened and why they had kept the boy inside. They said he had stolen some watches from the shop and he had already stolen some video games from this shop before. My brother-in-law called the boy and asked him what he had done. He said he had picked up some fancy watches from the shop which had scattered down [fallen down]. My brother-in-law gave him one slap and chastised him for shaming his parents' name. I asked the shop persons to release this boy since he belonged to our area. Instead they rang up the police, saying they were doing it to scare the boy. The shop staff told us not to bother since they would release him soon. I came back thinking they would release Satish Kumar. I did not meet Senthil that day, so I told him the next morning.*

No one had contact or knew the whereabouts of Satish until the next day, June 9, 1994, when a boy, Raju, told Satish's father, Kapali, that his son was in the police station. Raju had gone to the station to give food to another person detained in the station. At approximately 9:15 a.m., Kapali went to the police station to see his son and talk to the police. Kapali told the fact-finding team:

At that time my son came and cried to me. Then I asked the constable what had happened and why had they caught him. The policeman said that my son had stolen 5,000 rupees [$142.86] worth of articles from a fancy shop named Trillions and Trillions, together with a few other boys. They could not catch all the boys and only Satish Kumar got caught. The policeman said the boys had stolen some watches, video games, electronic goods, etc... He asked me to pay 2,000 rupees [$57.14] for the release of my son. When I asked my son what he did, he told me that some other boys might have taken something from the shop and instead he got caught. He told me he did not steal anything. I saw my son in lungi [a garment, similar to a sarong] and shirt and he was crying in pain. He said he was caught by the shop manager, Muthukrishnan, and handed over to the police. I told the policeman that if the boy had really done something wrong, they should leave him in the juvenile home because I did not have such a big amount to pay. But the policeman said, " If you have money come, otherwise we will look after him." So I came back home.

Later that day, two policemen came to Kapali's house with Satish Kumar to search for the stolen goods. Kapali told the fact-finding team that the police asked him whether any stolen items were in the house and that Satish was only wearing a lungi and his hands were tied with a rope. The police found a small penknife and a keychain on Satish's person, which they confiscated. According to Kapali, the police kept on pushing and threatening Satish which caused him to cry. Kapali said:

My son started weeping and said he did not have anything else. I asked the policemen why they were taking him back when no stolen goods were found. They told me to shut up and that they knew how to take care of my son.

That same afternoon, Kapali went to Satish Kumar's employer, Vijay Kumar, and told him that Satish Kumar was in the police station and that the police had demanded 2,000 rupees for his release. As a result of this, Vijay Kumar went to the police station at approximately 8:00 p.m. to see Satish Kumar and speak to the police. Vijay Kumar told the fact-finding team:

> *Thursday evening at eight, I went with another person to the Mylapore police station and met Sub-Inspector [SI] Gopinath. I saw Satish crying and asking me to release him. I requested the SI to reduce the amount [of the bribe] since they [Satish Kumar's family] were very poor people. The SI asked me to pay 500 rupees [$14.28]. Satish Kumar then requested me to pay 500 rupees and take him out and to deduct the amount from his salary. I noticed that Satish had been beaten up and he was crying in pain. Then I brought some tiffin [food] and gave it to him. I informed his father of the matter. But he said he did not have the money and if the boy had really done something wrong, he could be sent to the juvenile home for some time.*

During Satish Kumar's detention, he was severely beaten and kicked by police officers. This was alleged by Ravi, a seventeen-year-old boy, who was detained in the police station at the same time in relation to another case of theft. Ravi told the fact-finding team that he and four other boys (Venkatesan, Kannan, Ranjit, and Madhukar) were apprehended by the police and detained for fifteen days. He described what he saw in the police station:

> *On the evening of June 8, 1994, I saw this boy, Satish Kumar, being brought by the policemen to the station. The police usually beat us every day [He showed some open injuries on his hands]. Like that they beat Satish Kumar. Again on June 10, they took Satish Kumar into the SI's room and beat him severely. We could hear only the voice of the boy who was screaming loudly and crying. After sometime they brought Satish out and gave us all some iddlies [steamed rice cakes] to eat. We all sat together (including Satish) and had the food. After some time, we saw the boy [Satish] vomiting the food with blood. We called the policemen and told them. In front of us, a policeman immediately kicked the boy in the stomach with his boots. I saw the boy's eyes*

becoming yellow. Immediately the police shoved us into the lock-up. Afterwards, I do not know what happened to the boy.

According to the fact-finding report, the statements of the other three boys, Venkatesan, Kannan, Madhukar, and Ranjit were published in the June 22, 1994 issue of the Madras-based magazine Junior Vikatan. All of these boys were in custody from May 31, 1994 to June 11, 1994, the same day that Satish Kumar died.

According to Ranjit's statement:

Inspector Krishnamurthy and Sub-Inspector Gopinath beat Satish Kumar repeatedly with a big causarina [a type of wood] stick, "This is hockey style. How is it?" asked SI Gopinath, laughing. At twelve o'clock, they brought Satish Kumar to the lock-up, and Satish asked for water. The Inspector warned us not to give him water. After some time, Satish Kumar started vomiting blood. They immediately took him out. When some policemen asked for Satish Kumar, SI Gopinath said he had gone home. They also threatened me, "Pay ten thousand rupees [$285.71] or you will also vomit blood like Satish Kumar."

Venkatesan confirmed this, and said:

In front of me, SI Gopinath asked my mother to pay 20,000 rupees [$571.42] for my release. The whole night my mother stayed in the police station. Under the influence of liquor, SI Gopinath shouted at my mother, "If you don't have the money, then send me your daughters." My mother kept quiet, weeping to herself. The next day the police grabbed all the household articles and materials from my father's vulcanizing shop. In front of me, they hit my father and mother for money. They also grabbed my mother's one-fourth sovereign [gold] ring.

Kannan told the fact-finding team:

They [police] beat my brother and father for money, so that my father gave 1,000 rupees [$28.57]. They told my *father, "That is not enough, sell the cattle and bring money, otherwise we will not leave your son alive." Poor Satish Kumar was crying all the time saying, "I did not steal, I did not steal."*

The fact-finding team reported Madhukar's statement to the magazine:

Among the boys, they hit me severely and asked me to name the pawnbroker's shop where I had sold jewels. I refused to tell any shop's name. Afterwards they took my mother to my native village of Nugambal. On the way, they had some liquor and hit my mother. Due to the death of Satish, they remanded us to jail in a hurry. We were caught by the police ten days ago, but we were asked to tell the magistrate we were only caught the day before, otherwise we would have to meet the same fate as Satish.

Satish Kumar allegedly died in the early morning of June 11, 1994. According to the fact-finding report, earlier that evening an auto-rickshaw driver, C. Srinivasan, was asked by Sub-Inspector Gopinath to drive him around. Srinivasan initially refused, but he was threatened by Gopinath, two other policemen, and a man named Antony. He took these four people in his auto and told the fact-finding team what happened:

First we went to a slum in front of Stella Maris College. Antony showed the police the houses of some of his relatives sought by the police. Then they brought into the auto another man, about twenty-five years of age. I was asked to proceed to Mylapore and drop him at the police station. Then we again went to Visalatchi Thottam [the name of the slum]. From there the constables brought another man, aged around thirty-five, and pushed him into the auto. Again we dropped him at Mylapore PS [police station]. Then SI Gopinath and a constable asked me to drive to Hotel Samco at Alwarpet. The hotel was closed. SI Gopinath asked me to proceed to Hotel Select. SI Gopinath and the other constable had drinks at the hotel. The constable remained there. SI Gopinath asked me to take him to his house at Kottur. At this point the *meter showed 67.40 rupees [$1.93]. Gopinath said the fare would be paid at the police station the next day. Then I came back to Luz Corner.*

After fifteen minutes, about 1:30 a.m., early on Saturday, June 11, 1994, the two constables attached to Mylapore PS asked me to come along with them. I went with them to C.I.T. Colony [a housing project]. There were two constables there on patrol duty. They asked the patrol constables to come along, but they refused. Then we went to Srinivasapuram police quarters to call somebody, but no one came. They asked me to come to Triplicane, but since there wasn't sufficient petrol in my auto, I refused to go. They even called me to come to Bazaar Road. Again I refused. Then I dropped them at Mylapore PS.

While I was waiting for the fare, I had gone to the rear side of the police station. I heard somebody crying in pain. When I enquired about this with the constable, he said a boy was suffering from stomach pain, diarrhoea, and vomiting. I requested them to admit the boy to a hospital. The constable said permission from higher officials was required for that. They asked me to take him to a hospital, but I refused to take this risk. Then they asked me to take him to his house. At first I did not agree, but when they said they would also accompany me, I agreed to take the boy.

The boy, I noticed, could not walk. The constables had to lift him and drag him into the auto [rickshaw]. Two constables accompanied the boy in the auto. When we reached Kapali Thottam [Satish Kumar's neighborhood], they stopped in front of the boy's house. The three of us carried the boy out and laid him on a cycle-rickshaw we found nearby. Then I dropped them at the station again. They too told me to come the next morning for the fare. The next day they only gave me thirty rupees and threateningly asked me to leave.

A woman who lived in Kapali Thottam, Rajam, saw the driver and the two constables transporting Satish Kumar to the empty rickshaw. She told the fact-finding team:

I went to take some water from the outside [hand] pump. It would have been around 2:30 [a.m.]. It was dark. I saw an auto coming. Three persons from it carried a small boy and laid him on a rickshaw nearby and went off. Then the rickshaw man came and asked the boy to get up. The boy woke up and crawled to an auto just opposite the rickshaw and lay down inside it. I thought someone was not feeling well. I could not recognize the face of the boy because it was dark. Afterwards, I went inside and left for work early morning. That is all I know. When I came from work, I saw the boy's mother crying and came to know about this incident and told them what I had witnessed.

The owner of the cycle-rickshaw confirmed to the fact-finding team that he found Satish in his rickshaw at around 2:30 a.m. and asked Satish to move so that he could sleep. According to the fact-finding report, Satish woke up and crawled to a nearby rickshaw. At approximately 5:45 a.m., an unidentified woman told Satish Kumar's parents that their son was unconscious and lying outside. Kapali, Satish's father told the fact-finding team:

I immediately rushed down and saw Satish. His face was changed, his eyes were yellowish and he had some swelling underneath the stomach. I rushed him to Royapettah Government Hospital. The doctors took some time to respond to us. When the doctor examined Satish, he said that the boy had been dead for at least three hours. Then the body was taken for post-mortem.

The state government initially suspended four police officers, including Inspector Krishnamurthy, and then prosecuted them, but on February 15, 1996, all four officers were acquitted of any wrongdoing. The Hindu (Madras edition), a Madras-based national daily, described the verdict:

The Magistrate in his order said that it was clear from the report of the Forensic Department that the boy, Satish Kumar, had died of acute dehydration and there were no marks on his body to indicate that he was subjected to violence. There was lack of evidence to prove the guilt of the accused beyond a reasonable doubt, he pointed out and acquitted all the four accused, Krishnamurthy, Inspector, Gopinath, Sub-Inspector, and

> *Karuppaswamy Pandian and Jayabalan, Grade I constables.*

In response to widespread reports of human rights abuses throughout India, in 1993, the Congress (I) government created the National Human Rights Commission under the Protection of Human Rights Act of 1993. On December 14, 1993, the commission ordered all the State Governments and Union Territories to direct all district magistrates or superintendents of police to submit a report in any case of custodial death or custodial rape to the commission within twenty-four hours of the incident. The commission said that a failure to do so would "lead to a presumption by the Commission that an effort was being made to suppress knowledge of the incident." The effort has not been entirely effective, as the commission reported:

> *In response to these instructions and from the reports received, it appears that a keener sense of responsibility is being created, but much remains to be done to consolidate it.*

The commission does not have an independent investigative apparatus, but must rely on other government bodies and personnel to investigate cases of abuse. It does have the power to compel testimony as in a civil court, but statements made to the commission are not admissible in a trial. Moreover, the commission's decisions are non-binding and its findings are only recommendations. State governments and union territories have discretion to send reports to it but are not obligated to do so. For these reasons the commission relies on press reports and submissions by victims, lawyers, nongovernmental organizations, and state legal aid boards to provide information on cases of alleged abuse. Many cases of abuse go unreported because the victim is intimidated by police, unaware of how to complain, or unwilling to lodge a complaint. There are frequently no press reports of such incidents and organizations do not know about the allegations and cannot file complaints on the victims' behalf. As a result, the number of complaints is far less than the actual number of incidents of custodial abuse. Finally, the commission's investigations, by mandate, have a statute of limitation of one year from the time the alleged abuse occurred;

therefore, the commission is unable to initiate any investigation into incidents that are more than one year old although once initiated, investigations are not curtailed by any time limit). The most recent statistics and statements available from the commission, illustrate the problem of not having a truly independent investigative body. In its 1994-95 Annual Report, the commission reported that there were 1,660 "particularly grave cases" which the commission investigated. The commission noted:

> *It will be seen that 111 of these cases relate to death in police custody, fifty-one to death in judicial custody and nine to death while in the custody of other State agencies (the Armed Forces or the Forest Department). It will also be seen that 497 cases relate to allegations of various forms of police excesses, including the use of torture or third-degree methods in interrogation, while 114 cases allege illegal detention... While the cases relating to custodial death and rape invariably originated in reports from State agencies themselves... The other cases were generally based on complaints by those who were themselves victims of ill-treatment, or those representing them.*

On September 16, 1996, the commission reported that there were 444 reported deaths in custody throughout India from April 1995 to March 1996, almost triple the number of custodial deaths reported over the same period in 1994 to 1995. But the commission attributed this increase to "a greater honesty in reporting incidents" as opposed to an actual increase in custodial deaths. The commission said in its 1994-95 Annual Report that "the Commission is of the view that instances of custodial death and rape are now generally being reported to it, and not being covered-up..." which does not adequately explain how there could have been a three-fold increase in the number of custodial deaths in 1995-96, if the commission believed that custodial deaths were properly reported in 1994-95, and there was no real increase in custodial deaths in 1995-96.

The commission has frequently recommended payment of compensation to victims or victims' families in cases of state abuse. According to the Supreme Court of India, compensation is provided under Article 32 of the Indian Constitution and was made precedent in the case Nilabati Behara v. State of Orissa, 1993. But these recommendations are non-binding and cannot be enforced by the commission. Compensation can only be recommended after alleged abuses have been investigated and payment only occurs after the recommendation is agreed to by the state government. Compensation is not a measure designed to prevent abuses but a measure to alleviate the suffering of victims and their families.

The commission has also recommended prosecutions of abusers, but these recommendations are also non-binding. The case of Raja Murugan, a fifteen-year-old boy who died in police custody in the state of Tamil Nadu on January 30, 1994, provides an example of a successful intervention by the commission.

On February 2, 1994, the Tamil Nadu Legal Aid Board sent a letter to the commission notifying it that a newspaper report in The Hindu stated that Raja had disappeared after being taken into police custody. Upon receiving the letter, the commission issued a notice to the Hosur Police Station requiring it to provide the details of the incident. K. Radhakrishnan, Superintendent of Police (SP), responded to the commission's request by letter.

According to police, Raja was arrested by the Hosur police on October 10, 1993 and sent to the observation home at Dharmapuri for his involvement in the theft of unspecified items worth 765 rupees ($21.86). Raja escaped from the observation home on November 22, 1993 at approximately 3:00 a.m. Consequently, a magistrate in Hosur issued a warrant for the arrest and production (to the court) of Raja on January 18, 1994.

On January 28, 1994 at approximately 7:30 p.m., Raja was brought to the Hosur Police Station voluntarily by his brother and presented to Sub-inspector Muthamiah Muthalvan. Raja was not immediately sent to an observation home, but kept in police custody. On January 30 at approximately 3:30 p.m., Venkatammal, a suspect who was being interrogated by police in connection with a case of female infanticide, went to the toilet where he discovered Raja's body hanging from the ceiling. Sub-inspector Muthalvan then transported the body to a car and drove it to an unknown location. Muthalvan returned to police station at approximately 11:00 a.m. on January 31, 1994.

On the same day, Raja's father, Muniappan, submitted a written complaint to the Hosur Sub-collector alleging that his son was missing from the police station and asking that his son be found and returned to him. The sub-collector forwarded the request to Hosur's assistant superintendent of police who conducted an informal inquiry into the whereabouts of Raja. The inquiry revealed that Raja had committed suicide on January 30, 1994 by hanging himself and that Sub-inspector Muthalvan had disposed of the body. Based on the findings, Muthalvan and constables Duriasamy and Sharief were suspended, a missing persons case was registered, and a formal investigation was initiated.

Initially Muthalvan claimed that Raja had tried to hang himself and when police were transporting him to the hospital he jumped out of the car and escaped, but the formal investigation revealed that Raja had died of hanging in the police station and that Muthalvan along with constables Joseph and Ganesan took the body to a nearby wooded area, built a pyre, doused the body with gasoline and cremated it. This resulted in the arrest of Muthalvan and the case was transferred to the State Crime Branch CID (Crime Investigation Department) on February 5, 1994. The investigations led to the prosecutions of Muthalvan, Duriasamy and Sharief for illegally disposing of Murugan's body, and trying to conceal his death and cremation from the authorities. The National Human Rights Commission in a written decision dated May 5, 1994 stated:

> *In view of the fact that the prosecution had been ordered, the Commission expects that the matter may be pursued at their end in accordance with law. No further action by the Commission in that regard is necessary except keeping track of further development of the matter in Court.*

This seems to be a case where compensation should be paid to the next of kin of the deceased. The Commission is of the view that in the facts and circumstances appearing in the papers, compensation of Rs.50000/-[$1428.57] without prejudice to any other claim, may be paid within one month from now. The Commission would expect a report of compliance within that period. Send a copy of this order to the Secretary, Tamil Nadu State Legal Aid & Advice Board. The Commission would like to express commendation over the interest taken by the Tamil Nadu State Legal Aid & Advice Board in protecting the human rights in the area.

In a letter dated, August 23, 1994, the Krishnagiri District Legal Aid and Advice Committee notified the Tamil Nadu State Legal Aid and Advice Board that the state government had paid the parents of Raju the 50,000 rupees in compensation. The police officers involved confessed to the charges and were prosecuted.

The commission has strongly urged that the recommendations of the National Police Commission be implemented, as it stated in its 1994-1995 Annual Report:

> *The commission has recommended on more than one occasion that it is essential to revitalize the role of the civilian administration if the rule of law is to be effectively revived... [I]n almost all parts of the country there is a clear and increasing need to reform the police itself, to retrain and reorganize it and to restore to it the skills and the integrity that country so desperately needs if the function of preserving law and order is to be improved. It is for this reason that the Commission recommends that serious action be taken on the Report of the Police Reforms Commission [The National Police Commission] which in 1979, made a series of proposals that remain highly pertinent today... Without determined action being taken on that report, the Commission fears that the daily decisions of the Courts, no less than its own recommendations in respect of police high-handedness, will remain palliatives, the illness itself remaining unchecked.*

Constituted in 1979, the National Police Commission was originally charged with investigating abuses committed by the police during the Emergency of 1975, when then Prime Minister Indira Gandhi suspended the Constitution and declared a state of emergency. The suspension was followed by widespread arrests of opposition party members and massive human rights abuses by law enforcement agencies. The commission was formed to study the problem of police excesses and functioning and make recommendations to the central government. It investigated 76,444 complaints to police from the states of Harayana, Himachal Pradesh, Jammu and Kashmir, Karnataka, Madhya Pradesh, Maharashtra, Manipur, Meghalaya, Nagaland, Punjab, Rajasthan, Tamil Nadu, Uttar Pradesh, and Delhi. Based on their findings, the commission reported that deficiencies in the investigation of police abuse had led to an environment of impunity. In particular, the commission noted that inquiry officers would not properly investigate allegations of police abuse because they felt any negative findings would stigmatize the police, that frequent exposure of abuse would make the investigating officer unpopular with his peers, that investigation of otherwise professionally competent officers would unnecessarily harm those officers, that an already corrupt or abusive investigator does not wish to expose other officers' actions, that investigators do not take the time to conduct a thorough investigation, and that political pressure would undermine serious investigations.

The commission made specific recommendations to address these problems, including the formation of "complaint cells" to deal with police abuses. The first level of inquiry was to be a special complaint cell to be headed by a deputy superintendent of police with two or three inspectors and support staff to investigate complaints of police misconduct on a district level. A second cell was to be created to monitor the first at a multi-district level under a Range Inspector, a police officer with jurisdiction over several districts. A third cell, called the "police complaints board," was recommended to monitor and investigate police abuses at the state level.

The commission recommended a fourth body to be empowered to oversee the functioning of the other complaint boards. This body was to be constituted of police and qualified civilians, in order to provide civilian monitoring. This board would also be in charge of appointing members to the police complaints board.

In addition to the police monitoring and investigation of alleged abuses, the commission recommended that a mandatory judicial inquiry should take place in several instances, including alleged rape in custody and a death or "grievous hurt" in police custody. Grievous hurt was defined as castration, permanent blindness or deafness, fractures, dislocations, or permanent injury to any limb.

Senior police officers concerned about custodial abuse have endorsed the reforms. In 1994, Additional Director General of the Madras Police, R.K. Raghavan described the National Police Commission's recommendations as "[p]erhaps the most significant and practical guidelines in the area [of custodial abuse]..."

However, these recommendations have never been implemented, largely due to the lack of will on the part of India's national and state governments to do so. As recently as February 15, 1996, the chief minister of West Bengal, Jyoti Basu, stated that a mandatory judicial inquiry in the case of a custodial death would not be implemented on the grounds that there was no need for an inquiry because "beating or torture were not responsible for all such incidents." Ironically, the chief minister's decision was released on the same day that four policemen were acquitted in Madras for the death of Satish Kumar.

Another factor that was not addressed by the National Police Commission, but that contributes to environment of impunity is the fact that even if a complaint of abuse is registered, it rarely leads to prosecution or conviction of police officers. As a result, many observers, including the Law Commission of India, have advocated reforms to Indian penal law in order to facilitate prosecution of police officers. In a 1995 study on custodial deaths in Andhra Pradesh, the Andhra Pradesh Civil Liberties Committee (APCLC) commented:

> *The Supreme Court and the Law Commission have, in the past, acknowledged the special nature of custodial violence. The Supreme Court said in Ramsagar Yadav's*

case (1985) that since there can be no independent witnesses in a case of custodial violence, the onus of proof must be shifted to the policemen. The same opinion was reiterated by the Supreme Court in the case of Bhagwan Singh (1992). The Law Commission expressed the same opinion in its 113th report. Though a decade has passed since then, no action has been initiated by the Government to legislate this recommendation.

The recommendation the Law Commission made to facilitate prosecution of police officers was to amend the Indian Evidence Act by inserting Section 114B, which states:

(1) In a prosecution (of a police officer) for an offence constituted by an act alleged to have caused bodily injury to a person, if there is evidence that the injury was caused during the period when that person was in the custody of the police, the court may presume that the injury was caused by the police officer having custody of that person during that period.

(2) The Court, in deciding whether or not it should draw a presumption under sub-section (1), shall have regard to all the relevant circumstances, including, in particular, (a) the period of custody, (b) any statement made by the victim as to how the injuries were received, being a statement admissible in evidence, (c) the evidence of any medical practitioner who might have examined the victim's statement or attempted to record it.

In the absence of reforms to Indian law, prosecutions are rare, as the Andhra Pradesh Civil Liberties Committee reported:

Prosecutions are not being undertaken even under ordinary penal law, as they can very well be without any amendment of the law. Of the present 211 cases [of custodial deaths documented in the report], criminal prosecution has been launched in not more than 10 cases. To our knowledge, only three of them... have resulted in conviction at a trial court.

It is significant that of the three cases that resulted in conviction, the most recent case occurred in 1986. This means that 162 incidents of custodial death have occurred between 1986 and 1995 in Andhra Pradesh alone which have not resulted in prosecution of police officers. Fourteen of these 162 custodial deaths involved children. The following cases represent a sample of those incidents, as reported by the committee that took place between 1990 and 1994:

Solanki Maruti-Central Crime Station, Hyderabad, October 26, 1994

Solanki Maruti, a young man who belonged to an itinerant community of iron smiths, was taken into custody in the village of Bothi of Bhokar Taluk, Nanded district, Maharashtra, where he had gone to work on the laying of a road, in April 1994. He was arrested on the suspicion that he was making sharp nails for the use of highway robbers. For three months he and another eleven youths were detained illegally and beaten at Mamda police station, and later for another three months at the Central Crime Station in Hyderabad. When Maruti's condition deteriorated, the twelve youths were taken to the court at Nirmal, where the magistrate remanded them to jail without even looking at the prisoners. They were all then taken in a police van to the Nizamabad district jail, but Maruti died on the way. Police said he died of cardiac arrest.

Koora Narayana-Kosgi Police Station, Mahbubnagar District, Andhra Pradesh, September 6, 1994

Koora Narayana, a "head-load" worker with a criminal record, Narayana and five other youths were taken into custody on September 1 for a suspected theft in a grocery store. The parents of four of the children paid 1,000 rupees each to the police and got their sons released. Narayana and Yella Reddy, who remained, were beaten with sticks and given electric shocks for five days. Narayana died in the police station on September 6. Police said he died of an epileptic fit.

Kachanapalli Outpost-Khammam District, Andhra Pradesh, August 16, 1994

Orusu Narasamma of Kachanapalli was taken into custody on the evening of August 16 as she got off a bus at her village.

Police suspected her of selling illicit liquor. She had her one-month-old child in her arms. The mother was continuously beaten by the police until she reached the outpost, and was beaten further at the outpost. As she cringed and begged the police not to beat her, some of the blows hit the child and the child died in the mother's arms. Police disclaimed responsibility for the child's death.

Kakkarla Sudhakar Goud-Central Crime Station, Warangal, Warangal District, Andhra Pradesh, June 22, 1994.

Kakkarla Sudhakar Goud, an unemployed rural youth, was suspected of a theft in his own brother's house by the police. Goud knew that the police suspected him, so on June 15, he went with his brother to the police station and presented himself to the authorities. The police detained him and beat him regularly till he died on June 22. The police then called his brother, gave him the dead body and told him to tell everyone that his brother had come home and committed suicide. The police claimed that he committed suicide in his home after being released from custody.

Sudhakar-Yemmiganur Police Station, Kurnool District, Andhra Pradesh, November 19, 1993

Sudhakar, a fifteen-year-old rickshaw puller, was taken into custody on the night of November 10, after a customer who was traveling in Sudhakar's rickshaw saw some policemen coming and jumped out and ran away. The policemen caught hold of Sudhakar and took him into custody to question him about the customer. After four days of illegal custody and torture, the unconscious Sudhakar was sent home in another rickshaw on November 14. He never regained consciousness and died on November 19. Police said they let him off and he died later of natural causes.

Pochamma-Pochampally Police Station, Nalgonda District, Andhra Pradesh, September 16, 1993

Pochamma, a fifteen-year-old girl, was taken into custody along with her mother, Lachammma on September 14 because the police suspected they had links with "radicals." Both were beaten very badly, and when Pochamma complained of pain, she was taken to a local doctor by the police, who advised that she should be taken to Hyderabad. She died in a hospital at Hyderabad on September 16. The post-mortem report said she died of internal bleeding. Police said she died of natural causes.

Habibnagar Police Station-Habibnagar, Hyderabad, September 7, 1993

Sophia, a member of an itinerant community, who was at that time staying in Hyderabad, was arrested along with her mother, Radhabai, on suspicion of having committed a theft while they were staying at Warangal. When the Warangal police came to Hyderabad to arrest her, the whole community rebelled and beat up the police. The local police then entered the scene. When they took Sophia along with her five-month-old child to a police station on September 6, the inspector beat and kicked Sophia very badly. The blows struck the child who was in the mother's arms. As a result of the beating, the child fell and died. The police denied responsibility for the child's death.

K. Bhaskar-Railway Police Station, Kazipet, Warangal District, Andhra Pradesh, June 8, 1993

On the morning of June 7, K. Bhaskar, a thirteen-year-old student and talented athlete, went to the Kazipet Railway Stadium to practice, but he found the stadium locked and the RPF guarding it. When he tried to defy them and enter, they beat him. Bhaskar playfully picked up the bag of one of the constables and ran away.

Later, he sent word that he would return the bag, but police said it was Bhaskar they wanted and not the bag. On the evening of June 8, the railway policemen found Bhaskar and took him into custody. That very night his dead body was found on the railway tracks in the goods yard. In a second post-mortem examination conducted on public demand, it was found that the body had injuries apparently caused by beating and kicking. The police claimed his death was an accident or suicide.

Kanne Sammaiah-Mahadevpur Police Station, Karimnagar District, Andhra Pradesh, June 5, 1993

Kanne Sammaiah, an unemployed youth, was involved in a public quarrel with another youth, Penta Bapu, on June 3. Both were taken into custody by the police. Bapu was released but Sammaiah was not. His dead body was found, floating in the Godavari river. Police claimed that he was never in custody.

Babu Rao-Matwada Police Station, Warangal, Warangal District, Andhra Pradesh, January 17, 1993

On January 10, 1993, Babu Rao, an unemployed youth, had an altercation in the street, on behalf of a friend, with a man whom he did not know to be a plainclothes policeman. Babu Rao beat the man. When he learned that the man was a policeman, he hid. On January 13, his relatives took him to the policestation and handed him over to the police. The police beat him severely, for four days. They took him in an unconscious state to a hospital on January 17 and he died in the hospital that same day. Police claimed that he died a natural death.

Ramavath Badya Naik-Gurajala Police Station, Guntur District, Andhra Pradesh, September 26, 1992.

Ramavath Badya Naik, a tribal youth, was arrested on September 20 on suspicion of murdering his wife. He was tortured regularly for six days, and many contusions and cigarette burns were found on his body. He died on the morning of September 26. Police said he hanged himself in the lock-up.

Simhachalam-VIII Town Police Station, Vijayawada, Krishna District, Andhra Pradesh, July 26, 1991

Simhachalam, a thirteen-year-old picker of waste paper and old iron, was suspected by the police of being involved with a theft and taken into custody on July 20, along with another ragpicker, Sambaiah. Simhachalam was tortured very badly, with pins being stuck under his fingernails. He was repeatedly kicked in the stomach. The two were released on July 24, and Simhachalam, who was running a high fever by that time, died in the streets on July 26. Police said he died of natural causes after they released him.

Nelluri Babu Rao-Nagaram Police Station, Guntur District, Andhra Pradesh, February 19, 1990

Nelluri Babu Rao, a sixteen-year-old boy who made a living by pressing clothes, was taken into custody on February 10 on suspicion of theft. He was illegally detained and made to confess to several crimes while being tortured. He died in custody on the afternoon of February 19. Police said that he died of cardiac arrest.

No one has been prosecuted for any of these deaths. From January 4, 1994 to March 31, 1995, the most recent statistics which are available, the NationalHuman Rights Commission reviewed 152 cases of alleged custodial death. The commission determined that there was no wrongdoing by police in thirty-nine cases; decisions were pending in 107 cases; in three cases the commission recommended prosecution of police; and in two cases it recommended compensation.

The former Congress (I) government did not ratify the U.N. Convention against Torture. However, on June 6, 1996, India's fledgling United Front government announced in its platform that the Indian Penal Code, the Criminal Procedure Code and all other national laws "will be reviewed and amended to make their provisions consistent with the sanctity of human rights. The United Nations Convention on Torture will be adopted..." As of October 1996, these measures had not been implemented.

THE APPLICABLE LAWS

The arbitrary detention and physical abuse of children by police are prohibited under both international and national law. However, the Indian government has not abided by these standards.

International Laws

Arbitrary and illegal arrests and detention are forbidden by two basic international agreements to which India is a party, the International Covenant on Civil and Political Rights (ICCPR) and the Convention on the Rights of the Child. Illegal arrests and detentions are by definition "arbitrary"; such acts can also be arbitrary if not in conformity with international standards of human rights and procedural fairness, regardless of specific provisions of domestic law. Basic procedural rights of persons who are arrested include the right to know the reasons for arrest, the right to be brought promptly before a judge or other judicial officer following arrest, and the right to receive either a trial in a reasonable time of release. Victims of unlawful arrest also have an enforceable right to compensation.

The detention of children with adults is also specifically prohibited by these international agreements, in recognition of the special protection to which children are entitled.

According to the United Nations Convention against Torture and Other Forms of Cruel, Inhuman or Degrading Treatment or Punishment, torture is defined as:

> *...any act by which severe pain or suffering, whether physical or mental, is intentionally inflicted on a person for such purposes as obtaining from him or a third person information or a confession, punishing him for an act he or a third person has committed or is suspected of having committed, or intimidating or coercing him or a third person, or for any reason based on discrimination of any kind, when such pain or suffering is inflicted by or at the instigation of or with the consent or acquiescence of a public official or other person acting in an official capacity. It does not include pain or suffering only from, inherent in or incidental to lawful sanctions.*

Severe beatings of children by police are a form of torture and are prohibited by international standards. Torture is expressly prohibited in numerous international treaties and standards. The prohibition of torture can be considered customary international law, binding on all nations regardless of whether they are parties to the Convention against Torture. Even where physical and mental abuse does not cause severe pain or suffering, it may be prohibited as "cruel, inhuman or degrading treatment or punishment" under the International Covenant on Civil and Political Rights, the Convention on the Rights of the Child, and the Convention against Torture and

Other Forms of Cruel, Inhuman or Degrading Treatment or Punishment.

The Laws of India

Articles 21 and 22 of the Indian Constitution mandate that no one may be arbitrarily detained or arrested. Article 22 of the Indian Constitution and Sections 50, 56, 57, and 70 of the Code of Criminal Procedure specify that an arrested person must be told of the reason for his or her arrest, and must be presented before a magistrate within twenty-four hours, otherwise the detention is illegal.

To detain a person for a period greater than twenty-four hours, the police must obtain permission from a magistrate. In addition to these laws, Section 160 of the Code of Criminal Procedure states that neither males under the age of fifteen nor any women may be brought to a police station for questioning when a crime is investigated.

The Juvenile Justice Act was enacted in 1986 to address the treatment of juveniles by law enforcement officials. Sections 13 and 18 of the Juvenile Justice Act mandate that juveniles cannot be kept in a police station for more than twenty-four hours, and upon identification as a "neglected juvenile" or upon arrest (where the child is not released on bail) as a "delinquent juvenile," may not be remanded to a jail or police station, but must immediately be sent to an observation home or remand center. Juveniles charged with criminal offenses must be tried in juvenile courts and cannot be tried with adults. The act also mandates that arrested juveniles have the right to be informed of the charges against them, the right to remain silent, and the right to an attorney.

The Supreme Court has ruled in five decisions that Article 21 of the Indian constitution forbid torture, although the constitutional prohibition is not explicit. Section 24 of the Indian Evidence Act makes confessions made through "inducement, threat, or promise" inadmissible as evidence and sections 25 and 26 of the Indian Evidence Act make any confession to a police officer inadmissible unless it takes place in the presence of a magistrate. However, under section 27 of the Indian

Evidence Act, any evidence obtained by a police officer while a suspect is in custody is admissible in court. Torture by police is subject to criminal charges under the Indian Penal Code.

The Prevention of Corruption Act was enacted in 1988. Sections 7 and 11 forbid public servants to take money or property in discharge of official duties, outside of their normal remuneration. Section 13 of the Act considers any public servant habitually involved in corrupt practices to be guilty of "criminal misconduct." Corruption is a criminal offense in the Indian Penal Code. A beating used to propagate corruption constitutes a criminal offense under Section 329 of the code and calls for a prison term of up to ten years.

CONCLUSION

The detention, ill-treatment, and torture of street children by police in India has reached epidemic proportions. Torture has long been a routine part of police investigations, and despite widespread recognition of the problem, little has been done to address it. The victims typically represent the most vulnerable sectors of society: they are poor, members of low-caste groups or minorities, and have no political standing that would afford them protection from the lawlessness of the police. Street children, in addition, generally have no family members to intervene on their behalf.

Changing a police culture that not only tolerates but endorses torture is not easy. As a first step toward ending the abuse, the Indian government should implement all of the reforms of the National Police Commission, a step that is now at least fifteen years overdue. The recommendations of the commission include making judicial inquiries into cases of alleged rape, death, or grievous injury in police custody mandatory, and establishing investigative bodies whose members would include civilians as well as police and judicial authorities. Provisions prohibiting the detention of juveniles in police lock-ups should be strictly enforced, and a civilian review board comprised of former police, NGO representatives, judges, and lawyers should be established to monitor police stations. Complaints against law enforcement personnel should be promptly and thoroughly investigated by an independent agency with subpoena power and an adequately trained investigatory staff. This agency should be directly accessible to street children. Where the agency finds evidence of wrongdoing, prosecutions and trials should be pursued expeditiously.

These reforms will only work, however, if the state governments, for their part, agree to work with local NGOs and citizens' groups to monitor police behavior and enforce the law, and if the central government monitors the state governments' performance. No single agency can bring an end to police abuse. Most importantly, better police training and closer monitoring of police behavior must be linked to greater accountability, for as long as police feel assured of impunity, custodial violence will not end.

India must also change the laws that contribute to the problem. The Code of Criminal Procedure should be amended to require mandatory medical examinations and age verification at the time of detention. All laws relating to child labor as well as the Juvenile Justice Act should be revised to ensure that the implementation of both laws does not result in criminalizing children who are forced to work.

At the international level, the government of India should ratify the Convention Against Torture and Other Forms of Cruel, Inhuman and Degrading Treatment or Punishment, a pledge made by the current government of India in their platform. It should also invite the United Nations Special Rapporteur on Torture to India to investigate, and the U.N. Working Group on Arbitrary Detention to investigate, respectively, the torture and arbitrary detention of street children by police.

4

Government and Crime Against Children

Introduction

The problem of juvenile justice is, no doubt, one of tragic human interest so much so in fact that it is not only confined to this country alone but cuts across national boundaries. Juvenile delinquency laws are characterised by the feature that they prescribe many acts which are regarded as non-criminal if indulged by elder persons like drinking, smoking, viewing adult films or reading adult literature, etc. The extension of the concept of juvenile delinquency to wider limits has drawn adverse criticism on the ground that it is neither necessary nor desirable to use police and courts in private matters which can well be tackled by the family themselves.

The first legislation concerning children which came in 1850 was the Apprentice Act which provided that children in the age groups of ten to eighteen convicted by courts were intended to be provided with some vocational training which might help their rehabilitation. It was followed by the Reformatory Schools Act, 1897. The Indian Jail Committee (1919-1920) brought to the fore the vital need for fair trial and treatment for young offenders. Its recommendations prompted the enactment of the Children Act in Madras in 1920. This was followed by the Bengal and Bombay Acts in 1922 and 1924 respectively. The three pioneer statutes (i.e. Acts concerning Madras, Bengal and Bombay) were extensively amended between 1948 and 1959.

In 1960 at the second United Nations Congress on the Prevention of Crime and Treatment of Offenders at London, this issue was discussed and some therapeutic recommendations were adopted.

The Central enactment, the Children Act, 1960 was passed to cater to the heads of the Union Territories. To remove the same inherent lacunae of the above mentioned Act, the Children (Amendment) Act was passed in 1978. But the need of a uniform legislation regarding juvenile justice for the whole of the country had been expressed in various fora, including Parliament, but it could not be enacted on the ground that the subject matter of such legislation fell in the State List of the Constitution. To bring the operations of the juvenile justice system in the country in conformity with the UN Standard Minimum Rules for the Administration of Juvenile Justice, Parliament seems to have exercised its power under Article 253 of the Constitution read with Entry 14 of the Union List to make law for the whole of India to fulfill international obligations. On 22nd August, 1986, the Juvenile Justice Bill, 1986 was introduced in the Lok Sabha.

STATEMENT OF OBJECTS AND REASONS

A review of the working of the existing Children Acts would indicate that much greater attention is required to be given to children who may be found in situations of social maladjustment, delinquency or neglect. The justice system as available for adults is not considered suitable for being applied to juveniles. It is also necessary that a uniform juvenile justice system should be available throughout the country which should make adequate provision for dealing with all aspects in the changing social, cultural and economic situation in the country. There is also a need for larger involvement of informal systems and community based welfare agencies in the care, protection, treatment, development and rehabilitation of such juveniles.

In this context, the proposed legislation aims at achieving the following objectives:-

(i) to lay down a uniform legal framework for juvenile justice in the country so as to ensure that no child under any circumstances is lodged in a jail or a police lock-up. This is being ensured by establishing Juvenile Welfare Boards and Juvenile Courts;

(ii) to provide for a specialised approach towards the prevention and treatment of juvenile delinquency in its full range in keeping with the developmental needs of the child as found in any situation of social maladjustment;

(iii) to spell out the machinery and infrastructure required for the care, protection, treatment, development and rehabilitation of various categories of children coming within the purview of the juvenile justice system. This is proposed to be achieved by establishing observation homes, juvenile homes for neglected juveniles and special homes for delinquent juveniles;

(iv) to establish norms and standards for the administration of juvenile justice in terms of investigation and prosecution, adjudication and disposition and care, treatment and rehabilitation;

(v) to develop appropriate linkages and coordination between the formal system of juvenile justice and voluntary agencies engaged in the welfare of neglected or societally maladjusted children and to specifically define the areas of their responsibilities and roles;

(vi) to constitute special offences in relation to juveniles and provide for punishments therefore;

(vii) to bring the operation of the juvenile justice system in the country in conformity with the United Nations Standard Minimum Rules for the Administration of Juvenile Justice.

As its various provisions come into force in different parts of the country they would replace the corresponding laws on the subject, such as the Children Act, 1960 and other State enactments on the subject.

The Bill seeks to achieve the above objects.

ACT 53 OF 1986

The Juvenile Justice Bill, 1986 was passed by both the Houses of Parliament. After receiving the assent of the President it came on the Statute Book as the Juvenile Justice Act, 1986 (53 of 1986).

THE JUVENILE JUSTICE ACT, 1986

(53 of 1986)

[1st December, 1986]

An Act to provide for the care, protection, treatment, development and rehabilitation of neglected or delinquent juveniles and for the adjudication of certain matters relating to and disposition of, delinquent juveniles.

CHAPTER I

Preliminary

1. Short title, extent and commencement.:

(1) This Act may be called the Juvenile Justice Act, 1986.

(2) It extends to the whole of India except the State of Jammu and Kashmir.

(3) It shall come into force on such date as the Central Government may, by notification in the Official Gazette, appoint, and different dates may be appointed for different provisions of this Act and for different States.

2. Definitions.-In this Act, unless the context otherwise requires,-

(a) "begging" means-

(i) soliciting or receiving alms in a public place or entering into any private premises for the purposes of soliciting or receiving alms, whether under the pretense of singing, dancing, fortune-telling, performing tricks or selling articles or otherwise;

(ii) exposing or exhibiting, with the object of obtaining or extorting alms, any sore, wound, injury, deformity or disease, whether of himself or of any other person or of an animal;

(iii) allowing oneself to be used as an exhibit for the purpose of soliciting or receiving alms;

(b) "Board" means a Juvenile Welfare Board constituted under section 4;

(c) "brothel", "prostitute", "prostitution" and "public place" shall have the meanings respectively assigned to them in the Suppression of Immoral Traffic in Women and Girls Act, 1956 (104 of 1956);

(d) "competent authority" means, in relation to neglected Juveniles, a Board and, in relation to delinquent Juveniles, a Juvenile Court and where no such Board or Juvenile Court has been constituted, includes any court empowered under sub-section (2) of section 7 to exercise the powers conferred on a Board or Juvenile Court;

(e) "delinquent juvenile" means a juvenile who has been found to have committed an offence;

(f) "fit person" or "fit institution" means any person or institution (not being a police station or jail) found fit by the competent authority to receive and take care of a juvenile entrusted to his or its care and protection on the terms and conditions specified by the competent authority;

(g) "guardian" in relation to a juvenile, includes, any person who, in the opinion of the competent authority, having cognizance of any proceeding in relation to a juvenile, has, for the time being, the actual charge of, or control over, that juvenile;

(h) "juvenile" means a boy who has not attained the age of sixteen years or a girl who has not attained the age of eighteen years;

(i) "Juvenile Court" means a court constituted under section 5;

(j) "Juvenile home" means an institution established or certified by the State Government under section 9 as a juvenile home;

(k) "narcotic drug" and "psychotropic substance" shall have the meanings respectively assigned to them in the

Narcotic Drugs and Psychotropic Substances Act, 1985 (61 of 1985);

(l) "neglected juvenile" means a juvenile who-

(i) is found begging; or

(ii) is found without having any home or settled place of abode and without any ostensible means of subsistence and is destitute; or

(iii) has a parent or guardian who is unfit or incapacitated to exercise control over the juvenile; or

(iv) lives in a brothel or with a prostitute or frequently goes to any place used for the purpose of prostitution, or is found to associate with any prostitute or any other person who leads an immoral, drunken or depraved life; or

(v) who is being or is likely to be abused or exploited for immoral or illegal purposes or unconscionable gain;

(m) "observation home" means any institution or place established or recognised by the State Government under section 11 as an observation home;

(n) "offence" means an offence punishable under any law for the time being in force;

(o) "place of safety" means any place or institution (not being a police station or jail), the person in charge of which is willing temporarily to receive and take care of a juvenile and which, in the opinion of the competent authority may be a place of safety for the juvenile;

(p) "prescribed" means prescribed by rules made under this Act;

(q) "probation officer" means an officer appointed as a probation officer under this Act or under the Probation of Offenders Act, 1958 (20 of 1958);

(r) "special home" means an institution established or certified by the State Government under section 10;

(s) "supervision", in relation to a juvenile placed under the care of any parent, guardian, or other fit person or fit institution under this Act, means the supervision of that juvenile by a probation officer for the purpose of ensuring that the juvenile is properly looked after and that the conditions imposed by the competent authority are complied with;

(t) all words and expressions used but not defined in this Act and defined in the Code of Criminal Procedure, 1973 (2 of 1974), shall have the meanings respectively assigned to them in that Code.

3. Continuation of inquiry in respect of juvenile who has ceased to be a juvenile.-Where an inquiry has been initiated against a juvenile and during the course of such inquiry the juvenile ceases to be such, then, notwithstanding anything contained in this Act or in any other law for the time being in force, the inquiry may be continued and orders may be made in respect of such person if such person had continued to be a juvenile.

CHAPTER II

Competent Authorities and Institutions for Juveniles

4. Juvenile Welfare Boards:

(1) The State Government may, by notification in the Official Gazette, constitute for any area specified in the notification, one or more Juvenile Welfare Boards for exercising the powers and discharging the duties conferred or imposed on such Board in relation to neglected juveniles under this Act.

(2) A Board shall consist of a Chairman and such other members as the State Government thinks fit to appoint, of whom not less than one shall be a woman; and every such member shall be vested with the powers of a Magistrate under the Code of Criminal Procedure, 1973 (2 of 1974).

(3) The Board shall function as a Bench of Magistrates and shall have the powers conferred by the Code of Criminal Procedure, 1973 (2 of 1974), on a Metropolitan Magistrate

or, as the case may be, a Judicial Magistrate of the first class.

5. Juvenile Courts.-

(1) Notwithstanding anything contained in the Code of Criminal Procedure, 1973 (2 of 1974), the State Government may, by notification in the Official Gazette, constitute for any area specified in the notification, one or more Juvenile Courts for exercising the powers and discharging the duties conferred or imposed on such court in relation to delinquent juveniles under this Act.

(2) A Juvenile Court shall consist of such number of Metropolitan Magistrates or Judicial Magistrates of the first class, as the case may be, forming a Bench as the State Government thinks fit to appoint, of whom one shall be designated as the Principal Magistrate; and every such Bench shall have the powersconferred by the Code of Criminal Procedure, 1973 (2 of 1974), on a Metropolitan Magistrate or, as the case may be, a Judicial Magistrate of the first class.

(3) Every Juvenile Court shall be assisted by a panel of two honorary social workers possessing such qualifications as may be prescribed, of whom at least one shall be a woman, and such panel shall be appointed by the State Government.

6. Procedure, etc. in relation to Boards and Juvenile Courts.-

(1) In the event of any difference of opinion among the members of a Board or among the Magistrates of a Juvenile Court, the opinion of the majority shall prevail, but where there is no such majority, the opinion of the Chairman or of the Principal Magistrate, as the case may be, shall prevail.

(2) A Board or Juvenile Court may act notwithstanding the absence of any member of the Board or, as the case may be, any Magistrate of the Juvenile Court, and no order made by the Board or Juvenile Court shall be invalid by reason only of the absence of any member or Magistrate, as the case may be, during any stage of the proceeding.

(3) No person shall be appointed as a member of the Board or as a Magistrate in the Juvenile Court unless he has, in the opinion of the State Government, special knowledge of child psychology and child welfare.

7. Powers of the Board and Juvenile Court.-

(1) Where a Board or a Juvenile Court has been constituted for any area, such Board or Court, shall, notwithstanding anything contained in any other law for the time being in force but save as otherwise expressly provided in this Act have power to deal exclusively with all proceedings under this Act relating to neglected juveniles or delinquent juveniles, as the case may be:

Provided that a Board or a Juvenile Court may, if it is of opinion that it is necessary so to do having regard to the circumstances of the case, transfer any proceedings to any Juvenile Court or Board, as the case may be:

Provided further that where there is any difference of opinion between a Board and a Juvenile Court regarding the transfer of any proceedings under the first proviso, it shall be referred to the Chief Metropolitan Magistrate or, as the case may be, the Chief Judicial Magistrate for decision, and in a case where the District Magistrate is functioning as a Board or a Juvenile Court, such difference of opinion shall be referred to the Court of Session, and the decision of the Chief Metropolitan Magistrate or Chief Judicial Magistrate or, as the case may be, the Court of Session on such reference shall be final.

(2) Where no Board or Juvenile Court has been constituted for any area, the powers conferred on the Board or the Juvenile Court by or under this Act shall be exercised in that area, only by the following, namely:-

(a) the District Magistrate; or

(b) the Sub-Divisional Magistrate; or

(c) any Metropolitan Magistrate or Judicial Magistrate of the first class, as the case may be.

(3) The powers conferred on the Board or Juvenile Court by or under this Act may also be exercised by the High Court and the Court of Session, when the proceeding comes before them in appeal, revision or otherwise.

8. Procedure to be followed by a Magistrate not empowered under the Act.-

(1) When any Magistrate not empowered to exercise the powers of a Board or a Juvenile Court under this Act is of opinion that a person brought before him under any of the provisions of this Act (otherwise than for the purpose of giving evidence) is a juvenile, he shall record such opinion and forward the juvenile and the record of the proceeding to the competent authority having jurisdiction over the proceeding.

(2) The competent authority to which the proceeding is forwarded under sub-section (1) shall hold the inquiry as if the juvenile had originally been brought before it.

9. Juvenile homes.-

(1) The State Government may establish and maintain as many juvenile homes as may be necessary for the reception of neglected juveniles under this Act.

(2) Where the State Government is of opinion that any institution other than a home maintained under sub-section (1) is fit for the reception of the neglected juvenile to be sent there under this Act, it may certify such institution as a juvenile home for the purpose of this Act.

(3) Every juvenile home to which a neglected juvenile is sent under this Act shall not only provide the juvenile with accommodation, maintenance and facilities for education, vocational training and rehabilitation, but also provide him with facilities for the development of his character and abilities and give him necessary training for protecting himself against moral danger or exploitation and shall also perform such other functions as may be prescribed to ensure all round growth and development of his personality.

(4) The State Government may, by rules made under this Act, provide for the management of juvenile homes, including the standards and the nature of services to be maintained by them and the circumstances under which, and the manner in which, the certification of a juvenile home is granted or withdrawn.

10. Special homes.-

(1) The State Government may establish and maintain as many special homes as may be necessary for the reception of delinquent juveniles under this Act.

(2) Where the State Government is of the opinion that any institution other than a home established or maintained under sub-section (1) is fit for the reception of the delinquent juveniles to be sent there under this Act, it may certify such institution as a special home for the purposes of this Act.

(3) Every special home to which a delinquent juvenile is sent under this Act shall not only provide the juvenile with accommodation, maintenance and facilities for education, vocational training and rehabilitation, but also provide him with facilities for the development of his character and abilities and give him necessary training for his reformation and shall also perform such other functions as may be prescribed to ensure all round growth and development of his personality.

(4) The State Government may, by rules made under this Act, provide for the management of special homes, including the standards and the nature of services to be maintained by them, and the circumstances under which, and the manner in which, the certification of a special home may be granted or withdrawn.

(5) The rules made under sub-section (4) may also provide for the classification and separation of delinquent juveniles on the basis of age and nature of offences committed by them.

11. Observation homes.-

(1) The State Government may establish and maintain as many observation homes as may be necessary for the

temporary reception of juveniles during the pendency of any inquiry regarding them under this Act.

(2) Where the State Government is of opinion that any institution other than a home established or maintained under sub-section (1) is fit for the temporary reception of juveniles during the pendency of any inquiry regarding them under this Act, it may recognise such institution as an observation home for the purposes of this Act.

(3) Every observation home to which a juvenile is sent under this Act shall not only provide the juvenile with accommodation, maintenance and facilities for medical examination and treatment but also provide him with facilities for useful occupation.

(4) The State Government may, by rules made under this Act, provide for the management of observation homes, including the standards and the nature of services to be maintained by them, and the circumstances under which, and the manner in which, an institution may be recognised as an observation home or the recognition may be withdrawn.

12. After-care organisations.-The State Government may, by rules made under this Act, provide-

(a) for the establishment or recognition of after-care organisations and the powers that may be exercised by them for effectively carrying out their functions under this Act;

(b) for a scheme of after-care programme to be followed by such after-care organisations for the purpose of taking care of juveniles after they leave juvenile homes or special homes and for the purpose of enabling them to lead an honest, industrious and useful life;

(c) for the preparation or submission of a report by the probation officer in respect of each juvenile prior to his discharge from a juvenile home or special home, as the case may be, regarding the necessity and nature of after-care of such juvenile, the period of such after-care, supervision thereof and for the submission of a report by the probation officer on the progress of each such juvenile;

(d) for the standards and the nature of services to be maintained by such after-care organisations;

(e) for such other matters as may be necessary for the purpose of effectively carrying out the scheme of after-care programme of juveniles.

CHAPTER III

Neglected Juveniles

13. Production of neglected juveniles before Boards.-

(1) If any police officer or any other person or organisation authorised by the State Government in this behalf, by general or special order, is of opinion that a person is apparently a neglected juvenile, such police officer or other person or organisation may take charge of that person for bringing him before a Board.

(2) When information is given to an officer-in-charge of a police station about any neglected juvenile found within the limits of such station, he shall enter in a book to be kept for the purpose the substance of such information and take such action thereon as he deems fit and if such officer does not propose to take charge of the juvenile, he shall forward a copy of the entry made to the Board.

(3) Every juvenile taken charge of under sub-section (1) shall be brought before the Board without any loss of time but within a period of twenty-four hours of such charge taken excluding the time necessary for the journey from the place where the juvenile had been taken charge of to the Board.

(4) Every juvenile taken charge of under sub-section (1) shall, unless he is kept with his parent or guardian, be sent to an observation home (but not to a police station or jail) until he can be brought before a Board.

14. Special procedure to be followed when neglected juvenile has parents.-

(1) If a person, who in the opinion of the police officer or the authorised person or organisation is a neglected juvenile, has a parent or guardian who has the actual charge of, or control over, the juvenile, the police officer or the authorised person or the organisation may, instead of taking charge of the juvenile, make a report to the Board for initiating an inquiry regarding that juvenile.

(2) On receipt of a report under sub-section (1), the Board may call upon the parent or guardian to produce the juvenile before it and to show cause why the juvenile should not be dealt with as a neglected juvenile under the provisions of this Act and if it appears to the Board that the juvenile is likely to be removed from its jurisdiction or to be concealed, it may immediately order his removal (if necessary by issuing a search warrant for the immediate production of the juvenile) to an observation home or a place of safety.

15. Inquiry by Board regarding neglected juveniles.-

(1) When a person alleged to be a neglected juvenile is produced before a Board, it shall examine the police officer or the authorised person or the organisation who brought the juvenile or made the report and record the substance of such examination and hold the inquiry in the prescribed manner and may make such orders in relation to the juvenile as it may deem fit.

(2) Where a Board is satisfied on inquiry that a juvenile is a neglected juvenile and that it is expedient so to deal with him, the Board may make an order directing the juvenile to be sent to a juvenile home for the period until he ceases to be a juvenile:

Provided that the Board may, if it is satisfied that having regard to the circumstances of the case it is expedient so to do, for reasons to be recorded, reduce the period of stay to such period as it thinks fit.

Provided further that the Board may, if it is satisfied that having regard to the circumstances of the case it is expedient so to do, for reasons to be recorded, reduce the period of stay to such period as it thinks fit.

(3) During the pendency of any inquiry regarding a juvenile, the juvenile shall, unless he is kept with his parent or guardian, be sent to an observation home or a place of safety for such period as may be specified in the order of the Board:

Provided that no juvenile shall be kept with his parent or guardian if, in the opinion of the Board, such parent or guardian is unfit or unable to exercise or does not exercise proper care and control over the juvenile.

16. Power to commit neglected juvenile to suitable custody.-

(1) If the Board so thinks fit, it may, instead of making an order under sub-section (2) of section 15, for sending the juvenile to a juvenile home, make an order placing the juvenile under the care of a parent, guardian or other fit person, on such parent, guardian or fit person executing a bond with or without surety to be responsible for the good behaviour and well-being of the juvenile and for the observance of such conditions as the Board may think fit to impose.

(2) At the time of making an order under sub-section (1) or at any time subsequently, the Board may, in addition, make an order that the juvenile be placed under supervision for any period not exceeding three years in the first instance.

(3) Notwithstanding anything contained in sub-section (1) or sub-section (2), if at any time it appears to the Board, on receiving a report from the probation officer or otherwise, that there has been a breach of any of the conditions imposed by it in respect of the juvenile, it may, after making such inquiry as it deems fit, order the juvenile to be sent to a juvenile home.

17. Uncontrollable juveniles.-Where a parent or guardian of a juvenile complains to the Board that he is not able to exercise proper care and control over the juvenile and the Board is satisfied on inquiry that proceedings under this Act should be initiated regarding the juvenile, it may send the juvenile to an observation home or a place of safety and make such further inquiry as is may deem fit and the provisions of

section 15 and section 16 shall, as far as may be, apply to such proceedings.

CHAPTER IV

Delinquent Juveniles

18. Bail and custody of juveniles.-

(1) When any person accused of a bailable or non-bailable offence and apparently a juvenile is arrested or detained or appears or is brought before a Juvenile Court, such person shall, notwithstanding anything contained in the Code of Criminal Procedure, 1973 (2 of 1974), or in any other law for the time being in force, be released on bail with or without surety but he shall not be so released if there appear reasonable grounds for believing that the release is likely to bring him into association with any known criminal or expose him to moral danger or that his release would defeat the ends of justice.

(2) When such person having been arrested is not released on bail under sub-section (1) by the officer-in-charge of the police station, such officer shall cause him to be kept in an observation home or place of safety in the prescribed manner (but not in a police station or jail) until he can be brought before a Juvenile Court.

(3) When such person is not released on bail under sub-section (1) by the Juvenile Court it shall, instead of committing him to prison, make an order sending him to an observation home or a place of safety for such period during the pendency of the inquiry regarding him as may be specified in the order.

19. Information to parent or guardian or probation officer.- Where a juvenile is arrested, the officer-in-charge of the police station to which the juvenile is brought shall, as soon as may be after the arrest, inform-

(a) the parent or guardian of the juvenile, if he can be found, of such arrest and direct him to be present at the Juvenile Court before which the juvenile will appear; and

(b) the probation officer of such arrest in order to enable him to obtain information regarding the antecedents and family history of the juvenile and other material circumstances likely to be of assistance of the Juvenile Court for making the inquiry.

20. Inquiry by Juvenile Court regarding delinquent juveniles.-Where a juvenile having been charged with an offence appears or is produced before a Juvenile Court, the Juvenile Court shall hold the inquiry in accordance with the provisions of section 39 and may, subject to the provisions of this Act, make such order in relation to the juvenile as it deems fit.

21. Orders that may be passed regarding delinquent juveniles.-

(1) Where a Juvenile Court is satisfied on inquiry that a juvenile has committed an offence, then, notwithstanding anything to the contrary contained in any other law for the time being in force, the Juvenile Court may, if it so thinks fit,-

(a) allow the juvenile to go home after advice or admonition;

(b) direct the juvenile to be released on probation of good conduct and placed under the care of any parent, guardian or other fit person, on such parent, guardian or other fit person executing a bond, with or without surety as that court may require, for the good behaviour and well-being of the juvenile for any period not exceeding three years;

(c) direct the juvenile to be released on probation of good conduct and placed under the care of any fit institution for the good behaviour and well-being of the juvenile for any period not exceeding three years;

(d) make an order directing the juvenile to be sent to a special home,-

(i) in the case of a boy over fourteen years of age or of a girl over sixteen years of age, for a period of not less than three years;

(ii) in the case of an other juvenile, for the period until he ceases to be a juvenile:

Provided that the Juvenile Court may, if it satisfied that having regard to the nature of the offence and the circumstances of the case it is expedient so to do, for reasons to be recorded, reduce the period of stay to such period as it thinks fit:

Provided further that the Juvenile Court may, for reasons to be recorded, extend the period of such stay, but in no case the period of stay shall extend beyond the time when the juvenile attains the age of eighteen years, in the case of a boy, or twenty years, in the case of a girl;

(e) order the juvenile to pay a fine if he is over fourteen years of age and earns money.

(2) Where an order under clause (b), clause (c) or clause (e) of sub-section (1) is made, the Juvenile Court may, if it is of opinion that in the interests of the juvenile and of the public it is expedient so to do, in addition make an order that the delinquent juvenile shall remain under the supervision of a probation officer named in the order during such period, not exceeding three years, as may be specified therein, and may in such supervision order impose such conditions as it deems necessary for the due supervision of the delinquent juvenile:

Provided that if at any time afterwards it appears to the Juvenile Court on receiving a report from the probation officer or otherwise, that the delinquent juvenile has not been of good behaviour during the period of supervision or that the fit institution under whose care the juvenile was placed is no longer able or willing to ensure the good behaviour and well being of the juvenile it may after making such inquiry as it deems fit, order the delinquent juvenile to be sent to a special home.

(3) The Juvenile Court making a supervision order under sub-section (2), shall explain to the juvenile and the

parent, guardian or other fit person or fit institution, as the case may be, under whose care the juvenile has been placed the terms and conditions of the order and shall forthwith furnish one copy of the supervision order to the juvenile, the parent, guardian or other fit person or fit institution, as the case may be, the sureties if any, and the probation officer.

(4) In determining the special home, or any person or institution to whose custody a juvenile is to be committed or entrusted under this Act, the court shall pay due regard to the religious denomination of the juvenile to ensure that religious instruction contrary to the religious persuasion of the juvenile is not imparted to him.

22. Orders that may not be passed against the delinquent juvenile.-

(1) Notwithstanding anything to the contrary contained in any other law for the time being in force, no delinquent juvenile shall be sentenced to death orimprisonment, or committed to prison in default of payment of fine in default of furnishing security:

Provided that where a juvenile who has attained the age of fourteen years has committed an offence and the Juvenile Court is satisfied that the offence committed is of so serious a nature or that his conduct and behaviour have been such that it would not be in his interest or in the interest of other juveniles in a special home to send him to such special home and that none of the other measures provided under this Act is suitable or sufficient, the Juvenile Court, may order the delinquent juvenile to be kept in safe custody in such place and manner as it thinks fit and shall report the case for the orders of the State Government.

(2) On receipt of a report from a Juvenile Court under sub-section (1), the State Government may make such arrangement in respect of the juvenile as it deems proper and may order such delinquent juvenile to be detained at such place and on such conditions as it thinks fit:

Provided that the period of detention so ordered shall not exceed the maximum period of imprisonment to which the juvenile could have been sentenced for the offence committed.

23. Proceeding under Chapter VIII of the Code of Criminal Procedure not competent against juvenile.-Notwithstanding anything to the contrary contained in the Code of Criminal Procedure, 1973 (2 of 1974), no proceeding shall be instituted and no order shall be passed against a juvenile under Chapter VIII of the said Code.

24. No joint trial of juvenile and person not a juvenile.-

(1) Notwithstanding anything contained in section 223 of the Code of Criminal Procedure, 1973 (2 of 1974), or in any other law for the time being in force, no juvenile shall be charged with or tried for, any offence together with a person who is not a juvenile.

(2) If a juvenile is accused of an offence for which under section 223 of Code of Criminal Procedure, 1973 (2 of 1974), or any other law for the time being in force, such juvenile and any person who is not a juvenile would, but for the prohibition contained in sub-section (1), have been charged and tried together, the court taking cognizance of that offence shall direct separate trials of the juvenile and the other person.

25. Removal of disqualification attaching to conviction.-Notwithstanding anything contained in any other law, a juvenile who has committed an offence and has been dealt with under the provisions of this Act shall not suffer disqualification, if any, attaching to a conviction of an offence under such law.

26. Special provision in respect of pending cases.-Notwithstanding anything contained in this Act, all proceedings in respect of a juvenile pending in any court in any area on the date on which this Act comes into force in that area, shall be continued in that court as if this Act had not been passed and if the court finds that the juvenile has committed an offence, it shall record such finding and instead of passing any sentence in respect of the juvenile, forward the juvenile to the

Juvenile Court which shall pass orders in respect of that juvenile in accordance with the provisions of this Act as if it had been satisfied on inquiry under this Act that the juvenile has committed the offence.

CHAPTER V

Procedure of Competent Authorities Generally and Appeals and Revision from Orders of Such Authorities

27. Sittings, etc. of Boards and Juvenile Courts.-

(1) A Board or a Juvenile Court shall hold its sittings at such place, on such day and in such manner, as may be prescribed.

(2) A Board or, as the case may be, a Juvenile Court under sub-section (2) of section 7 shall, while holding any inquiry regarding a juvenile under this Act, as far as practicable, sit in a building or room different from that in which the ordinary sittings of Civil and Criminal Courts are held, or on different days or at times different from those at which the ordinary sittings of such courts are held.

(3) An inquiry regarding a juvenile under this Act shall be held expeditiously and shall ordinarily be completed within a period of three months from the date of its commencement, unless, for special reasons to be recorded in writing, the competent authority otherwise directs.

28. Persons who may be present before competent authority.-

(1) Save as provided in this Act, no person shall be present at any sitting of a competent authority, except-

(a) any officer of the competent authority, or

(b) the parties to the inquiry before the competent authority, the parent or guardian of the juvenile and other persons directly concerned in the inquiry including police officers and legal practitioners, or

(c) such other persons as the competent authority may permit to be present.

(2) Notwithstanding anything contained in sub-section (1), if at any stage during an inquiry a competent authority considers it to be expedient in the interest of the juvenile or on grounds of decency or morality that any person including the police officers, legal practitioners, the parent, guardian or the juvenile himself should withdraw, the competent authority may give such direction, and if anyperson refuses to comply with such direction, the competent authority may have him removed and may, for this purpose, cause to be used such force as may be necessary.

(3) No legal practitioner shall be entitled to appear before a Board in any case or proceeding before it, except with the special permission of that Board.

29. Attendance of parent or guardian of juvenile.-Any competent authority before which a juvenile is brought under any of the provisions of this Act may, whenever it so thinks fit, require any parent or guardian having the actual charge of, or control over, the juvenile to be present at any proceeding in respect of the juvenile.

30. Dispensing with attendance of juvenile.-If, at any stage during the course of an inquiry, a competent authority is satisfied that the attendance of the juvenile is not essential for the purpose of the inquiry, the competent authority may dispense with his attendance and proceed with the inquiry in the absence of the juvenile.

31. Committal to approved place of juvenile suffering from dangerous disease and his future disposal.-

(1) When a juvenile who has been brought before a competent authority under this Act is found to be suffering from a disease requiring prolonged medical treatment or physical or mental complaint that will respond to treatment, the competent authority may send the juvenile to any place recognised to be an approved place in accordance with the rules made under this Act for such period as it may think necessary for the required treatment.

(2) Where a juvenile is found to be suffering from leprosy or is of unsound mind, he shall be dealt with under the provisions of the Lepers Act, 1898 (3 of 1898), or the Indian Lunacy Act, 1912 (4 of 1912), as the case may be.

32. Presumption and determination of age.-

(1) Where it appears to a competent authority that a person brought before it under any of the provisions of this Act (otherwise than for the purpose of giving evidence) is a juvenile, the competent authority shall make due inquiry as to the age of that person and for that purpose shall take such evidence as may be necessary and shall record a finding whether the person is a juvenile or not, stating his age as nearly as may be.

(2) No order of a competent authority shall be deemed to have become invalid merely by any subsequent proof that the person in respect of whom the order has been made is not a juvenile, and the age recorded by the competent authority to be the age of the person so brought before it shall, for the purposes of this Act, be deemed to be the true age of that person.

33. Circumstances to be taken into consideration in making orders under the Act.-In making any order in respect of a juvenile under this Act, a competent authority shall take into consideration the following circumstances, namely:-

(a) the age of the juvenile;

(b) the state of physical and mental health of the juvenile;

(c) the circumstances in which the juvenile was and is living;

(d) the reports made by the probation officer;

(e) the religious persuasion of the juvenile;

(f) such other circumstances as may, in the opinion of the competent authority, require to be taken into consideration in the interest of the welfare of the juvenile: Provided that in the case of a delinquent juvenile, the above circumstances shall be taken into consideration after the Juvenile Court has recorded a finding against the juvenile that he has committed the offence: Provided further that if no report of the probation officer is received within ten weeks of his being informed under section 19, it shall be open to the Juvenile Court to proceed without it.

34. Sending a juvenile outside jurisdiction.-In the case of a neglected or delinquent juvenile whose ordinary place of residence lies outside the jurisdiction of the competent authority before which he is brought, the competent authority may, if satisfied after due inquiry that it is expedient so to do, send the juvenile back to a relative or other person who is fit and willing to receive him at his ordinary place of residence and exercise proper care and control over him, notwithstanding that such place of residence is outside the jurisdiction of the competent authority; and the competent authority exercising jurisdiction over the place to which the juvenile is sent shall in respect of any matter arising subsequently have the same powers in relation to the juvenile as if the original order had been passed by itself.

35. Reports to be treated as confidential.-The report of the probation officer or any circumstance considered by the competent authority under section 33 shall be treated as confidential:

Provided that the competent authority may, if it so thinks fit, communicate the substance thereof to the juvenile or his parent or guardian and may give such juvenile, parent or guardian an opportunity of producing such evidence as may be relevant to the matter stated in the report.

36. Prohibition of publication of names, etc. of juveniles involved in any proceeding under the Act.-

(1) No report in any newspaper, magazine or news-sheet of any inquiry regarding a juvenile under this Act shall disclose the name, address or school or any other particulars calculated to lead to the identification of the juvenile nor shall any picture of any such juvenile be published:

Provided that for reasons to be recorded in writing, the authority holding the inquiry may permit such disclosure, if in its opinion such disclosure is in the interest of the juvenile.

(2) Any person contravening the provisions of sub-section (1) shall be punishable with fine which may extend to one thousand rupees.

37. Appeals.-

(1) Subject to the provisions of this section, any person aggrieved by an order made by a competent authority under this Act may, within thirty days from the date of such order, prefer an appeal to the Court of Session:

Provided that the Court of Session may entertain the appeal after the expiry of the said period of thirty days if it is satisfied that the appellant was prevented by sufficient cause from filing the appeal in time.

(2) No appeal shall lie from-

(a) any order of acquittal made by the Juvenile Court in respect of a juvenile alleged to have committed an offence; or

(b) any order made by a Board in respect of a finding that a person is not a neglected juvenile.

(3) No second appeal shall lie from any order of the Court of Session passed in appeal under this section.

38. Revision.-The High Court may, at any time, either of its own motion or on an application received in this behalf, call for the record of any proceeding in which any competent authority or Court of Session has passed an order for the purpose of satisfying itself as to the legality or propriety of any such order and may pass such order in relation thereto as it thinks fit:

Provided that the High Court shall not pass an order under this section prejudicial to any person without giving him a reasonable opportunity of being heard.

39. Procedure in inquiries, appeals and revision proceeding.-

(1) Save as otherwise expressly provided by this Act, a competent authority while holding any inquiry under any of the provisions of this Act, shall follow such procedure as may be prescribed and subject thereto, shall follow, as far as may be, the procedure laid down in the Code of Criminal Procedure, 1973 (2 of 1974), for trials in summons cases.

(2) Save as otherwise expressly provided by or under this Act, the procedure to be followed in hearing appeals or revision proceedings under this Act shall be, as far as practicable, in accordance with the provisions of the Code of Criminal Procedure, 1973 (2 of 1974).

40. Power to amend orders.-

(1) Without prejudice to the provisions for appeal and revision under this Act, any competent authority may, either on its own motion or on an application received in this behalf, amend any order as to the institution to which a juvenile is to be sent or as to the person under whose care or supervision a juvenile is to be placed under this Act.

(2) Clerical mistakes in orders passed by a competent authority or errors arising therein from any accidental slip or omission may, at any time, be corrected by the competent authority either on its own motion or on application received in this behalf.

CHAPTER VI

Special Offences in Respect of Juveniles

41. Punishment for cruelty to juvenile.-

(1) Whoever, having the actual charge of, or control over, a juvenile, assaults, abandons, exposes or wilfully neglects the juvenile or causes or procures him to be assaulted, abandoned, exposed or neglected in a manner likely to cause such juvenile unnecessary mental or physical suffering shall be punishable with imprisonment for a term which may extend to six months, or with fine, or with both.

(2) No court shall take cognizance of an offence punishable under sub-section (1) unless the complaint is filed with the previous sanction of the State Government or an officer authorised by it in this behalf.

42. Employment of juveniles for begging.-

(1) Whoever employs or uses any juvenile for the purposes of begging or causes any juvenile to beg shall be punishable with imprisonment for a term which may extend to three years and shall also be liable to fine.

(2) Whoever, having the actual charge of, or control over, a juvenile abets the commission of the offence punishable under sub-section (1), shall be punishable with imprisonment for a term which may extend to one year and shall also be liable to fine.

(3) The offence punishable under the section shall be cognizable.

43. Penalty for giving intoxicating liquor or narcotic drug or psychotropic substance to a juvenile.-Whoever gives, or causes to be given, to any juvenile any intoxicating liquor in a public place or any narcotic drug or psychotropic substance except upon the order of a duly qualified medical practitioner or in case of sickness shall be punishable with imprisonment for a term which may extend to three years and shall also be liable to fine.

44. Explanation of juvenile employees.-Whoever ostensibly procures a juvenile for the purpose of any employment and withholds the earnings of the juvenile or uses such earnings for his own purposes shall be punishable with imprisonment for a term which may extend to three years and shall also be liable to fine.

45. Alternative punishments.-Where an act or omission constitutes an offence punishable under this Act and also any other Central or State Act, then, notwithstanding anything contained in any law for the time being in force, the offender found guilty of such offence shall be liable to punishment only under such Act as provides for punishment which is greater in degree.

CHAPTER VII

Miscellaneous

46. Power of State Government to discharge and transfer juveniles.-

(1) The State Government may, notwithstanding anything contained in this Act, at any time, order a neglected or delinquent juvenile to be discharged from the juvenile home or special home, either absolutely or on such conditions as it may think fit to impose.

(2) The State Government may, notwithstanding anything contained in this Act, order-

(a) a neglected juvenile to be transferred from one juvenile home to another;

(b) a delinquent juvenile to be transferred from one special home to another or from a special home to a borstal school where such school exists or from a special home to a juvenile home;

(c) a neglected juvenile or a delinquent juvenile to be transferred from a juvenile home or a special home to a fit person or a fit institution;

(d) a juvenile who has been released on licence which has been revoked or forfeited, to be sent to the special home or juvenile home from which he was released or to any other juvenile home or special home or borstal school:

Provided that the total period of the stay of the juvenile in a juvenile home or a special home or fit institution or under a fit person shall not be increased by such transfer.

(3) The State Government may, notwithstanding anything contained in this Act, at any time, discharge a juvenile from the care of any person under whom he was placed under this Act either absolutely or on such conditions as may think fit to impose.

47. Transfers between juvenile homes, etc. under the Act, and juvenile homes, etc. of like nature in different part of India.-

(1) The Government of a State may direct any neglected juvenile or delinquent juvenile to be transferred from any juvenile home or special home within the State to any other juvenile home, special home, or institution of a like nature in any other State with the consent of the Government of that State.

(2) The Government of a State may, by general or special order, provide for the reception in a juvenile home or special home with the State of a neglected juvenile or delinquent juvenile detained in a juvenile home or special home or institution of a like nature in any other State where the Government of that State makes an order for such transfer, and upon such transfer the provisions of this Act shall apply to such juvenile as if he had been originally ordered to be sent to such juvenile home or special home under this Act.

48. Transfer of juveniles of unsound mind or suffering from leprosy or addicted to drugs.-

(1) Where it appears to the State Government that any juvenile kept in a special home or juvenile home or institution in pursuance of this Act is suffering from leprosy or is of unsound mind, or is addicted to any narcotic drug or psychotropic substance, the State Government may order his removal to a leper asylum or mental hospital or treatment centre for drug addicts or other place of safe custody for being kept there for such period not exceeding the period for which he is required to be kept in custody under the orders of the competent authority or for such further period as may be certified by the medical officer to be necessary for the proper treatment of the juvenile.

(2) Where it appears to the State Government that the juvenile is cured of leprosy or of unsoundness of mind or drug addiction it may, if the juvenile is still liable to be kept in custody, order the person having charge of the juvenile to send him to the special home or juvenile home or institution from which he was removed or, if the juvenile is no longer liable to be kept in custody order him to be discharged.

49. Placing out on licence.-

(1) When a juvenile is kept in a juvenile home or special home, the State Government may, if it so thinks fit, release the juvenile from the juvenile home or special home and grant him a written licence for such period and on such conditions as may be specified in the licence permitting him to live with, or under the supervision of, any responsible person named in the licence willing to receive and take charge of him with a view to educate him and train him for some useful trade or calling.

(2) Any licence so granted under sub-section (1) shall be in force for the period specified in the licence or until revoked or forfeited by the breach of any of the conditions on which it was granted.

(3) The State Government may, at any time, by order in writing, revoke any such licence and order the juvenile to return to the juvenile home or special home from which he was released or to any other juvenile home or special home, and shall do so at the desire of the person with whom or under whose supervision the juvenile has been permitted to live in accordance with a licence granted under sub-section (1).

(4) When a licence has been revoked or forfeited and the juvenile refuses or fails to return to the special home or juvenile home to which he was directed so to return, the State Government may, if necessary, cause him to be taken charge of and to be taken back to the special home or juvenile home.

(5) The time during which a juvenile is absent from a special home or juvenile home in pursuance of a licence granted under this section shall be deemed to be part of the time for which he is liable to be kept in custody in the special home or juvenile home:

Provided that when a juvenile has failed to return to the special home or juvenile home on the licence being revoked or forfeited, the time which elapses after his failure so to return shall be excluded in computing the time during which he is liable to be kept in custody.

50. Provision in respect of escaped juveniles.- Notwithstanding anything to the contrary contained in any other law for the time being in force, any police officer may take charge without warrant of a juvenile who has escaped from a special home or a juvenile home or from the care of a person under whom he was placed under this Act and shall send the juvenile back to the special home or the juvenile home or that person, as the case may be; and no proceeding shall be instituted in respect of the juvenile by reason of such escape but the special home, juvenile home or the person may, after giving the information to the competent authority which passed the order in respect of the juvenile, take such steps against the juvenile as may be deemed necessary.

51. Contribution by parents.-

(1) The competent authority which makes an order for sending a neglected juvenile or a delinquent juvenile to a juvenile home or a special home or placing the juvenile under the care of a fit person or fit institution may make an order requiring the parent or other person liable to maintain the juvenile to contribute to his maintenance, if able to do so, in the prescribed manner.

(2) The competent authority before making any order under sub-section (1) shall inquire into the circumstances of the parent or other person liable to maintain the juvenile and shall record evidence, if any, in the presence of the parent or such other person, as the case may be.

(3) The person liable to maintain a juvenile shall, for the purposes of sub-section (1), include in the case of illegitimacy, his putative father:

Provided that where the juvenile is illegitimate and an order for his maintenance has been made under section 125 of the Code of Criminal Procedure, 1973 (2 of 1974), the competent authority shall not ordinarily make an order for contribution against the putative father, but may order the whole or any part of the sums accruing due under the said order for maintenance to be paid to such personas may be named by the competent authority and such sum shall be paid by him towards the maintenance of the juvenile.

(4) Any order made under this section may be enforced in the same manner as an order under section 125 of the Code of Criminal Procedure, 1973 (2 of 1974).

52. Fund.-

(1) The State Government may create a Fund under such name as it thinks fit for the welfare and rehabilitation of the juveniles dealt with under this Act.

(2) There shall be credited to the Fund such voluntary donations, contributions or subscriptions as may be made by any individual or organisation.

(3) The fund created under sub-section (1) shall be administered by such officers or authority in such manner and for such purposes as may be prescribed.

53. Advisory Board.-

(1) The State Government may constitute an Advisory Board to advise it on matters relating to the establishment and maintenance of homes, mobilisation of resources, provision of facilities for education, training and rehabilitation of neglected and delinquent juveniles and co-ordination among the various official and non-official agencies concerned.

(2) The Advisory Board shall consist of such number of officers and other persons as the State Government thinks fit and may also include experts and the representatives of voluntary organisations engaged in the relevant areas.

54. Visitors.-

(1) The State Government may nominate not more than three non-officials to be Visitors for each of the homes established under this Act.

(2) A Visitor nominated for a home under sub-section (1) shall periodically visit such home and make a report to the State Government.

55. Control of custodian over juvenile.-Any person in whose custody a juvenile is placed in pursuance of this Act shall, while the order is in force, have the like control over the juvenile as

he would have if he were his parent, and shall be responsible for his maintenance, and the juvenile shall continue in his custody for the period stated by the competent authority, notwithstanding that he is claimed by his parent or any other person: Provided that no juvenile while in such custody shall be carried except with the permission of the competent authority.

56. Delinquent juvenile undergoing sentence at commencement of the Act.-In any area in which this Act is brought into force, the State Government may direct that a delinquent juvenile who is undergoing any sentence of imprisonment at the commencement of this Act shall, in lieu of undergoing such sentence, be sent to a special home or be kept in safe custody in such place and manner as the State Government thinks fit for the remainder of the period of the sentence; and the provisions of this Act shall apply to the juvenile as if he had been ordered by a Juvenile Court to be sent to such special home or, as the case may be, ordered to be detained under sub-section (2) of section 22.

57. Appointment of officers.-

(1) The State Government may appoint as many probation officers, officers for the inspection of special homes, juvenile homes, observation homes or after care organisations and such other officers as it may deem necessary for carrying out the purposes of this Act.

(2) It shall be the duty of the probation officer-

(a) to inquire, in accordance with the direction of a competent authority, into the antecedents and family history of any juvenile accused of an offence, with a view to assist the authority in making the inquiry;

(b) to visit neglected and delinquent juveniles at such intervals as the probation officer may think fit;

(c) to report to the competent authority as to the behaviour of any neglected or delinquent juvenile;

(d) to advise and assist neglected and delinquent juveniles and, if necessary, endeavour to find them suitable employment;

(e) where a neglected or delinquent juvenile is placed under the care of any person or institution on certain conditions to see whether such conditions are being complied with; and

(f) to perform such other duties as may be prescribed.

(3) Any officer empowered in this behalf by the State Government may enter any special home, juvenile home, observation home or after-care organisation and make a complete inspection thereof in all its departments and of all papers, registers and accounts relating thereto and shall submit the report of such inspection to the State Government.

58. Officers appointed under the Act to be public servants.- Probation officers and other officers appointed in pursuance of this Act shall be deemed to be public servants within the meaning of section 21 of the Indian Penal Code, 1860 (45 of 1860).

59. Procedure in respect of bonds.-The provisions of Chapter XXXIII of the Code of Criminal Procedure, 1973 (2 of 1974), shall, as far as may be, apply to bonds taken under this Act.

60. Delegation of powers.-The State Government may, by general or special order, direct that any power exercisable by it under this Act shall, in such circumstances and under such conditions, if any, as may be specified in the order, be exercisable also by an officer subordinate to that Government.

61. Protection of action taken in good faith.-No suit or other legal proceeding shall lie against the State Government or any probation officer or other officer appointed under this Act in respect of anything which is in good faith done or intended to be done in pursuance of this Act or of any rules or orders made thereunder.

62. Power to make rules.-

(1) The State Government may, by notification in the Official Gazette, make rules to carry out the purposes of this Act.

(2) In particular and without prejudice to the generality of the foregoing power, such rules may provide for all or any of the following matters, namely:-

(a) the places at which, the days on which, the time at which, and the manner in which, a competent authority may hold its sittings;

(b) the procedure to be followed by a competent authority in holding inquiries under this Act, and the mode of dealing with juveniles suffering from dangerous diseases or mental complaints;

(c) the circumstances in which, and the conditions subject to which, an institution may be certified as a special home or a juvenile's home or recognised as an observation home, and the certification or recognition withdrawn;

(d) the internal management of special homes, juvenile homes and observation homes and the standards and the nature of services to be maintained by them;

(e) the functions and responsibilities of special homes, juvenile homes and observation homes;

(f) the inspection of special homes, juvenile homes, observation homes and after-care organisations;

(g) the establishment, management and functions of after-care organisations; the circumstances in which, and the conditions subject to which an institution may be recognised as an after-care organisation and such other matters as are referred to in section 12;

(h) the qualifications and duties of probation officers;

(i) the recruitment and training of persons appointed to carry out the purposes of this Act and the terms and conditions of their services;

(j) the conditions subject to which a girl who is neglected or delinquent juvenile may be escorted from one place to another, and the manner in which a juvenile may be sent outside the jurisdiction of a competent authority;

(k) the manner in which a contribution for the maintenance of a juvenile may be ordered to be paid by a parent or guardian;

(l) the officers or authorities by whom, the manner in which and the purpose for which the Fund created under section 52 shall be administered;

(m) the conditions under which a juvenile may be placed out on licence and the form and conditions of such licence;

(n) the conditions subject to which juveniles may be placed under the care of any parent, guardian or other fit person or fit institution under this Act and the obligations of such persons or institutions towards the juveniles so placed;

(o) any other matter which has to be, or may be, prescribed.

(3) Every rule made by a State Government under this Act shall be laid, as soon as may be after it is made, before the legislature of that State.

63. Repeal and savings.-If, immediately before the date on which this Act comes into force in any State, there is in force in that State, any law corresponding to this Act, that law shall stand repealed on the said date: Provided that the repeal shall not affect-

(a) the previous operation of any law so repealed or anything duly done or suffered thereunder; or

(b) any right, privilege, obligation or liability acquired, accrued or incurred under any law so repealed; or

(c) any penalty, forfeiture or punishment incurred in respect of any offence committed against any law so repealed; or

(d) any investigation, legal proceeding or remedy in respect of any such right, privilege, obligation, liability, penalty, forfeiture or punishment as aforesaid, and any such investigation, legal proceeding or remedy may be instituted, continued or enforced and any such penalty, forfeiture or punishment may be imposed, as if this Act had not been passed.

5

Crime Against Children in Bihar

The report "904 children abducted in Bihar since 2001" may look grim, but the overall facts tell a different story about Bihar regarding the crimes against children vis-à-vis other Indian states, at least in the year 2005.

Let us examine the National Crime Record Bureau' Crimes in India-2005 report, as an example. A total number of 14,975 cases of crime against children were committed in 2005 compared to 14,423 cases in 2004 (an increase of 3.8%) and 11,633 cases in 2003. Out of this, Bihar records only 115 incidents (17th position out of 28 states and 7 union territories) of crimes against children with a percentage contribution of 0.8% only to All-India total of 100% compared to 3721 case in Madhya Pradesh (24.8% and 1st rank), 2305 cases in Maharashtra (15.4& and 2nd rank) and 1801 case in Uttar Pradesh (12% and 3rd rank. The overall crime rate against children has marginally increased from 1.3% in 2004 to 1.4% in 2005.

Crimes against children have been steadily rising over the last few years-from 832 cases registered in 2000 to 2,281 in 2004. From 2003 to 2004 alone, crimes against children rose by 3.63% though Bihar has shown continuous decline in overall crimes against children, except kidnapping.

Out of the 35 notorious cities covered the crime chart, Patna, the capital of Bihar recorded only 4 cases off crime against children with a low percentage of 0.1% compared to Indore, which recorded the highest incidents of 448 with a whopping percentage of 14.6% and ranked second after Delhi that leads the graph with 852 case and 27.7% of the total crimes. Even the high-tech city, Pune recorded 314 cases in 2005. Under the major cities (out of the 35), even Jharkhand has a better record with only two cities e.g. Dhanbad and Jamshedpur in the list with a total of 5 cases. However, Delhi tops the chart.

Among the crimes, rape tops the list with a total 4026 cases were reported in the country in 2005 as compared to 3542 in 2004 accounting for an increase of 13.7%. During 2005, Madhya Pradesh has recorded the highest number of rape cases i.e. 780 followed by Maharashtra with 634 cases of child rape. In fact, the number of rapes of children in the age group of 10-18 has almost doubled from 2000 to 2004.

Kidnapping and abduction comes next on the crime chart with a total of 3518 cases of criminal acts against children were reported in 2005 as compared to 3196 cases in the preceding year, which is an increase of 10.1%. In kidnapping and abduction, Uttar Pradesh, not Bihar, leads the crime graph with 749 cases, which is 21.3% at the national level.

Homicide is another criminal act meted out against children with a total of 1327 cases were reported in country against 1304 in 2004 with an increase of 1.8% in 2005. Uttar Pradesh leads in child homicide with 390 cases (29.4% of the total cases).

However, the cases of child marriage showed a decline of 31.2% with 93 incidents in 2005 as compared to 122 in 2004. The evil of child marriages were reported from Gujarat (25 cases), Maharashtra (22 cases) and Madhya Pradesh (18 cases), which accounted for 20.5%, 18% and 14.8% respectively. Here also, Bihar has no record.

A total of 28 cases of buying of girls and 50 cases of selling of girls for prostitution were reported in the country during 2005 against 21 and 19 such cases in the preceding year. While Delhi and Andhra Pradesh with 32.1% each along with 21.4% of Maharashtra accounted for 85.6% of total cases of buying of girls, West Bengal accounted for 88% of the total selling of girls. In addition, there were 145 incidents of procuration of minor girls did take place in 2005, which shows a decrease of 29.3% compared to 2004 with 205 such cases.

In 2005, a total of 108 cases of infanticide were reported in country in 2005, which is also a marginal increase from 102 cases in 2004 and 203 cases in 2003.

The state wise crime graph shows a rather surprising trend, as Madhya Pradesh is leading with 3721 cases of crime against children followed by Maharashtra (2305 cases), Uttar Pradesh (1801 cases) and Delhi (1026 cases) respectively.

In spite of forceful legal provisions, such Section IPC (for rape), Section 372 & 373 IPC (selling and buying girls for prostitution), Section 315 & 316 IOC (crime against a foetus) apart from various IPCs (Section 360-369) for different forms of kidnapping and Section 302 IPC for homicide, the prosecution has been inadequate. For example, out of the 19,728 persons arrested for various crimes against children, the police could manage to provide charge-sheet against 16,669 persons only and out of the these charge-sheeted persons, only 4475 could be convicted.

The good news is that Mizoram, Nagaland and Lakshadweep have no record of crime against children. When will we see Bihar in this category? In all our hope against hope, we can expect a better Bihar, probably in near future where children are safe and secure.

The continuous rise in crimes against children is an abject failure of the law enforcement agencies, government and civil society who have not been able to play their respective roles in an efficient manner. In addition, the growing rate of incidents also indicate young children have a high exposure to criminal elements in the society, not only in Metros but also cities like Indore and Pune. Above all, the sensitisation of the police force besides different government measures to protect children from violence have so far proved ineffective. A complete failure on the part of criminal justice system in delivering the desired results in punishing the culprits is perhaps the most important reason that a large number of criminals are at large.

A criminal-police-politician nexus is often cited as the primary reason, at least in the case of Bihar, aided and abetted with the teeming unemployed youths taking to anti-social activities with a view to become rich overnight. TV channels, including soap operas laden with sophisticated life style and luxurious houses where big business tycoons plan strategies to outwit the rivals by hook or by crook to stay at the top, are playing critical role in swaying the young minds.

However, the reporting of high incidence of crime against children is a sign of the proactive role of police. It can be hoped that the police personnel across the country would study these data and analyse the causes and take steps to curb such cases of violence against children. As a society, our efforts to prevent crimes committed against children have not kept pace with the increasing vulnerability of our children.

Children, the most precious commodity, are most vulnerable in our society. Hence, every needs protection right from his or her own home to school to market place because the predator could be anyone-close relatives, teachers, elder colleagues in school, strangers, among others. Children need protection from physical harm, protection from exploitation and gender-biased violence both inside and outside home

A recent home ministry approved draft has been circulated among states, which would, after a due process, become laws to protect Indian children from various types of abuses. There is an urgent need for the draft on Offences Against Children Act 2006 to be made comprehensive. In addition, Child Protection Units (CPUs) and Children Protection Courts (CPCs), which would deliver these new laws effectively and speedily, should be establish without delay. "The children of India need their rights and their legal protection from Parliament if they are to function as responsible future citizens", writes Pinki Virani.

The rising trend in crimes against children is disturbing, not only for Bihar, but also for whole of India, which needs urgent attention because India has the largest population (340 million or 340419115 to be exact) of children in the age group of 0-14 in the world exceeding those of China, which has 320 million (320866959 to be exact) children by about 19.5 million i.e. 5.75% (Census of India, 2001). Cyber crime is the latest in the list of scores of heinous abuses against children. Studies have shown that about 60 per cent of all websites are sexual in content. About 20% of them solicited their visitors, 13% went voluntarily and the rest were pictorially lured. An estimated 100,000 pornographic websites generate revenues in the region of US$1 billion annually. The increasing popularity of chat rooms and the vulnerability of personal data to criminal access makes children the easiest targets for a range of culpable crimes.

With the development in economy and IT, crime has also been on the rise, especially those that victimise innocent children. Each year, crime against children in India are increasing and becoming more heinous. Due to factors like age and physical as well as mental strength, children are the easiest prey to the violent crimes and vulnerable to all possible abuses the modern world has been witnessed to. Sometimes, even minors of three to four years old are not spared. In fact, the crime against children is a pervasive phenomenon that knows no political, social, cultural and economic boundaries except human lust, anger and evil business. Nature of crimes against children includes abduction, homicide, rape, assault, and physical and sexual abuse, kidnapping, buying and selling for prostitution, early marriages, infanticide and foeticide etc.

TRADING CHILDREN

The proposed Offences Against Children Bill, 2005, attempts to address the legal loopholes through which child traffickers slip.

Child Rights Activists demand that the draft under consideration be made into law.

MALA is barely 11. Clad in tattered clothes, hands and feet grimy with continuous rummaging through garbage in and around New Delhi railway station, she is often subjected to beating by her 'uncle' for not picking up enough after a day's work. She is often forced to go begging to compensate for the deficit. Mala and her nine-year-old brother Sonu go through life in the same mechanical way day in and day out. Nobody knows where the children came from, or who their parents are. The children themselves say nothing except that they are "looked after" by their chacha (uncle), who brought them to the city from the village after a big flood. Try probing them more about the uncle and they scamper away. Mala and Sonu are among thousands of such children who can be seen roaming the streets begging, asking for alms in the name of shani devta, rummaging at garbage dumps, or selling cheap books and other things at traffic signals. One also comes across small children doing back-breaking chores at dhabas, restaurants and hotels as domestic servants. Has anyone ever stopped to wonder who these children are, where they come from, or why they are here? They rarely beg or sell wares for themselves. The awful truth is that children are bought and sold like commodities and used for commercial purposes, making cheap profits and facilitating illegal acts.

Child-trafficking, traditionally associated with only trafficking for commercial sex, is growing fast in India. The authorities, apparently unaware of the magnitude of the problem, have made no attempt to mitigate it. No wonder then that there is no reliable data available on the issue in India.

According to the National Human Rights Commission (NHRC), every year an average of 44, 476 children go missing. Of these 11,008 are never traced. The NHRC, in its report "Action Research on Trafficking in Women and Children in India" (2002-03), suggests that many of the missing children are not really missing but are instead trafficked. Most end up in adoption, marriage, labour markets or working in the entertainment industry, of which sex tourism is the most recent aspect. Unfortunately, if activists are to be believed, many victims are pushed into this murky world by their own parents or guardians.

According to figures provided by the National Crime Records Bureau, in 2004, as many as 2,265 cases of kidnapping and abduction of children qualified as forms of trafficking and were reported to the police. Of these, 1,593 cases were of kidnapping for marriage, 414 were for illicit sex, 92 for unlawful activity, 101 for prostitution and the rest for various other things like slavery, begging and even selling body parts. Most of these children (72 per cent) were between 16 and 18 years of age. Twenty-five per cent were children aged 11-15 years. This is the tip of the iceberg; the malaise runs much deeper and many cases go unreported. India's poor track record in this regard has drawn flack from the United States government. Its Trafficking in Persons Report (June 2005) described India as a "source, transit, and destination country for women, men, and children trafficked for the purposes of sexual and labour exploitation". It also criticised India for its lackadaisical attitude to implementing laws.

The report said, "The Government of India does not fully comply with the minimum standards for the elimination of trafficking... the quality and magnitude of the government's anti-trafficking response, particularly in the law enforcement area, are seriously insufficient relative to India's huge trafficking in persons problem." The U.S. report placed India on its Tier 2 Watch List for a second consecutive year "for its inability to show evidence of increased efforts to address trafficking in persons, particularly its lack of progress in forming a national law enforcement response to inter-State and transnational trafficking crimes."

While one may or may not agree with the premises on which the U.S. department made these observations, one cannot argue with the lack of comprehensive law on human trafficking in India. According to a report prepared by HAQ: Centre for Child Rights, a non-governmental organisation (NGO) spearheading the national Campaign Against Child Trafficking, the "absence of law and inability to register a case as an offence of trafficking make it difficult to assess the magnitude of the problem as well as maintain statistics for investigation, arrest, prosecutions and convictions in the context of human trafficking".

There are no laws that specifically target child-trafficking. Child abuse cases are handled under various sections of the Indian Penal Code, which are laws meant for adults. Commercial sex-trafficking offences are handled under the Immoral Traffic (Prevention) Act. Labour-trafficking offences are handled under the Child Labour Act for those hazardous industries in which child labour is considered an offence. There is no law prohibiting employment of children in work outside the definition of "hazardous".

As a result, many cases of trafficking are not booked by the police. "Begging or giving alms or selling wares at traffic signals is an offence, but has even one single conviction taken place so far?" asks Praveen Bhatt, secretary, HAQ: Centre for Child Rights.

One positive development in this regard has been the preparation of a draft by the Ministry of Women and Child Development. The Offences Against Children Bill, 2005, in circulation since January this year, is hailed by child rights activists as a landmark document; it is the first time that a law specifically aimed at protecting children's rights has been under debate.

"So far there was not a single law aimed at safeguarding children and protecting them against abuse. Offences against children were so far booked under laws under the IPC, which at times failed to result in prosecution and conviction simply for the reason that crimes involving children need to be handled with different tools," said Rajmangal Prasad, director, Pratidhi, another NGO active in the field of child rights. According to him, if the proposed draft does become law, it will go a long way to check child trafficking because specific sections in the draft deal with precisely this issue.

Furthermore, the definition of trafficking goes beyond trafficking for commercial sex. The proposed document has specific sections dealing with various offences against children, including sale/transfer, sexual assault, sexual/physical/emotional abuse, commercial sexual exploitation, child pornography, grooming for sexual purpose, incest, corporal punishment, bullying and economic exploitation. The document makes it clear that provisions in this law will be in addition to other legislation within the IPC and the Juvenile Justice Act because these laws do not separately cover persons who commit crimes against children and some other categories of children under various circumstances of abuse, exploitation and neglect.

Child rights activists are calling for the draft under consideration to be made into a law so that the suffering children have some hope. As the first paragraph of the document states, "although India has the second largest child population in the world, there is no separate legislation to deal with offences against children". It is high time it was enacted.

CHILD TRAFFICKING: AMENDMENT PROPOSED IN IMMORAL TRAFFIC (PREVENTION) ACT 1956

Section Existing Provision Amendments proposed 2(aa) "Child" means 'a person who has not completed the age of sixteen years' "Child" means a person under the age of eighteen years. 2(ca) "major" means 'a person who has completed the age of eighteen years' May be deleted

2(cb) "minor" means 'a person who has completed the age of sixteen years but who has not completed the age of eighteen years' May be deleted

2(k)

After the existing entries after 2(j) add clause 2(k)

(a) "Trafficking in persons" shall mean the recruitment, transportation, transfer, harbouring or receipt of persons, by means of the threat or use of force or other forms of coercion, of abduction, of fraud, of deception, of the abuse of power or of a position of vulnerability or of the giving or receiving of payments or benefits to achieve the consent of a person having control over another person, for the purpose of exploitation. Exploitation shall include, at a minimum, the exploitation of the prostitution of others or other forms of sexual exploitation, forced labour or services, slavery or practices similar to slavery, servitude or the removal of organs;

(b) The consent of a victim of trafficking in persons to the intended exploitation set forth in subparagraph (a) shall be irrelevant where any of the means set forth in subparagraph (a) have been used;

(c) The recruitment, transportation, transfer, harbouring or receipt of a child for the purpose of exploitation shall be considered "trafficking in persons" even if this does not involve any of the means set forth in subparagraph (a);

3(1)

Punishment for keeping a brothel or allowing premises to be used as a brothel Punishment for keeping a brothel or allowing premises to be used as a brothel Any person who keeps or manages, or acts or assists in the keeping or management of a brothel shall be punishable on first conviction with RI for a term of not less than one year and not more than three and also with fine which may extend to two thousand rupees and in the event of a second or subsequent conviction, with RI for a term of not less than two years and not more than five years and also with fine which may extend to two thousand rupees. Any person who keeps or manages or acts or assists in the keeping or management of a brothel shall be punishable on first conviction with RI for a term of not less than three years with fine which may extend to ten thousand rupees and in the event of second or subsequent conviction with RI for a term of not less than seven years and also with fine which may extend to two lakh of rupees.

7(1A). Where an offence committed under Sub-section (1) is in respect of a child or minor, the person committing the offence shall be punishable with imprisonment of either description for a term which shall not be less than seven years but which may be for life or for a term which may extend to ten years and shall also be liable to fine. Where an offence committed under Sub-section (1) is in respect of a person of less than 18 years, the person committing the offence shall be punishable with imprisonment of either description for a term which shall not be less than seven years but which may be for life or for a term which may extend to ten years and shall also be liable to fine.

8. Seducing or soliciting for purpose or prostitution whoever, in any public place or within sight of, and in such manner as to be seen or heard from, any public place, whether from within any building or house or not-May be deleted.

(a) by words, gestures, willful exposure of her person (whether by sitting by a window or on the balcony of a building or a house or in any other way) or otherwise tempts or endeavours to tempt, or attracts or endeavours to attract the attention of any persons for the purpose of prostitution; or

(b) solicits or molests any person, or loiters or acts in such manner as to cause obstruction or annoyance to persons residing nearly or passing by such public places or to offend against public decency, for the purpose of prostitution, May be deleted

Shall be punishable on first conviction with imprisonment for a term which may extend to six months, or with fine which may extend to five hundred rupees or with both, and in the event of a second or subsequent conviction, with imprisonment for a term which may extend to one year and also with fine which may extend to five hundred rupees.

Detention in a corrective institution

May be deleted

Detention in a corrective institution. 10(a)

Where-----

(a) a female offender is found guilty of an offence under Sec.7 or Sec.8 and

(a) a female offender is found guilty of an offence under Sec. 7; and

(b) the character, state of health and mental condition of the offender and

(b) the character, state of health and mental condition of the offender and the other circumstances of the case are such that it is expedient that she should be subject to detention for such term and such instructions and discipline as are conducive to her correction, It shall be lawful for the Court to pass, in lieu of a sentence of imprisonment, an order for detention in corrective institution for such term, not being less than two years and not being more than five years as the Court thinks fit. It shall be lawful for the Court to pass, in lieu of a sentence of imprisonment, an order for detention in corrective institution for such term not being less than two years and not being more than seven years.

13(2): The Special Police Officer shall not be below the rank of an inspector of police The special police officer shall not be below the rank of a sub-inspector/ inspector of police. 13(3)(b).

The State Government may associate with the special police officer a non-official advisory body consisting of not more than five leading social welfare workers of that area (including women social welfare workers, wherever practicable) to advise him on questions of general importance regarding the working of this Act The State Government shall associate with the special police officer or officers a non-official advisory body consisting of not more than five leading social welfare workers of that area (including women social welfare workers, wherever practicable) to advise him/them on questions of general importance regarding the working of this Act. New provision proposed.

(i) Provisions for confiscation of property and assets of traffickers and agents of organized prostitution/flesh trade as under:

   (1) As from the commencement of the amended act, it shall be lawful for any person to hold any illegally acquired property either by himself or through any other person on his behalf;

   (2) Where any person holds any illegally acquired property in contravention of the provision of Sub-section (1), such property shall be liable to be forfeited to the Central/State Governments in accordance with the provisions of this Act.

(ii) A provision providing protective mechanisms, immunities and safeguards for the members of voluntary agencies who take initiatives for preventing, trafficking, facilitating rescue or carrying out victims protection activities to be included in consultation with the Ministry of Law and Justice.

Consequential changes in various sections where the term 'his' or 'her' has been used. The words 'his' and 'her' wherever occur in the Act should be substituted by a gender neutral word for example 'person' so as to cover both sexes.

CHILD ABUSE

Article 34 and 35 of the Convention state that the States parties shall undertake to protect the child from all forms of sexual exploitation and sexual abuse. Child abuse and neglect within the family have been highlighted as a part of advocacy under the Convention. Another obligation of significance that has been included is safeguarding children from sexual exploitation and abuse, and action to prevent the abduction and sale of children in any form. At the same time, the Convention assigns the primary responsibility to both parents for children's upbringing. In India, Child abuse is increasingly coming out in the open and is drawing more attention, concern and condemnation. There is also an acknowledgment of the importance of a specific focus on the problems of children, especially of girl children, related to their abuse and neglect.

Traditionally, the family and community in India have been insular, authoritarian and patriarchal, with parents(s)/ guardians/caretakers having full right over their children, to treat them in whichever way they deem fit. Traditional child rearing practices accept physical force or punishment as means of disciplining. Child beating and corporal punishment by the parents/guardians or even teachers are considered to be in the "interest of the child".

The term "Child abuse" encompasses a broad and wide range of acts and maltreatment of children. Various attempts to define child abuse have not achieved a consensus. There is also no consensus about its various forms, which can include child battering, extreme punishment, hard labour, emotional abuse, sexual abuse, including incest and exploitation, and abandonment. There is inadequate data with regard to child abuse. However, statistics of children admitted to institutions due to abandonment, after running away from home, of children apprehended under the Juvenile Justice Act or of cases of exploitation, victimisation as well as the increasing population of child beggars and reports of minor girls becoming victims of prostitution and of sexual assaults, indicate that child abuse remains a series problem in the country.

Physical Violence and Sexual Abuse

Child battering and injuring the child physically by the parents, teachers and others in authority is very much prevalent in India as observed by social workers and reported in the newspapers. Sexual abuse of the child is defined as any sexual relation between an adult and a child. Its legal definition includes child molestation, incest and rape. It is the least reported form of child abuse despite its high incidence and the fact of its occurring in all economic and ethnic groups. Some estimates show that in 30% to 50% incidents, the offenders are family members, close relatives, neighbours and friends and 80% of children know their at attackers.

According to the Report of the National Crime Records Bureau, CRIME IN INDIA (1994), child rape victims in the age groups of 0-10 and 10-16 years went on increasing from 1988 to 1991 but declined in 1992. Out of 301 cases reported in all Union Terriories, Delhi recorded 276 (19.7%) cases while Lakshadweep has the unique distinction of being free from this form of crime. The incidence of rape, torture and sexual harassment recorded increased in 1994 over its previous year, while cases of kidnapping, abduction and molestation have decline.

Policy and Provisions

The National Policy for Children, 1974 states that "children shall be protected against neglect, cruelty and exploitation". The National Decadal Plan of Action for the Girl Child (1991-2000 A.D.) recognises the rights of the girl child to protection from exploitation, assault and physical abuse. The Plan aims to utilise intervention strategies to sensitise various agencies on the need to protect the girl child from assault and physical abuse and exploitation, and adolescent girls from prostitution and rape through legislation, proper enforcement and speedy legal remedies through family courts (Family Courts Act, 1984) and special courts.

Though the National Policy on Education 1986, recommends "firm exclusion" of corporal punishment to children in schools, it is found to be continuing as all State Education Acts and Rules have not banned corporal punishment in schools. The Indian Penal Code considers the following as serious offenses; kidnapping or maiming a child for the purposes of begging (Se. 363-A), selling a child for the purposes of prostitution (Se. 372-373), exposure and abandonment of child under

12 years by parents or persons having care of the child (Se. 317) and sexual harassment (Section 509). Child prostitution and child rape are also covered. The Juvenile Justice Act has provisions for prostitution from and punishment for cruelty and indignity to children as also for care, protection and rehabilitation of neglected and abused children. The Immoral Traffic Prevention Act, 1956 (amended) deals with the punitive as also preventive aspects of prostitution including child prostitution.

Rape is covered under Section 375, 376 of Indian Penal Code (1860). Offences of kidnapping and abduction for different purposes are covered by Sec. 363-373, IPC. Sexual intercourse with a women with or without her consent when she is under 16 years of age amounts to rape and the offender is punishable with imprisonment for life (Section 375 of the IPC). The National Commission for Women, a statutory and autonomous body constituted by the Government of India under the Department of Women and Child Development has prepared a draft ordinance with the aim of raising the age of consent (majority) from mere 16 years to 18 years so as to bring it at par with International Conventions. The proposed bill is under the consideration of the Government.

Procedural details are great hurdles in the speedy trial of the cases of child rape. It is estimated that for cases in which trials were completed, only 41.5% ended in conviction during 1990, 34.2% in 1991 and 33.8% in 1992. Thus the percentage of cases acquitted is showing an upward trend over the years. The rate of disposal of cases in courts was 23.9% in 1990, 18.6% in 1991 and 18.1% in 1992. On an average, 80% of the cases remained pending.

The Supreme Court has directed the State Governments to immediately implement the provisions of the Indian Penal Code on the issue of child rape in a strict manner, in particular the provisions that the act of sexual intercourse with a child (below the age of 16 years) with or without her consent should be treated as an offence of rape under Sec. 375 of IPC. In the procedure of conviction, this responsibility is transferred to the police. In this process the offender often manipulates acquittal.

There are numerous cases to support this observation. The three major changes that have been brought about in the legislation and evidence aspect of child rape are:

- the definition of rape to include oral penetration in the meaning of sexual penetration;
- the onus of proof of not committing rape is now on the rapist; and
- the section on "consent or no consent" has been made irrelevant.

Child Prostitution

Prostitution in India has manifested itself in various forms with varying degrees of social sanction. There is now increasing concern about children being inducted for commercial purposes into the trade and becoming subjects of shocking sexual abuse and sexual diseases. Thee are no reliable statistics available about the number of prostitutes-least of all about child prostitutes, but according to newspaper reports thee are around 0.4 million prostitutes. Reports and some studies on prostitutes and prostitution point out that there are some social groups and communities in various pockets of the country in which family based prostitution is traditionally practiced but statistics about their numbers is also not available. No estimates are available even about the number of child Devadasis and Jogins though these systems have been traditionally in existence as a socially sanctioned form of exploitation of women particularly those from lower socio-economic groups in the States of Karntaka, Maharashtra and Andhra Pradesh. With the aim of curbing child prostitution and rehabilitating child prostitutes, an Expert Committee has been formed by the National Commission for Women. More police personnel as well as judges are being sensitised through seminars and workshops on this issue.

The Supreme Court of India in a 'Public Interest Litigation' in 1990 on the subject of child prostitution had directed that the Central and State Governments should set up Advisory Committees to suggest measures to be taken in eradicating child prostitution. Government of India has accordingly constituted a Central Advisory Committee which includes representatives of the Ministries of Welfare, Home Affairs, Legal Affairs, National Commission for Women, National Institute of Social Defiance, Indian Council of Child Welfare, Association for Social Health in India and three voluntary Organisations. A sub-committee was constituted to frame recommendations/plan of action for legal and non-legal approaches for the rescue and rehabilitation of child prostitutes. The Plan of Action has been finalised and accepted. The implementation machinery is being set up.

Legal Provisions

The Government of India enacted the Suppression of Immoral Traffic in Women and Girls Act, 1956. In 1986 this Act was amended and provided enhanced penalties for offences involving children and minors. It continued to prohibit prostitution in its commercialised form without rendering prostitution per se an offence. Along with contemplating specialised machinery for enforcement, the Act envisages a comprehensive scheme for rescue, protection and treatment of prostitutes.

The Substantive Law also has several provisions which have a bearing on curbing conditions responsible for prostitution. The Indian Penal Code includes sexual offences procurement of minor girls (Sec. 366A), importation of minor girl from foreign country (Section 366B), selling minors for purposes of prostitution (Section 372), buying minors, for purpose of prostitution (Section 373) as punishable by law. The Juvenile Justice Act, 1986 has elaborate provisions for the care, protection, treatment, education, vocational training, development and rehabilitation of children rescued from those procuring, inducing and taking persons for the sake of prostitution.

The various provisions of the Immoral Traffic Prevention Act (ITPA) 1986 are to be enforced through the local police. As the Police already have many duties relating to the general criminal law, they have not been effective to take action under ITPA. There are reports also about protection money being paid by the prostitutes/brothel keepers to the local mafia and also to the local police. This along with vested interests ensure the continuance of this exploitative system. There is a need for special police officers to be notified for proper coordination between the enforcement and the welfare machineries.

Drug Abuse

According to Article 33 of the Convention, the 'State shall take appropriate measures to protect children from the illicit use of narcotic drugs and psychotropic substances and to prevent the use of children in the illicit production and trafficking of such substances.

Drug abuse and drug trafficking has become a global phenomenon. Various studies reveal that teenage children are falling prey to drug abuse knowingly or unknowingly. The Government of India has adopted a two-pronged strategy to tackle the problem of drug abuse. This includes supply-control and demand reduction. The supply-control aspect is taken care of by various Central Agencies like Customs, Excise, Central Bureau of Narcotics, C.B.I. etc. The Narcotics Control Bureau, established under Sec. 4 of the Narcotics Drugs and Psychotropic Substance Act, 1985 coordinates action taken by various Departments and Agencies in respect of matters relating to drug abuse control. It is the implementing authority in respect of various international conventions on drugs. The Ministry of Welfare has been given the responsibility of looking after the social welfare and educational aspects of drug addiction.

The Narcotics Control Bureau is considering a proposal to amend the Narcotics Drugs and Psychotropic Substances Act to protect the children from illicit use of drugs and to award the highest level of punishment under the following situations i.e., when minors are affected by the offence or minors are used for commission of the offence, and when the offence is committed in an educational institution or social service facility or in their immediate vicinity or in other places to which school children and students resort for educational, sports and social activities.

For achieving and above objectives, a Scheme of Assistance to Voluntary Organisations for Prohibition and Drug Abuse Prevention has been formulated. In this scheme grant-in-aid to the extent of 90 per cent of the total approved expenditure is provided to the voluntary organisations for providing a variety of services by setting up counseling centers, de-addiction centers, after-care centers de-addiction camps and organising awareness generation programs.

The fundamental principal that a juvenile delinquent, more so a juvenile drug addict requires protective custody and not punitive custody has been recognized. Such protective measures have been incorporated in the legislation and are further being strengthened.

A lot of work is being done on social awareness through mass-media including the traditional medium of puppet shows, street plays and television programmes and advertisement, pamphlets hoarding, handouts, booklets etc. The work of sensitising and creating social awareness specially among children has been taken up as a part of advocacy under CRC.

Drug Abuse Control (Demand Reduction)

In addition to the above supply reduction measures, strategy is also being formulated to bring about demand reduction though anti-drug campaigns and particularly through the National Master Plan for Drug Abuse Control. This is an outcome of close co-operation between the Ministry of Welfare, Ministry of Health and Family Welfare and the Narcotics Control Bureau with financial assistance for United Nations Drug Control Programme (UNDCP).

Coordination Committee of Secretaries

A Narcotics Coordination Committee of Secretaries has been functioning with representation at Secretary level from Ministry of Home Affairs, Ministry of Welfare, Ministry of Health and Family Welfare and Ministry of Finance to take a holistic view of the problem of narcotics control and take suitable measures in this regard.

CONCLUSION

The preceding chapters have presented the situation of children in India with reference to the provisions contained in various Articles of the Convention. India, presently, has an infrastructure available for translating the Convention's Provisions into reality in a phased manner, despite there being gaps in provisions available to the Indian Child under many Articles.

The efforts in the field of Child Development are a testimony to the Government of India's commitment to the cause of children. These mandates have resulted in planning of appropriate actions aimed at child-centred development, where children are just not recipients of benefits of services and programmes but the focus of development itself.

The National Plan of Action for children is an important tool with the government, to monitor the progress of its own commitment. Concerted measures are being taken to achieve targets within the stipulated time frame. Some of the goals are well within reach, while in case of others much more needs to be done. With competitive demands from other sectors, resource scarcity is going to impose a serious constraint in achieving goals. Optimal utilisation and mobilisation of internal and external resources is thus being attempted. The measures to be adopted for achieving these goals require multi-pronged strategies to be initiated simultaneously. The process has already begun; it includes sharpening of strategies, strengthening of the implementation process, convergence of services, coordination and decentralisation of development activities.

"Unless the life of the child in the family and community improves, all development efforts would be meaningless. There is, therefore, a need to raise awareness and create an ethos of respect for the rights of the child in society to meet his/her basic developmental needs. Advocacy and social mobilisation are two crucial processes which are being emphasised to achieve this end. With India's ratification of the UN Convention on the Rights of the Child, the 'rights approach' to child development is gradually gaining importance and will, henceforth, form the basis of Government's strategy towards child development."

6

CHILDREN AND GOVERNMENT POLICY

ERADICATION OF CHILD PROSTITUTION

The public concern on the issue of child prostitution originated in a land mark judgement of the Hon'ble Supreme Court of India in 1990. In response to Public Interest Litigation (PIL) on the subject, the Court ruled that the States and Central Government should initiate comprehensive measures for the rehabilitative care of such children and elimination of this social menace. The Court directed the Government to form a Central and State Advisory Committees. As per the directives of the Supreme Court, a Central Advisory Committee was constituted to eradicate child prostitution. Further a SubCommittee has been set up to frame recommend-ations/ plan of action for the rescue and rehabilitation of all child prostitutes. The SubCommittee has submitted its report.

The report of the Central Committee (1994) was deliberated upon in the national consultations held in 1994 at Mumbai. Predictably, it was felt that regional consultations were essential to document and understand the problem. Accordingly, a number of regional workshops were held at Calcutta, Goa, Hyderabad, Patna, Chandigarh and Bangalore with assistance from UNICEF. A report has been prepared and submitted in August, 1996.

ERADICATION OF COMMERCIAL SEXUAL EXPLOITATION OF WOMEN & CHILDREN

The Government has finalized a Plan of Action to combat trafficking and commercial sexual exploitation of women and children. The State Governments and UT Administrations have been requested to implement the Plan of Action. The Central Advisory Committee on Child Prostitution proposed certain amendments in the Immoral Traffic (Prevention) Act to make it more stringent and effective, which was referred to the Department of Legal Affairs who have concurred with the same. A draft Cabinet Note on the same lines has been prepared and will be sent to the Cabinet Secretariat after circulating it to concerned Ministries/ Departments.

India has drafted a Regional Convention on prevention and combating trafficking of women and children for the purposes of prostitution. The Convention seeks to take measures and encourage cooperation among the SAARC member countries to prevent the incidence of trafficking; this is specially relevant because Nepal and Bangladesh are the major source areas. The Convention is expected to be signed in the next SAARC Summit.

A Work Plan under the GOI-UNICEF MPO has been finalized. Funds have been earmarked for various activities such as projects for rehabilitation of victims of prostitution, preparation of manual for senstisation of police officers, building of a data base on the subject matter of prostitution and trafficking, holding of regional level meet for interaction with State Governments close to source areas and NGOs.

DIMENSIONS OF CHILD ABUSE

Protection without Rights?

Child sexual abuse cuts across class, caste, cultural and economic backgrounds. But there is no specific law to make it an offence. The recent disclosure of the Nithari killings may prompt the government to pass the much-awaited and long-needed Offences against Children Bill, 2005. But more laws may not ensure more rights for children

When Pinki Virani wrote Bitter Chocolate in 2000, the book sent shockwaves through the 'Happy Indian Family'. For the first time, popular consciousness started questioning what was understood to be the most secure space for children. We were aware of children's vulnerability to sexual abuse--but were convinced that it happened to 'bad' children, from 'bad' families, in 'bad' places. In case a 'good' child, from a 'good' family was abused, the abuser would invariably be a 'bad' stranger. Bitter Chocolate shattered this myth and laid bare the fact that sexual abuse of children cuts across class, caste, cultural and economic backgrounds; and that there was no specific law to make Child Sexual Abuse (CSA) an offence.

In 2007, while we are trying hard to recover from the horrors of the Nithari case--in which many of the 38 children who have been reported missing in the small urban village on the outskirts of Delhi were allegedly brutally abused and murdered--we still don't have a specific law on CSA. Perhaps Nithari will be the impetus for the much-awaited and long-needed Offences against Children Bill, 2005 to become an Act.

In this article we will briefly look at the inadequacies of existing criminal laws in India that address CSA, trace the progress (or lack of it) of the law through some debates that have emerged out of the demand for a law on CSA, and, finally, look closely at the provisions of the Offences against Children Bill, 2005 to gauge its transformative potential and point out that the offence of CSA cannot be prevented only through legal means.

Criminal law and CSA

The Indian Penal Code (IPC) does not recognise CSA as an offence. It is through the application of certain other provisions in the IPC that a child sexual offender is criminalised--these are, inter alia, the offences of rape (Section 375), outraging the modesty of a woman (Section 354), and 'unnatural offences' (Section 377). None of the above sections define in legal terms what constitutes CSA.

Section 375 defines the offence of rape as sexual intercourse committed by a man on a woman against her will or without her consent. The section goes on to provide certain other circumstances where the standard of will or consent does not apply. Among these, intercourse with a girl under 16 years of age, even with her consent, is rape. The section provides an explanation that "penetration is sufficient to constitute the sexual intercourse necessary to the offence of rape". Thus, only

CSA of girl-children where peno-vaginal penetration has taken place falls within the ambit of this section. Most often CSA does not take this form, but ranges from exhibitionism, touching, to all forms of penetration (including penile-anal, penile-oral, object-vaginal, and finger-vaginal). Penetration of the vagina with any other object, even if life-threatening, does not amount to rape.

In cases of CSA concerning girl-children, where penetration of the vagina has not taken place, Section 354 comes into operation. This section punishes the offence of assault or use of criminal force to outrage the modesty of a woman. And 'modesty' of a woman remains ambiguously defined through judicial interpretation. Especially in the case of CSA, it becomes even more confusing because the 'victim' is a child and whether as a child she can be said to possess modesty is a point of argument in court. In the 1967 Supreme Court (SC) judgment of State of Punjab v Major Singh, the judges deliberated on whether a female child of seven-and-a-half years could be said to be possessed of 'modesty', which can be 'outraged'. Another major inadequacy of this provision is its quantum of punishment. For CSA amounting to the gravest forms of molestation just falling short of penetration, it stipulates a maximum of two years imprisonment, as against a minimum of seven years imprisonment for 'rape'.

The most controversial provision of the IPC, Section 377, is purportedly meant to be applied in cases of CSA where penetration is not peno-vaginal in nature--defined as 'unnatural offences' by the law. This section is gender-neutral. While it addresses the sexual abuse of boys, when the abuse does not include penetration it escapes the ambit of the section. This means that there is no provision in the IPC to criminalise molestation of boys. Section 377 is also inadequate because it is not a law designed to criminalise CSA, and thus fails to cover the majority of forms that the abuse might take.

Demands for a Law on CSA

Child rights activists demanding a specific law on CSA have been facing many hurdles in the course of their engagements with the judiciary and State. On most occasions, the responses have either addressed procedural aspects of the law or have been ridden with conservative sexual morality.

The 1999 Supreme Court case of Sakshi v Union of India and Others was the first attempt to challenge inadequacies of the provisions in the IPC to make CSA an offence. Sakshi, a women's resource centre working with victims of sexual abuse, filed the PIL in 1997 after the Delhi High Court declared that the case of an eight-year-old child, penetrated in three orifices by her father, could not be considered either rape or an 'unnatural offence'.

The PIL questioned the legal procedures during trial and urged the apex court to alter the definition of sexual intercourse, with reference to Section 375 of the IPC, to mean all kinds of sexual penetration on any type of orifice of the body, not just intercourse understood in the traditional sense. So that sexual abuse other than what is defined as rape could also be included.

The 2004 judgment in this case, instead of broadening the definition of 'rape' (as was sought by the PIL) only focused on reducing the trauma of the victim by directing that she cannot be forced to answer insensitive and crude questions during court trials, and that a screen may be used so that the victim did not have to undergo the trauma of seeing the perpetrator.

Interestingly, in this judgment the court admitted the wide prevalence of CSA, yet it failed to clearly define sexual abuse and stated: "An exercise to alter the definition of rape... by a process of judicial interpretation is bound to result in a good deal of chaos and confusion and will not be in the interest of society at large..."

Naina Kapur, Director of Sakshi, responding to the judgment pointed out: "What is the point of (introducing) procedural changes if the abuse doesn't fall within the definition of rape or outrage of modesty or 'unnatural acts' as laid down by our law? I think this was a chance to really get justice for victims of sexual abuse by widening the definition of sexual abuse. But the judge (G P Mathur) has missed the opportunity and, by letting the law remain as it is, has rendered the whole exercise purposeless."

Pursuant to the order passed by the Supreme Court in the Sakshi case, the Law Commission of India (LCI) has reviewed the laws with regard to CSA and recommended amendments in consultation with Sakshi and other organisations. The major amendments recommended in the 172nd Report of the LCI were that the offence of 'rape' be substituted by 'sexual assault', which would make it gender-neutral and bring into its fold a range of sexual offences and not merely forced peno-vaginal penetration. The report also recommended the deletion of Section 377.

The issue of CSA was again raised in the legal arena when, in 2001, Naz Foundation, a Delhi-based organisation working on issues of HIV/AIDS, filed a petition in the Delhi High Court asking for the 'reading down' of Section 377. The petition demanded that adult, consensual and private sex be taken out of the purview of this section. A demand for reading down was made instead of a complete repeal of the section by the petitioners, keeping in mind the lacunae in the IPC regarding CSA. However, in response to the petition, the government sought the dismissal of the petition on exactly the same grounds, stating that it complements the lacunae in rape laws for prosecuting child sexual offenders. Thus we found the government hiding behind the fig leaf of Section 377 to absolve itself of the responsibility of passing a separate law on CSA, and perpetuating homophobia in the process.

As has been noted in a report titled 'Rights for All' (RFA) by the coalition Voices Against 377: "...we have here not a mere oversight on the part of the government but a deliberate attempt to confuse issues... to pit child rights against gay and lesbian rights. There is little evidence... that the government is in fact concerned about the child's search for justice. The government has itself acknowledged the need for a separate law to deal with CSA in its First Periodic Report to the UN Committee on the Rights of the Child. The government's actions however fail to match the stated intention..." RFA further notes that despite demands by groups from all over the country, working on child rights, women's rights and sexual rights, and even the National Commission for Women, the government has sought to ignore the demand for a law on CSA, and instead of proactively legislating on the issue has been creating hurdles in the way of these civil society pursuits.

OFFENCES AGAINST CHILDREN BILL, 2005

In 2005, the Ministry of Women and Child Development (MWCD) of the government, in consultation with NGOs, legal experts and social workers, drafted the Offences Against Children Bill, 2005. According to the MWCD website: "After wide consultations a draft Bill for Offences Against Children was prepared and circulated to the State Governments for their comments and views. After obtaining the comments of concerned Ministries and Departments a draft Cabinet Note has been referred to Law Ministry for their vetting. The proposal will be placed before the Cabinet shortly." The passing of this Bill would further India's obligation to meet the standards in the UN Convention on the Rights of the Child, which it ratified in 1992.

In a post-Nithari situation, this Bill might actually get passed. However, the government's response to CSA through the Bill is again laden with interpretive discrepancies and 'protectionist' approaches that do not necessarily enhance or create enabling conditions for the realisation of child rights.

This Bill defines CSA and makes 'consent' of the child the qualifying ground for ascertaining abuse when the child is between 16-18 years of age (Section 2 [c]). The law deems children below 16 years of age incapable of giving consent to any of the sexual acts mentioned in the Bill. The problem with such a provision is that it could actually lead to criminalising consensual sexual acts between young people. Under this law, if a child of 14 years has consensual sex with another child of 17 years, the 17-year-old, who is capable of consent, would have committed a crime against the other child, as he is deemed incapable of giving consent. Interestingly, in a situation where both are under 16, they are both guilty of committing sexual assault since their consent is invalid according to the law!

"The Offences Against Children Bill will create yet another provision which can be used to harass and penalise teenagers for victimless crimes, only to serve public morality," observes lawyer Tarunab Khaitan. "The importance of protecting children from sexual abuse by adults cannot be over-emphasised. However, to criminalise children under a legislation ostensibly meant to protect them solely on the basis of a prudish denial of child sexuality is simply moral policing," he adds.

As pointed out earlier, the IPC stipulates the age of criminal responsibility at 7 years. It's paradoxical that by virtue of this law the age at which a child can be held responsible for a sexual offence (should this be changed to sexual act?) is 16 years and above--in effect meaning that children are capable of scheming and executing murder and rape at 7 years, but not capable of consenting to sex with someone of the same age till they are 16!

The punitive measures provided in the Bill also do not seem to adhere to standards of parity between offence and punishment. Section 10 states that any person who prepares, produces, facilitates, distributes or knowingly abets in the creation of child pornography will be liable to rigorous imprisonment of not less than seven years, but which may extend to 10 years, and a fine. While for distribution of child pornography the Bill stipulates a minimum punishment of seven years, according to Section 6, if a person is guilty of sexual abuse of a child between 16-18 years, the minimum punishment is imprisonment of not less than six months. This disparity allows a child sexual offender to get away with only six months' imprisonment, whereas a distributor of child pornography--who has not physically abused a child--can be booked for seven years.

Though the framers of the Bill have given considerable attention to punitive measures, a glaring omission in the Bill is the absence of any provision for children with disabilities whose vulnerability to sexual abuse may be higher compared to other children.

Looking ahead...

The Offences Against Children Bill is indeed a useful piece of legislation on CSA (in the absence of any) and other forms of child abuse. But there is a need to be careful about an over-reliance on the law, believing that it will fulfil the promise of phenomenal transformation. Law reform demands by the women's movement and the queer movement in India have not always reaped the desired results. Gaining from this experience, we need to remember that more laws may not ensure more rights for children. State accountability should also extend to creating enabling conditions where existing rights can be realised and enjoyed. The same responsibility lies with parents and teachers who are an integral part of the world around them. One of the major reasons for CSA continuing unabated is the culture of silence and shame that prevails in India--an environment where stringent legal measures (as and when they come) become less useful.

A law like this will be relevant when it is able to move beyond merely criminalising acts that it identifies as CSA, but stipulates mechanisms that are in real terms accessible to children. A model can be found in the anti-sexual harassment cells set up at workplaces on the directives of the Vishakha guidelines. Similar cells in schools could address CSA--the provision of 'mandatory reporting' under Section 32 in the Bill is a move in that direction as it makes persons in positions of trust or authority responsible for reporting abuse. The recent committee set up by the National Human Rights Commission (NHRC) to suggest guidelines to stop violations of child rights--a response to the Nithari case--will hopefully assist the State in its endeavour to guarantee child rights.

Given that the Commissions for Protection of the Child Rights Act 2005 has been passed, and we have in hand the draft Bill, we have an opportunity to capitalise on these documents by involving more child rights groups to fine tune and build on the provisions of the Bill. More importantly, any move towards making laws on child rights must involve the voices of children themselves, as stakeholders and active participants instead of mute and passive beneficiaries.

INDIAN CHILDREN FACE SEXUAL ABUSE

A disturbing new study on child abuse, carried out by the government and civil society organisations, puts Assam at the top of the list of states where children face sexual abuse, followed closely by Andhra Pradesh and Delhi.

A landmark study by the Indian government along with two civil society organisations--Prayas and Save the Children--and backed by the United Nations Children's Fund admitted on April 9, 2007, that two-thirds of children in India are physically abused while more than half have faced some form of sexual abuse.

The first ever national-level study by the Ministry of Women and Child Development covered 13 of India's 29 states with a sample size of 12,447 children in the 5-12 age-group, and 2,324 young adults. The survey didn't have a margin of error.

The survey divided abuse into three categories: physical, sexual and emotional abuse. Some disturbing data from the survey:

- Over 50% of children have experienced physical abuse, which includes slapping and corporal punishment. 88.6% of these children face physical abuse from their parents; 45.68% of them are boys.
- Nearly 65% of schoolchildren reported being beaten by their teachers, mostly in government schools.
- A shocking 53.22% of children have faced sexual abuse. The report says that most children do not report the matter to anyone. Half of the cases of sexual abuse (50%) were committed by people known to the child or in a position of trust and responsibility.
- Every second child reported emotional abuse, in an equal number of girls and boys.
- While 41.17% of children in the 5-12 age-group complained of being forcibly kissed, the figure came down to 25.73% in the 13-14 age-group. Similarly, around 25.86% of teenagers reported being forced to exhibit their private parts; the relevant figure for those below 12 was 35.86%.
- Around 37.25% of children in the younger age-group, and 27.61% of teenagers, were sexually abused during

travel. As much as 41.33% of children in the 5-12 age-group and 25.29% in the 13-14 age-group reported abuse during marriages and other family ceremonies.

- What's worse, the report says, "around 70% of abused children have never reported the matter to anyone".
- While Assam (86.26%) topped the list of states where children faced sexual abuse, Andhra Pradesh and Delhi followed closely at 72.83% and 72.26% respectively. Rajasthan reported the lowest complaints--29.36%.
- Likewise, the percentage of sexually abused young adults (13-14 age-group) is high in Assam, at 77.5%, followed by Delhi at 69.11%. Goa reported the least complaints--23.01%. Kerala had the lowest incidence of child abuse.

Child rights activists have welcomed the study, saying it was positive that the government was waking up to the reality. "Homes, schools and neighbourhoods are not safe for our children as most people don't even believe that hitting or sexually abusing a child is a serious crime," says Kailash Sathyarthi of Bachpan Bachao Andolan (Save Childhood Movement). Activists say the existing laws must be strengthened and mindsets changed.

CHILDREN AS CITIZENS

Childhood in India is not homogeneous; several childhoods co-exist. Social and economic status, physical and mental ability, geographical location and other differences determine the degree of vulnerability of India's children. The bitter core of this diversity is the wide inequality between various sections of society.

The child in India is discriminated against by virtue of these inequalities, in addition to being subjugated by the hierarchy of age. Thus, all children in India suffer certain violations on account of their status as a child. The recently published study on child abuse by the Ministry of Women and Child Development bears testimony to this. Several campaigns, policies and demands for laws later, children in India are still at the receiving end of the most egregious forms of human rights abuse.

And yet, children's issues get peripheral and often superficial political attention in India. On most occasions this attention is triggered by tragedies such as the recent killings of more than 30 children in Nithari, on the outskirts of Delhi, the knee-jerk reaction to which was immediate consensus on the passing of the Offences Against Children Bill, 2005. But everyday cases of child exploitation or neglect are rarely recognised as violations or registered as offences. The State infrastructure and services for children in need are poor both in terms of number and quality; the infrastructure is crumbling thanks to skewed budgetary allocations of funds for child rights.

The government's responses to child rights have until recently been erected through a welfarist approach--where children are looked at as passive recipients, and the State as the benevolent giver. The State therefore came up with policy formulations, rather than non-discriminatory and accountable delivery systems for the realisation of child rights.

In 1974, India adopted a National Policy for Children (NPC), declaring children to be the nation's most precious asset. Hence, from the Fourth Five-Year Plan (1969-74) onwards, children have found mention in national development plans, but there has been insufficient attention in terms of investment. In the wake of the 1990 World Summit for Children, the Government of India adopted a National Plan of Action for Children in 1992, with goals for the decade. In the same year, it also ratified the United Nations Convention on the Rights of the Child (UNCRC) and thereafter in its Periodic Country Reports submitted to the UN Committee on the Rights of the Child, India has dwelt at length on the measures taken to ensure children's rights. These reports and the India Report on the World Summit for Children undoubtedly record some positive changes in the situation of children in India. But there are significant problems and performance gaps too.

We still do not have a law against child sexual abuse; child marriage is rampant in spite of amendments to the law; although education is a fundamental right, the process of delivery of this most vital right faces major funds constraints and administrative hurdles; and the huge increase in the number of missing girls has not yet been arrested despite the Pre-Conception and Pre-Natal Diagnostic Techniques (Prohibition of Sex Selection) Act.

However, there has been a recent spurt of legislative action on child rights issues. Take, for example, the recent Protection of Child Rights Act 2005, the Juvenile Justice (Care and Protection of Children) Act 2006, the proposed Immoral Traffic (Prevention) Amendment Bill 2006, Offences Against Children Bill, and the Child Marriage Bill that has recently been passed by the Rajya Sabha. Surely this decade is seeing the highest rate of legislative action on any one constituency or issue in the history of India, and a definitive shift from addressing children's issues as a matter of charity to a matter of justiciable and deliverable entitlements.

This issue of InfoChange Agenda explores the fallout of the systemic malaise that denies children guarantees to the protection of their rights, and profiles some civil society interventions, including governmental schemes, that challenge this malaise.

The issue brings together essays by practitioners, policy experts and activists who provide an insider's view of the processes of implementation of government commitments. It looks at some civil society initiatives that are both innovative and effective in guaranteeing the realisation of child rights and creating enabling conditions for such realisation. And, most importantly, it foregrounds the voices of the primary stakeholders, the children--through their narratives of triumph and creativity.

We have two children from Kolkata's Sonagachi red-light area talking about their experiences as children of sex workers and as young activists who have now set up an organisation called Padatik to fight for the rights of their mothers. And Vicky Roy, a destitute child who was rehabilitated by the Salaam Balak Trust, reflects his own experiences as a street child through his defining images of street children in Delhi.

Thus, even as this issue lays bare the unavoidable reality of the suffering of children in India, it looks at children as active agents of change and citizens who demand participation in the processes of policy/law-making.

The following four-point agenda might help us formulate policies and legislation on child rights issues that ensure maximum positive impact:

1. The rights of the child must be articulated as non-negotiable and universal to ensure that the State does not use the rhetoric of 'progressive realisation' to de-prioritise child rights on the basis of economic inability.
2. The stress must be on enabling rights rather than on policy formulations only, with the State made accountable not only for the recognition of a particular right but also for putting in place a non-discriminatory delivery system.
3. The civil and political rights of children, such as the right against abuse and exploitation, must be connected with their economic, social and cultural rights, such as education and work. The disjuncture exists because children are not recognised as full citizens due to their inability to consent, which reduces them to non-citizens.
4. Children should have special rights, but at the same time their rights should not be isolated from larger rights issues. This will ensure that they are also considered citizens and guaranteed all existing constitutional rights. Respecting children as citizens is a step towards recognising their voices as stakeholders and as participants, not just mute beneficiaries.

7

STATUS OF CHILDREN IN INDIA

INTRODUCTION

With more than a third of its population below the age of 18, India has the largest child population in the world. This backgrounder explores the levels of health, nutrition, education and social security of children, and government policy and action on child rights

India has made some significant commitments towards ensuring the basic rights of children. There has been progress in overall indicators: infant mortality rates are down, child survival is up, literacy rates have improved and school dropout rates have fallen. But the issue of child rights in India is still caught between legal and policy commitments to children on the one hand, and the fallout of the process of globalisation on the other.

Over the last decade, countries across the world have been changing their existing economic models in favour of one driven by the free market, incorporating processes of liberalisation, privatisation and globalisation.

The direct impact of free trade on children may not leap to the eye, but we do know that globalised India is witnessing worsening levels of basic health, nutrition and shelter. Children are suffering as a result of social sector cutbacks/policies and programmes and development initiatives that deprive communities and families of access to and control over land, forest and water resources they have traditionally depended on. The negative fallout is visible: children are being deprived of even the scarce social benefits once available; they are displaced by forced and economic migration, increasing the number of children subsisting on the streets; more and more children are being trafficked within and across borders; and rising numbers of children are engaged in part-or full-time labour.

Ground realities:

- With more than one-third of its population below 18 years, India has the largest young population in the world.
- Only 35% of births are registered, impacting name and nationality.
- One out of 16 children die before they attain the age of 1, and one out of 11 die before they are 5 years old.
- 35% of the developing world's low-birth-weight babies are born in India.
- 40% of child malnutrition in the developing world is in India.
- The declining number of girls in the 0-6 age-group is cause for alarm. For every 1,000 boys there are only 927 females--even less in some places.
- Out of every 100 children, 19 continue to be out of school.
- Of every 100 children who enrol, 70 drop out by the time they reach the secondary level.
- Of every 100 children who drop out of school, 66 are girls.
- 65% of girls in India are married by the age of 18 and become mothers soon after.
- India is home to the highest number of child labourers in the world.
- India has the world's largest number of sexually bused children, with a child below 16 raped every 155th minute, a child below 10 every 13th hour, and at least one in every 10 children sexually abused at any point in time.

GOVERNMENT POLICY ON CHILDREN

On November 20, 1989, the UN General Assembly adopted the Convention on the Rights of the Child (CRC). On January 26, 1990, the opening day of the session, 61 countries signed it. The CRC covers all children under the age of 18 years, regardless of sex, colour, language, religion or race. India ratified the CRC in 1992.

Several constitutional provisions protect children in India. Among them:

- Article 15 affirms the right of the State to make special provision for women and children.
- Article 24 provides that no child below the age of 14 shall be employed to work... in any hazardous employment.
- Article 39 (e) of the Directive Principles of State Policy provides that children of tender age should not be abused and that they should not be forced by economic necessity to enter vocations unsuited to their age or strength.
- Article 39 (f) requires children to be given opportunities and facilities to develop in a healthy manner and in conditions of freedom and dignity, and that childhood and youth be protected against exploitation and moral and material abandonment.
- Article 45 of the Directive Principles of State Policy provides for free and compulsory education for all children until they complete the age of 14.

Prior to the Fifth Five-Year Plan, the government's focus was on child welfare through the promotion of basic minimum services for children. This culminated in the adoption of the National Policy for Children, in 1974.

The Fifth Five-Year Plan (1974-79) saw a shift of focus from welfare to development and the integration and co-ordination of services after the Integrated Child Development Services (ICDS) 1975.

The Sixth Five-Year Plan strengthened child welfare and development. It led to the spatial expansion and enrichment of child development services through a variety of programmes. The focus of the Eighth Five-Year Plan (1992-97) shifted to human development through advocacy, mobilisation and community empowerment.

The Government of India declared its commitment to every child in the Ninth Five-Year Plan (1997-2002).

The Tenth Five-Year Plan advocated a convergent/integrated rights-based approach to ensure the survival, development, protection and participation of children. It set targets for children: all children to complete five years of schooling by 2007; reduction in gender gaps in literacy and wage rates by at least 50%, by 2007; reduction in Infant Mortality Rate (IMR) to 45 per 1,000 live births by 2007, and 28 by 2012; reduction of Maternal Mortality Rate (MMR) to 2 per 1,000 live births by 2007 and to 1 per 1,000 live births by 2012; arresting the decline in the child sex ratio; and universalisation of the ICDS scheme.

The draft approach paper of the Eleventh Five-Year Plan (2007-2012) prepared by the Planning Commission emphatically stated that 'Development of the child is at the centre of the Eleventh Plan'. While continuing with the rights-based approach to child development, the plan recognises the importance of a holistic approach, focusing both on outcomes and indicators for child development as well as macro-perspective trends and governance issues.

Despite these laws, policies and commitments, however, what is the actual situation for India's children vis-à-vis health, education, early childhood care and protection?

SURVIVAL

The very survival of the Indian child is a matter of concern. Around 2.5 million children die in India every year, accounting for one in five deaths in the world, with girls being 50% more likely to die. Eighty-seven children of every 1,000 born still have the probability of dying between birth and 5 years of age. According to a report on the state of India's newborns, the health challenges faced by a newborn child in India are bigger than those experienced by any other country. Although India's

Neonatal Mortality Rate (NMR) witnessed a significant decline in the 1980s (from 69 per 1,000 live births in 1980 to 53 per 1,000 live births in 1990), it has remained static since then (only dropping four points from 48 to 44 per 1,000 live births between 1995 and 2000).

FOOD INSECURITY: MALNUTRITION AND STARVATION

One in every three malnourished children in the world lives in India. Child malnutrition is generally caused by a combination of inadequate or inappropriate food intake, gastrointestinal parasites and other childhood diseases, and improper care during illness. Is it not ironical that in a nation with soaring GDP rates and Sensex indices, marking India's entry into the global market, children continue to die of malnutrition and starvation?

The major cause is lack of public health services in remote and interior regions of the country, poor access to subsidised healthcare facilities, declining State expenditure on public health, and lack of awareness about preventive child healthcare.

According to the Planning Commission, 50% of below the poverty line (BPL) families are out of the purview of the targeted public distribution system. The very method of identifying the poor using the official poverty line defined at an absolutely low level of income corresponding to the expenditure required to purchase the bare minimum of calories, is contentious. Therefore, in reality, many more people are living in food insecurity.

Ironically, the Supreme Court of India has had to intervene to ensure that children in this country get adequate and nutritious food--the most basic of rights for all citizens to stay alive and healthy.

TO BE BORN A GIRL: PLUMMETING SEX RATIO

The very existence of the girl-child is under threat. Defying the normal male-female balance, the higher survival capacity of girl babies, and greater life expectancy of women to men prevalent in human populations, the female-male balance in India has been adverse to females for at least 100 years. The

1901 National Census recorded a female-male ratio of 972 to 1,000 males, for all ages. Virtually every subsequent census showed a decline.

While the overall female-male ratio for all ages rose slightly from the 1991 figure of 927 females per 1,000 males to 933 females per 1,000 males in 2001, the juvenile sex ratio in the 0-6 age-group fell from 945 girls per 1,000 boys to 927 girls per 1,000 boys. This is a decline of 18 points in just one decade! The Government of India, in its report to the UN Committee on the rights of the Child said: "Every year, 12 million girls are born--3 million of whom do not survive to see their 15th birthday. About one-third of these deaths occur in the first year of life and it is estimated that every sixth female death is directly due to gender discrimination."

Sex-selective abortion, more commonly known as foeticide, and what appears to be a re-emergence of infanticide, is taking a heavy toll, even as neglect of 'survivors' of this weeding out process persists.

Unlike all the other social evils attributed to poverty, the killing of female foetuses through sex-selective abortion cannot be attributed to poverty and ignorance. Indeed, it is the economically affluent states of Punjab, Haryana, districts of Gujarat, and Delhi that have the dubious distinction of having more people who can pay for expensive tests to help choose male children over females. Census figures based on 2001 data from 640 cities and towns across 26 states and union territories reveal that posh metropolitan India, with 904 girls per 1,000 boys, has a lower sex ratio for children below 6 years than overcrowded slums where there are 919 girls per 1,000 boys. The capital city Delhi has 919 and 859 for slum and non-slum areas respectively. Clearly it is those who can "afford to choose," who use the technology to do so.

Almost all government health policies seem to have an underlying family planning agenda. Health activists say that with its emphasis on population control, the Rural Health Mission is no different. Over the years it has become quite clear that if people are forced to limit the size of their families, they shall do so at the cost of the girl baby, even it means that they have to "import" brides from outside their states or communities. Commenting on the serious decline in the 0-6 sex ratio in India, leading demographer Ashish Bose says that the government's policies are all wrong. The two-child policy has got mixed up with female foeticide. Government slogans like 'Beti ya beta, dono ek hain' ('Girl or boy, both are equal') make little sense. And financial sops for couples having a girl-child make no dent in the traditional preference for sons in India. If India closes the gender gap between girls and boys aged 1-5 years, 1.3 lakh lives will be saved and, overall, the child mortality rate will go down by 5%.

There is no guarantee that the girl-child who escapes foeticide, infanticide and is in the 0-6 age-group will escape the cycle of deliberate neglect that may even result in death because she is less fed, less encouraged to explore the world, more likely to be handed jobs to do and given less healthcare and medical attention. Out-patient data from hospitals in northern Indian cities shows lower admissions of girl-children, and girls who are in a more serious condition than boys when brought for treatment. An August 2004 spot-check at one hospital showed 25,538 boy-children and 12,645 girl-children in the OPD records, 3,822 boy-babies as against 3,160 girl-babies born in hospital, and 1,954 boy-children admitted to a paediatric ward as compared to 1,091 girls.

ELEMENTARY EDUCATION

While enrolment levels propelled by the flagship Sarva Shiksha Abhiyan show an increase, levels of retention in schools remain a matter of concern. There has been a marginal improvement in the percentage of students who stay in school until Class 5--from 61.2% to 62%--but this is way below the global average of 83.3% (10). There is a sharp decline in the enrolment ratio at the upper primary level. Also, the dropout rate increases cumulatively as it proceeds towards higher levels. Although showing improvement, the enrolment of girls is still below that of boys. The dropout rate for girls too is higher. Children belonging to scheduled castes and scheduled tribes continue to face discrimination in schools and have lower enrolment and higher dropout rates. Despite the promise of education for all, 46% of children from scheduled tribes and 38% from scheduled castes continue to be out of school, as against 34% in the case of others. (11) This is not surprising considering the discrimination that these children face at school. The same can be said of the discrimination faced by disabled children.

The Constitution of India fails to even recognise education as a 'right' for those aged 15-18 years. Many children drop out after the elementary level. Indeed, the system is designed to push children out of education--there is a lack of adequate school infrastructure, the quality of education is poor, the educational system is gender-unfriendly, disabled-unfriendly, caste-discriminatory and violent because of a high degree of corporal punishment.

A Model Education Bill has been developed and circulated to the states for adoption into state law. There will thus be no central legislation on education, only state legislation since education is a state subject. If states decide to adopt the Model Education Bill as it is, they will be eligible for 75% assistance from the Centre for education programmes. But if they modify the Model Bill in their formulation of the state education law, they will only be eligible for 50% of central government assistance. The Model Education Bill is not available for public scrutiny, posing serious questions about the government's accountability and transparency.

CHILD LABOUR AND RIGHT TO EDUCATION: A CONTRADICTION

India has the highest number of child labourers in the world.

- Census reports clearly point to an increase in the number of child labourers in the country, from 11.28 million in 1991 to 12.59 million in 2001.
- Reports from the M V Foundation in Andhra Pradesh reveal that nearly 400,000 children, mostly girls between 7 and 14 years of age, toil for 14-16 hours a day in cotton seed production across the country. Ninety percent of them are employed in Andhra Pradesh alone.

- According to Yamina de Laet of the International Chemical, Energy and Mine Workers' federation (ICEM), children aged 6-14 years represent 40% of the labour force in the precious-stone-cutting sector.
- Rescue operations in Mumbai and Delhi in 2005-2006 highlight the employment of children in zari and embroidery units.
- Although the number of children employed in the agricultural sector, in domestic work, roadside restaurants, sweetmeat shops, automobile mechanic units, rice mills, Indian Made Foreign Liquor (IMFL) outlets and most such sectors considered to be 'non-hazardous' is unknown, there is ample evidence to suggest that more and more children are entering the labour force and are being exploited by their employers.

The existing law on child labour that allows children to work in occupations that are not part of the schedule of occupations that are considered harmful to children contradicts the right of every child to free and compulsory education. And yet no attempt is made to resolve this contradiction. How can children be at work and at school at the same time? Surely this means that any attempt to give them access to education will be second-rate, parallel non-formal education.

The Social Jurist, HAQ: Centre for Child Rights and M V Foundation have filed a joint PIL with the Supreme Court of India challenging the validity of the Child Labour Act in the wake of the constitutional guarantee to right to education for children in the 6-14 age-group. In the meantime, vide a notification in the official gazette dated October 10, 2006, the Centre has expanded the list of hazardous occupations banning employment of children under 14 years as domestic help or in restaurants and the entertainment industry.

THE DISABLED CHILD: ALWAYS ON THE PERIPHERY

Census 2001 reports that 2.19 crore (2.13%) of the total population of the country are persons living with disability, and that 1.67% of the total population within the age-group 0-19 years (46,38,26,702) are disabled (see table below).

Disabled population within the age-group 0-19 by type of disability, age and sex (Census 2001)

		Type of disability				
		In seeing	In speech	In hearing	In movement	Mental
Total disabled population	21906769	10634881	1640868	1261722	6105477	2263821
Disabled population in 0-19 age-group	7732196	3605553	775561	90452	2263941	796689
Disabled children as per cent of total population in 0-19 age-group	1.67%	0.78%	0.17%	0.01%	0.48%	0.17%
Disabled children as per cent of total disabled population	35.29%	33.9%	47.26%	23.02%	37.08%	35.19%
Source: Census of India 2001: Table C20 India						

Of all persons living with disability, 35.9% are children and young adults in the 0-19 age-group. Three out of five disabled children in the age-group 0-9 years are reported to be visually impaired. Movement disability has the highest proportion (33.2%) in the 10-19 age-group. This is largely true of 'mental' disability also.

Barely 50% of disabled children reportedly reach adulthood, and no more than 20% survive to cross the fourth decade of life. Although there is very little information regarding the nutritional status of children with disabilities, disabled children living in poverty are among the most deprived in the world. Those who suffer mental disorders are much worse off, as there is still very little recognition of the problem.

Poor enforcement of the Persons With Disabilities Act and the Mental Health Act means that disabled people in India continue to be discriminated against in terms of access to basic services and opportunities. There are few special services for disabled children. Paediatric wards at government hospitals are incapable of dealing with children with disabilities, particularly in terms of infrastructure and resources.

GOVERNMENT ACTION

Over the last few years, the government has taken a number of measures related to children. The most important has been the setting up of a full-fledged Ministry of Women and Child Development as against the Department of Women and Development that used to function as part of the Human Resource Development Ministry. Among the policy and law initiatives that were undertaken was the formulation of the National Charter for Children 2003, the National Plan of Action for Children 2005, and enforcement of the National Commissions for Protection of Child Rights Act 2006. However, the National Policy for Children 1974 has not been repealed, nor does the charter override it. Thus, the status of the charter is not very clear. The government announced the much-discussed and long-delayed National Plan of Action 2005 only in August 2005. Led by the Ministry of Women and Child Development, the government has completed a study on child abuse in India and is in the process of drafting a law on Offences Against Children. It has also initiated the process of amending the present law on child marriage.

Parliament has recently passed the Prohibition of Child Marriage Bill 2006, which enhances punishment for those involved in these practices, and people abetting or attending child marriages. It also declares all child marriages null and void. This is also the main criticism against the legislation that will come into force as a law applicable retrospectively-i.e., all child marriages that have taken place in the past will be declared null and void and the status of children born out of such marriages will come under question.

The Juvenile Justice (Care and Protection) Act 2000 was amended in 2006 and the Central Model Rules in this regard are being formulated.

The Model Right to Education Bill is not available for public scrutiny/comment, as is also the case with the Offences against Children Bill. The Offences against Children Bill has drawn criticism based on drafts available through various sources. The first is that it is too vast in terms of the kind of offences it seeks to address under one umbrella legislation. The second is that, unlike the Immoral Traffic Prevention Act (ITPA) that extends to the whole of India, the proposed legislation keeps the State of Jammu and Kashmir out of its scope. The third, and most important, criticism is that since many of the offences dealt with under the proposed Bill are of a very serious nature, the criminality of those offences should be established through the main criminal law of the land, i.e the Indian Penal Code and not through a social legislation. India already has a strong juvenile justice law to deal with social and reformatory aspects of a crime; that law could be strengthened further to ensure that human rights standards of child protection are met whilst rehabilitating a child victim. Moreover, both the Home Ministry and the Law Ministry are working on amendments in the Criminal Procedure Code, and many activists feel that this is the right time to seek appropriate amendments to ensure child-friendly legal procedures within the CrPC and the Indian Evidence Act.

The government has set up a National Coordination Group on the Rights of the Child for implementation of child rights in the country, and has instituted a Chair on the theme of Protection of Child Rights as part of the 10 Rajiv Gandhi Chairs in Contemporary Studies in central and state universities. These mechanisms, however, are not functional.

Recognising the importance of child budget analysis, the Ministry of Women and Child Development has institutionalised child budgeting and has included it in the new National Plan of Action for Children, 2005.

All of the above are important measures. However, what is required is a complete re-examination of the legal framework for children as whole, identification of gaps and reconciliation of existing anomalies within the law and the implementation of policies, programmes and schemes meant for children.

Only a recognition of children as individuals with rights can pave the way for future action. In the absence of this, all efforts will be sporadic, addressing only some symptoms and not the root cause of the problems that affect the children of this country.

8

NARROW MEANING OF CHILD

INTRODUCTION

The trouble with child rights begins with the very definition of a child in law. A child domiciled in India attains majority at the age of 18. But there are several grey areas in the law here. Under the child labour regulations, for instance, a child is a person under 14 years

Who is a child? When does childhood cease or begin? These simple questions have complex answers. Most of the old world's civilisations did not consider children human beings with full human value. Thus, childhood was not an independent social category until the beginning of the 18th century. Legislation did not deal with childhood as a period of life that needs special measures of protection until the early-19th century. In his book, L'enfant ET la vie familiale sous l'Ancien Regime, Philippe Aries said that the child in the Middle Ages did not exist as an independent anthropological category and therefore children did not need to be taken into consideration.

The law, policy and practice of child welfare have undergone significant changes from an historical perspective. Before 1839, authority and control was important. It was an established common law doctrine that the father had absolute rights over his children. After this, the welfare principle was reflected in the dominant ideology of the family. Victorian judges, who developed the welfare principle, favoured one dominant family form. The traditional Indian view of welfare is based on daya, dana, dakshina, bhiksha, ahimsa, samya-bhava, swadharma and tyaga, the essence of which were self-discipline, self-sacrifice and consideration for others. It was believed that the well-being of children depended on these values. Children were recipients of welfare measures.

It was only during the 20th century that the concept of children's rights emerged. This shift in focus from the 'welfare' to the 'rights' approach is significant. Rights are entitlements. They also imply obligations and goals. The rights approach is primarily concerned with issues of social justice, non-discrimination, equity and empowerment. The rights perspective is embodied in the United Nations Convention on the Rights of the Child (CRC), 1989, which is a landmark in international human rights legislation. India ratified the Convention on the Rights of the Child in December 1992.

According to Article 1 of the CRC, "a child means every human being below the age of 18 years unless, under the law applicable to the child, majority is attained earlier". The Article thus grants individual countries the discretion to determine by law whether childhood ceases at 12, 14, 16 or whatever age is found appropriate.

Today, nearly all cultures share the view that the younger the child the more vulnerable she/he is physically and psychologically and the less able to fend for herself/himself. Age limits are a formal reflection of society's judgement about the evolution of children's capacities and responsibilities. Almost everywhere, age limits formally regulate children's activities: when they can leave school; when they can marry; when they can vote; when they can be treated as adults by the criminal justice system; when they can join the armed forces; and when they can work. But age limits differ from activity to activity, and from country to country.

LEGAL AGE OF THE CHILD IN INDIAN LAW

Several provisions in the Constitution of India impose on the State the primary responsibility of ensuring that all the needs of children are met and that their basic human rights are fully protected. Article 21 A of the Constitution of India says that the State shall provide free and compulsory education to all children within the ages of 6 and 14 in such manner as the State may by law determine. Article 45 of the Constitution specifies that the State shall endeavour to provide early childhood care and education for all children until they complete the age of 6. Article 51 (k) lays down a duty that parents or guardians provide opportunities for education to their child/ward between the age of 6 and 14 years.

The age at which a person ceases to be a child varies under different laws in India. Under the Child Labour Prohibition and Regulation Act, 1986, a child is a person who has not completed 14 years of age. The Constitution of India protects children below the age of 14 from working in factories and hazardous jobs. But below 14, they can work in non-hazardous industries. An area of concern is that no minimum age for child labour has been specified. But for the purposes of criminal responsibility, the age limit is 7 and 12 under the Indian Penal Code, 1860. For purposes of protection against kidnapping, abduction and related offences, it's 16 years for boys and 18 for girls. For special treatment under the Juvenile Justice (Care and Protection of Children) Act 2000, the age is 18 for both boys and girls. And the Protection of Women from Domestic Violence Act 2005 defines a child as any person below the age of 18, and includes an adopted step-or foster child.

Some provisions relating to age under different laws are:

AGE OF MAJORITY

Under the Age of Majority Act 1875, every person domiciled in India shall attain the age of majority on completion of 18 years and not before. The Indian Majority Act was enacted in order to bring uniformity in the applicability of laws to persons of different religions. Unless a particular personal law specifies otherwise, every person domiciled in India is deemed to have attained majority upon completion of 18 years of age. However, in the case of a minor for whose person or property, or both, a guardian has been appointed or declared by any court of justice before the age of 18 years, and in case of every minor the superintendence of whose property has been assumed by the Court of Wards, age of majority will be 21 years and not 18.

The Hindu Minority and Guardianship Act (HMGA), 1956, in Section 4 (a), defines a 'minor' as a person who has not completed the age of 18 years.

The age of majority for the purposes of appointment of guardians of person and property of minors, according to the Dissolution of Muslim Marriages Act, 1939, is also completion of 18 years.

Christians and Parsis also reach majority at 18. Significantly, under the Child Marriage Restraint Act, 1929, which is a secular law, the age of marriage is 21 years for males and 18 years for females. But the age of marriage in Muslim personal law is the age of puberty (around 14 years). It was held that Muslims are not exempted from this law. If the marriage of a Muslim girl is performed while she is a minor, the marriage cannot be void, but the persons who participated in the marriage are not immune from the legal punishment provided under Sections 4, 5 and 6 of the Child Marriage Restraint Act. A Muslim girl can marry on attaining the age of puberty, and her marriage cannot be declared void because she is below the age of 18, according to the Child Marriage Restraint Act.

JUVENILE JUSTICE AND CLAIM OF JUVENILITY

The Juvenile Justice (Care and Protection of Children) Act 2000 is a legislation that conforms to the United Nations Minimum Standards for Administration of Justice to Children. It is an Act to consolidate and amend the law relating to juveniles in conflict with the law and children in need of care and protection, by providing for proper care, protection and treatment by catering to their development needs, and by adopting a child-friendly approach in the adjudication and disposition of matters in the best interest of children and for their ultimate rehabilitation through various institutions established under this enactment. Under the 2000 Act, juvenile means a boy or a girl who has not attained the age of 18 years.

Under the Juvenile Justice (Care and Protection of Children) Amendment Act, 2005, the following amendments were introduced and applicable to all cases involving detention, prosecution or sentence on imprisonment of juveniles under any such law:

- "Juvenile in conflict with law" means a juvenile who is alleged to have committed an offence and has not completed his 18th year as on the date of the offence being committed.
- Whenever a claim of juvenility is raised before any court, or a court is of the opinion that the accused person produced before it was a juvenile on the day the offence was committed, the court shall make an inquiry, take such evidence as may be necessary (but not an affidavit) so as to determine the age of the person, and shall record a finding as to whether or not the person is a juvenile or a child, stating his age as nearly as may be
- An important provision is that a claim of juvenility may be raised before any court and it shall be recognised at any stage even after disposal of the case in terms of the provisions. If the court finds a person to be a juvenile on the day the offence was committed, it shall forward the juvenile to the Board.

It has been observed that, in many instances, if the police that takes a child 'into custody' finds the child well-built he is considered an 'adult' and denied the beneficial provisions of the juvenile justice system.

MINIMUM AGE OF CRIMINAL RESPONSIBILITY (MACR)

The legal definition of a child will also affect how the courts deal with offenders, so age is very significant here. A person who is a minor or a child cannot be convicted in the same manner as an adult.

For instance, if a juvenile is accused of an offence under the provisions of the Narcotic Drugs and Psychotropic Substances (NDPS) Act, he is entitled to necessary benefits under the special enactment of the Juvenile Justice Act.

If there is legislation dealing with the criminal liability of minors, the accused should not be tried under the ordinary law for adults. Children have to be dealt with under the juvenile justice system and not the adult criminal justice system. Children can never be imprisoned or given the death sentence.

AGE VERIFICATION OF RESCUED VICTIMS OF TRAFFICKING

The age of a rescued victim is an important factor in law enforcement and justice delivery. Anyone under 18 years is a child under the Juvenile Justice Act 2000 and cannot be sent to jail. He has to be looked after in a home and treated according to the provisions of the Juvenile Justice Act.

There are several anomalies relating to the issue of age verification of trafficked minor girls after rescue. The Indian Penal Code, 1860, states that sexual intercourse with a girl-child under 16 years of age, even with her consent, constitutes an offence of rape under Section 375 of the IPC. Under Section 366 (A), procurement of a minor girl below 18 years of age is an offence. Under Section 366 (B), importation of girls less than 21 years of age from the state of Jammu and Kashmir to any other state, or from a foreign country to anywhere in India, is an offence. Under Section 372 and 373 of the IPC, selling/ buying of minor girls below 18 years of age for purposes of prostitution, etc, is an offence.

It has been found, however, that traffickers, brothel owners, etc, make sure that the age of the rescued minor is entered as 18 years or above, making her an adult in the records. So, when they are sent to jail, the traffickers/brothel owners bail them out and the victims are returned to their effective confinement.

There is a need to ensure the accountability of doctors who carry out age verification. Also of police officers who record the age immediately after a rescue. Age verification reports usually place the victims within an age bracket. There are countless police records where the age of the girl is recorded as "appears to be of 18-19 years of age". Even medical examinations place the age within a bracket. The Supreme Court has held that when the expert's opinion is given in an age bracket, the lower age in the bracket should be the one taken into consideration, so that the benefit of the doubt favours the victim. Therefore, if the age verification report says that the girl is in the age bracket 17-19 years, for the purposes of law enforcement the age has to be taken as 17 years.

AGE OF CONSENT FOR SEXUAL INTERCOURSE

In India, the law considers anyone less than 18 years to be a child/minor, not competent to take major decisions affecting herself or others for the purposes of the Indian Majority Act, Contract Act, Juvenile Justice Act, Child Marriage Restraint Act, or Representation of Peoples Act. However, under Section 375 of the Indian Penal Code, the girl (aged 16-18) is given the right of consent to sexual intercourse. Yet, she cannot marry at that age even with the consent of her parents. She cannot be taken out of the keeping of her lawful guardian, even with her consent, for lesser purposes. But she can consent to sexual intercourse so long as she does not go out of the keeping of her lawful guardian. The Law Commission of India did attempt, in its 84th report, to bring the age of consent in rape to 18 years, in tune with other enactments and consistent with refined and modern notions regarding the concern and compassion that society should bestow on its younger members. But this was not accepted. As a result, the age of consent in an offence of rape continues to be 16 years even today. Raising the age of consent for sexual intercourse to 18, consistent with the stipulations in subsequent enactments, appears to be the unavoidable imperative before the system.

CHILD WITNESSES

The courts have held that evidence from a child witness, if found competent to depose facts, could be the basis for a conviction. In other words, even in the absence of an oath, the evidence of a child witness can be considered under Section 118 of the Evidence Act, provided such a witness is able to understand the answers thereof. The evidence of a child witness and credibility would depend on the circumstances of each case. The only precaution the court should bear in mind whilst assessing the evidence of a child witness is that the witness must be reliable, his/her demeanour must be like that of any other competent witness, and that there is no likelihood of him/

her being tutored. Further, Section 118 of the Evidence Act envisages that all persons shall be competent to testify, unless the court considers that they are prevented from understanding the questions put to them, or from giving rational answers to the questions, because of their young age, extreme old age, or disease--whether of mind or any other similar cause. However, a young child can be allowed to testify if he/she has the intellectual capacity to understand questions and provide rational answers.

While the law recognises the child as a competent witness, a child who is around 6 years old, who is unable to form a proper opinion about the nature of the incident because of immaturity of understanding, is not considered by the court as a witness whose sole testimony can be relied on without other corroborative evidence. The evidence of a child must be evaluated carefully because he/she is easy prey to tutoring.

The word 'child' has therefore been used in law as a term denoting relationship; as a term indicating capacity; and as a term of special protection. Underlying these alternative specifications are very different concepts about the child. These include considering a child a burden, which invokes the right to maintenance and support; regarding children as individuals with temporary disabilities, making for rights to special treatment and special discrimination; treating children as specially vulnerable, to ensure rights to protection; and recognising children as resources for the country's development, necessitating nurturing and advancement.

Thus there do not appear to be any criteria or scientific parameters for determining a child: the age limit in some laws appear arbitrary or based on socio-cultural perceptions. The Indian Mines Act defines children as those below 18 years, and the various state Shops and Establishment Acts define the age as between 12-15 years.

It is necessary that the definition of 'child' be brought in line with the Convention on the Rights of the Child--viz all those below 18 years of age. If the best interest of the child is the guiding norm, one can err on the side of a higher age limit for protective care and a lower age limit with respect to civil and cultural matters. A review of the definition of 'child', in light of Article 1 of the CRC, has been referred to the Law Commission of India as part of a comprehensive review of the Code of Criminal Procedure, the Indian Evidence Act and the Indian Penal Code.

STUMBLING FROM THE START

The Achievements of Babies and Children (ABC) Index measures four very basic aspects of child well-being-survival, immunisation, nutrition and schooling. India scores no more than 66% overall.

But states such as Tamil Nadu and Himachal Pradesh, and even Sri Lanka and Bangladesh, have made rapid strides in child development. What is the key? The rights-based approach and outstanding records of active state involvement in the provision of health, nutrition and education services. It has been suggested that the first question the Indian prime minister should ask his ministers is not "How is the economy growing," but "How are children growing".

The ministers, however, would probably rather answer the former, for the state of Indian children is nothing short of a humanitarian emergency. Few countries, in fact, have worse indicators of child development. Progress in this field has been very slow, with countries like Bangladesh 'overtaking' India during the last few years. This crisis casts a deep shadow on India's progress in other fields.

The average Indian child gets a rather poor start in life. Even before birth, he or she is heading for disaster due to poor antenatal care and maternal undernutrition. About one-third of expectant mothers in India are deprived of tetanus vaccinations, an important defence against infection at birth. Similarly, about one-fourth of pregnant women do not have a single antenatal checkup, and a majority of deliveries take place without the assistance of a health professional (Table 1).

Worse, the average Indian mother is frail and anaemic. This is likely to result in low birth weight, a major cause of child undernutrition.

After birth, life continues to be precarious. About one-third of all newborn babies in India weigh less than the acceptable minimum of 2.5 kg. Undernutrition levels continue to increase during the first two years of life, largely due to poor breastfeeding and faulty weaning. About half of all children below 3 are undernourished, more than half are deprived of full immunisation, and a large majority suffer from anaemia (Table 2). Illness is also widespread, with a fifth of all children suffering from diarrhoea and almost a third suffering from fever. A substantial proportion of Indian children (about one-tenth) never reach the age of 5.

India: Maternal health and related indicators

	1998-99 (NFHS-2)	2005-06 (NFHS-3)
Proportion (%) of mothers who had*:		
No tetanus immunisation during pregnancy	33	NA
No antenatal checkup	34	*
No iron or folic supplement	42	NA
No assistance from a health professional during delivery	58	*
Proportion (%) of adult women with:		
Anaemia	52	*
Body Mass Index (BMI) below 18.5	36	*
* *Data pertains to births during three years preceding the survey*		
Source: National Family Health Survey 1998-99 (NFHS-2) and National Family Health Survey 2005-06 (NFHS-3) data presented in the International Institute for Population Sciences (2000, 2006); also available at www.nfhsindia.org. The figures apply to ever-married women in the age-group 15-49 years		

As children grow up, poor nutrition and ill health affects their learning abilities and preparedness for schooling. In 1998-99, almost one-third of all children in the 15-19 age-group failed to complete Class 5, and half did not complete Class 8. So much for the 'fundamental right to education'! By the time Indian children are supposed to complete upper primary school, many of them have actually been pushed into the labour force, further ruining their health by working long hours in harsh conditions.

In short, millions of Indian children are condemned to stumble right from the start. During the first six years of life, and especially the first two, they sink into a dreadful trap of undernutrition, ill health and poor learning abilities. This burden is extremely difficult to overcome in later years.

SLOW PROGRESS

Another disturbing aspect of this situation is that the rate of improvement over time is also very slow. Extreme forms of hunger and undernutrition, such as marasmus and kwashiorkor, have sharply declined over the years. But the general progress of nutrition indicators (such as the height and weight of Indian children) is sluggish.

The findings of the third National Family Health Survey (NFHS-3), released just a few days before the completion of this abridged report, are quite alarming in this regard. For instance, the proportion of undernourished children, based on standard weight-for-age criteria, was virtually the same in 2005-06 as in 1998-99: in both years, nearly half of all Indian children were underweight. Even the decline of stunting in that period, from 45% to 38%, is far from impressive--about one percentage point per year. If the incidence of stunting continues to decline at this rate, it will take another 25 years or so to reach levels similar to those in China today.

State of India's children

	1998-99 2005-06 (NFHS-2) (NFHS-3)	
Proportion (%) of young children with the following characteristics:		
Low birth weight (about 30)		
Not breastfed within an hour after birth	84	*
Undernourished*	47	46
Stunted*	45	*
Wasted*	16	*
Not fully vaccinated+	58	56
Not vaccinated at all+	14	NA
Birth was not preceded by any antenatal checkup	34	*
Suffer from anaemia	74	79

Proportion (%) of young children who suffered from the following, during the last two weeks:		
Fever	30	NA
Diarrhoea	19	NA
Acute respiratory infection	19	NA

* Based on standard anthropometric indicators: weight-for-age for 'undernourished', height-for-age for 'stunted', weight-for-height for 'wasted'

+ Age: 12-23 months

Source: National Family Health Survey (see Table 2.1). Unless stated otherwise, the reference group consists of children aged below 3 years (excluding children aged below 6 months, if appropriate). For 'low birth weight', the estimate is from Human Development Report 2006

Health-related indicators from the third National Family Health Survey are no less disturbing. For instance, they suggest that child immunisation rates were much the same in 2005-06 as in 1998-99 (Table 2). The incidence of anaemia among children was also similar in both years; in fact, it was a little higher in 2005-06, according to the available NFHS-3 data. While some indicators have improved, the general pace of change is excruciatingly slow--much slower, for instance, than in neighbouring Bangladesh.

Similar concerns arise if we look at mortality indicators. In India, as in most other countries, the infant mortality rate has steadily declined during the last 50 years or so: from about 150 per 1,000 live births in the late-1950s, to 60 or so per 1,000 today. However, the decline in infant mortality slowed down significantly in the '90s, compared with earlier decades. Although the rate of decline seems to have picked up again during the last few years, the overall progress made since 1990 is limited compared to many other countries.

This slow progress in the field of child health and nutrition is all the more striking as the Indian economy is one of the fastest-growing economies in the world. In the last 15 years, India's GDP has been growing at around 6% per year, on average, and per-capita income has more than doubled. Few countries have had it so good as far as economic growth is concerned. Yet, progress on child development indicators has been much slower in India than in many countries with comparable or even much lower rates of economic growth.

INDIA AND SOUTH ASIA

When India is compared with other countries, the comparison is usually made with 'big' countries--say China or the United States. Yet there is a great deal to learn from looking around us within South Asia, especially in matters of nutrition and health. Far from being 'backward' in comparison with India, other South Asian countries are generally doing better than India in this field (see Table 3). It may come as a shock to learn that India has the lowest child immunisation rate in South Asia. For instance, the proportion of children who have not had a BCG vaccine in India is twice as high as in Nepal, more than five times as high as in Bangladesh, and almost 30 times as high as in Sri Lanka! Turning to child undernutrition, India emerges in a poor light again, with only Nepal doing worse. And despite its sophisticated medical system and vast army of doctors, India has not been able to achieve higher rates of child survival than any of its neighbours except Pakistan. Almost any 'summary index' of these child development indicators would place India at the bottom of this list of countries.

Some aspects of this picture are relatively well-known. For instance, Sri Lanka's outstanding achievements in the field of child health have been widely noted. In spite of being almost as poor as India, in terms of per-capita income, Sri Lanka has an infant mortality rate of only 12 per 1,000--less than one-fifth of India's (about 62 per 1,000). Similarly, child immunisation is virtually universal in Sri Lanka, in sharp contrast with India where this is still a distant goal (Table 3).

What is less well known is that Sri Lanka's success in this field is largely based on public intervention. Free and universal provision of essential services, especially in health and education, became an important feature of social policy in Sri Lanka at an early stage of development. For instance, most children in Sri Lanka have been integrated in a common schooling system of reasonable quality, under government auspices. In fact, private schools have been banned since the 1960s, up to the secondary level. Indian readers may also be surprised to hear that in Sri Lanka "few people live more than 1.4 km away from the nearest health centre" (Oxfam International, 2006). The fact that Sri Lankan children are doing so well in comparison with their Indian siblings is no accident--it reflects highly divergent levels of public commitment to the well-being of children in these two countries.

Child deprivation in India and South Asia, 2004

	Bangla-desh	Bhutan	India	Nepal	Pakis-tan	Sri Lanka
Immunisation						
(% of children under 3 years who						
have not received the stated vaccine)						
BCG	5	8	27	15	20	1
DTP3	15	11	36	20	35	3
MCV	23	13	44	27	33	4
Pol3	15	10	30	20	35	3
Child undernutrition						
(% of children with						
the stated condition)						
Underweight	48	19	47	48	38	29
Stunting	43	40	46	51	37	14
Wasting	13	3	16	10	13	14
Infant and child						
mortality						
(per 1,000 live births)						
Infant mortality rate	56	67	62	59	80	12
Under-5 mortality						
Rate	77	80	85	76	101	14

Source: UNICEF (2006), 'State of the World's Children'. In each row, the 'worst' figure is highlighted

No less interesting is the contrast between Bangladesh and India. In spite of being poorer (much poorer) than India, Bangladesh has better indicators of child development in many respects, as Tables 3 and 4 illustrate. The contrast in immunisation rates is particularly sharp: the proportion of children who have not been vaccinated is two to five times as high in India as in Bangladesh, depending on which vaccine one looks at. Similarly, infant and child mortality rates are significantly lower in Bangladesh than in India. It is worth noting that this pattern is a relatively recent development: it is during the last 15 years or so that Bangladesh has 'overtaken' India in this field. While Bangladesh had a much higher infant mortality rate than India in 1990 (91 and 80 per 1,000 live births, respectively), today the positions are reversed: 56 per 1,000 in Bangladesh compared with 62 per 1,000 in India. India has been neatly leapfrogged, that too during a period when economic growth was much faster in India than in Bangladesh.

India and Bangladesh: Children's well-being and related indicators, 2004

	India	Bangladesh
Infant mortality rate		
(per 1,000 live births)	62	56
Proportion (%) of 1-year-olds immunised		
BCG	73	95
Measles	56	77
Proportion (%) of undernourished children, 1995-2003*		
Based on weight-for-age	49	48
Based on height-for-age	45	43
Estimated maternal mortality rate, 2000		
(per 100,000 live births)	540	380
Net primary enrolment ratio (female) (%)	87	95
GDP per capita		
(PPP US $)	3,139	1,870

* Data refers to the most recent year for which estimates are available during this period

Source: Human Development Report 2006. Unless stated otherwise, the reference year is 2004

It is also worth noting that the contrast between India and other South Asian countries would be even sharper if we were to focus on deprived regions or communities in each country, instead of national averages. This is because internal inequalities are typically larger in India. Other South Asian countries tend to be less 'heterogeneous', not only in terms of regional differences but also in terms of socio-economic inequalities. It is doubtful whether any country in South Asia (other than India) has substantial pockets where children live in such dreadful conditions as, say, among the Musahars of Bihar or the Sahariyas of Madhya Pradesh. And it is worth remembering that the Musahars alone represent a population of about 2.5 million-more than the entire population of Bhutan, or for that matter of 45 of the 177 countries listed in the latest Human Development Report.

CHILDHOOD AMONG THE SAHARIYAS

In May 2006 Dilli Dakha lost her first child, a girl aged one-and-a-half years. After that she had a boy, Sugreev, who is now two. The couple then lost their twin daughters Ganga and Jamuna. According to Dakha, she was unable to feed them as there was no milk. She says she eats one roti with onion, once a day. Her family's diet does not include any pulses or vegetables because they cannot afford it. Her husband earns around Rs 20 per day, on the few days he goes out to work. Subsequent to her third delivery she has started losing her sight, largely due to Vitamin A deficiency.

The deaths of children like Ganga and Jamuna are, unfortunately, not new to the district. Dilli Dakha and her husband are Sahariya tribals.

It is claimed that the Sahariyas were the first tribals in the country. For generations they depended on the forests for their survival, living a subsistence life with limited needs. Agriculture, gathering forest produce and hunting were traditional ways of earning a livelihood.

Life has not been easy for the Sahariyas after their eviction from the forests. Sahariya children are the worst affected due to poverty, lack of livelihood resources and an indifferent government policy. According to the regional medical research centre for tribals in Jabalpur, the Infant Mortality Rate (IMR) among Sahariyas is 88 per 1,000 live births, and 93.5% of Sahariya children are severely malnourished. According to the same sources, the average life-span of a Sahariya is only 45 years; 74.3% of Sahariya children are underweight, and 75.4% stunted. Data from the state government's Bal Sanjeevani Abhiyan (8th Report) indicates that 58% of children in the age-group 0-6 years, in the district, suffer from malnutrition. Nearly 86.5% of Sahariya women are anaemic because of the non-availability of nutritious food. These indicators show that the Sahariyas are one of the poorest and most deprived communities in the country.

REGIONAL CONTRASTS

National averages often hide major disparities between regions and socio-economic groups. This is particularly the case in a country like India, which is so large and so diverse. To illustrate, consider the immunisation rates as reported in the second National Family Health Survey (1998-99). For a child born in Tamil Nadu, the chance of being fully immunised by age one is around 90% (even higher among privileged Tamil families). But, chances of being fully immunised are only 42% for the average Indian child, dropping further to 26% for the average 'scheduled tribe' child, and a shocking 11% for the average Bihari child. When different sources of disadvantage (relating, for instance, to class, caste and gender) are combined, immunisation rates dip to abysmally low levels. For instance, among 'scheduled tribe' children in Bihar, only 4% are fully immunised and 38% have not been immunised at all. Startling disparities can also be observed in other aspects of child development.

Regional disparities are further explored in Table 5, based on NFHS-2 data. The table focuses on four crucial aspects of the well-being of children: survival, immunisation, nutrition and schooling (their SINS, if you like). For each of these, a standard indicator has been chosen (other indicators could have been used, but the choice does not matter much for our purpose). Each indicator is measured in percentage terms, and can be roughly interpreted as the 'probability' that an average child in the relevant state achieves a particular goal: survival until age 5, full immunisation, adequate nourishment, and school participation, respectively. In the last column, we present a simple 'summary index' of child development, based on these four indicators. This index is an average of the four indicators. To stress the vital importance of the achievements reflected in this index, we call it the 'Achievements of Babies and Children' (ABC) index.

In interpreting the index, it is useful to remember that we are focusing here on very basic achievements of Indian children, as the acronym indicates. Ideally, we would like every child (or almost every child--nothing is perfect!) to survive until the age of 5, be fully immunised, well nourished, and go to school. In that case, the ABC index would be close to 100%--full marks. As Table 5 shows, however, this ideal situation is nowhere near being realised in any Indian state, even Kerala, the trailblazer in this field.

At the bottom of the scale, the ABC index is barely 50% for the states formerly known (somewhat unkindly) as BIMARU states--Bihar, Madhya Pradesh, Rajasthan and Uttar Pradesh. Roughly speaking, this corresponds to a situation where the average child in these states achieves only half of the four elementary goals examined in Table 5.

One will perhaps not be surprised to see Kerala at the top of this ranking, since Kerala is well known for its achievements in the fields of health and education, which have a long history. However, it is interesting to note that Kerala is no longer "way ahead" of all the other states, as it once used to be. Further, the states that are "catching up" with Kerala do not seem to be doing it on the basis of economic growth alone. If the achievements of babies and children were driven by economic success, we would expect Punjab and Haryana (India's most prosperous states) to be ahead of the other states. But, in fact, Punjab and Haryana rank fourth and sixth, respectively, in terms of the ABC index. Both have been overtaken by Tamil Nadu and Himachal Pradesh, which are now quite close to Kerala as far as child development is concerned.

Regional contrasts in child development, 1998-99

State	Selected child development indicators*				'Achievements of Babies and Children' (ABC) index
	Survival (% of children who survive to age 5)	Immunisation (% of children who are fully immunised)	Nutrition (% of children who are not underweight)	Schooling (% of children who attend school)	
Kerala	98.1	80	73	97	87.0
Tamil Nadu	93.7	89	63	92	84.4
Himachal Pradesh	95.8	83	56	98	83.2
Punjab	92.8	72	71	91	81.7
Maharashtra	94.2	78	50	93	78.8
Haryana	92.3	63	65	89	77.3
Jammu and Kashmir	92.0	57	66	84	74.8
Karnataka	93.0	60	56	80	72.3
Andhra Pradesh	91.6	59	62	76	72.2
Gujarat	91.5	53	55	78	69.4
West Bengal	93.2	44	51	87	68.8
INDIA	90.5	42	53	79	66.1
Orissa	89.6	44	46	79	64.7
Assam	91.1	17	64	77	62.3
Uttar Pradesh+	87.8	21	48	77	58.5
Rajasthan	88.5	17	49	76	57.6
Madhya Pradesh+	86.2	22	45	76	57.3
Bihar+	89.5	11	46	63	52.4

**Age-groups: 12-23 months for immunisation; below 3 years for nutrition; 6-14 years for schooling*

+ Undivided (for example, including Jharkhand in the case of Bihar)

Note: The ABC Index is an unweighted average of the four indicators (for further discussion, see text). States are ranked in descending order of the index

There is an important pointer here to the role of public action in this field. Indeed, both Tamil Nadu and Himachal Pradesh have made serious efforts to ensure that all citizens have access to basic health, nutrition and education services. In Himachal Pradesh, for instance, a "schooling revolution" of sorts has taken place in the last few decades. Widely considered as an educationally "backward" state not so long ago, Himachal Pradesh has rapidly caught up with Kerala, based on active state promotion of elementary education. In 1998-99, school attendance rates in the 6-14 age-group were as high as 99% and 97% for boys and girls respectively, compared with 97% for both, in Kerala.

This schooling revolution, together with related social initiatives, has not only led to a dramatic increase in education levels, it has also (more recently) paved the way for rapid advances in other fields including health and nutrition. Himachal Pradesh's high ABC index is one manifestation of this general pattern of accelerated social progress based on public intervention.

Though Tamil Nadu has not been as successful as Himachal Pradesh in the field of elementary education, it has an outstanding record of active state involvement in the provision of health and nutrition services. For instance, Tamil Nadu was the first state to introduce cooked midday meals in primary schools, way back in 1982--almost 20 years before the Supreme Court nudged other states in the same direction.

Tamil Nadu also has an outstanding network of anganwadis. Here again it is not an accident that Tamil children are doing relatively well; nor is it due primarily to economic growth. Rather, it reflects concerted efforts to provide children with the 'opportunities and facilities' that are due to them under the Constitution.

At the other end of the scale, the dismal levels of child development in Bihar, Madhya Pradesh, Rajasthan and Uttar Pradesh reflect a long history of public apathy towards the well-being of children in these states. In some of these states, or their 'offspring' (Chhattisgarh, Jharkhand and Uttaranchal), there have been positive signs of change in recent years. For instance, Chhattisgarh launched an innovative community health programme (the Mitanin programme) in 2001-02 and recent evidence suggests that this programme may be having a significant impact on child health. However, the general level of attention to children's rights and well-being in these states remains abysmally low.

CHILDCARE AS A SOCIAL RESPONSIBILITY

The rights approach, which led to wider acknowledgment of elementary education as a fundamental right, contributed to the rapid expansion of school education in the 1990s. The rights approach should also be used to ensure the survival and well-being of children under 6, by demanding universalisation of the Integrated Child Development Services, the only major national programme aimed at this age-group

Most Indian children are left to their own devices until the age of 6, when they are finally herded into school. Yet the first six years of life (and especially the first two years) have a decisive and lasting influence on a child's health, well-being, aptitude and opportunities. The consequences of this neglect are staring us in the face: about half of all Indian children are undernourished, more than half suffer from anaemia, and a similar proportion escape 'full immunisation'. Few countries have such disastrous indicators of child well-being. According to the latest Human Development Report, India has the highest proportion of undernourished children in the world, along with Bangladesh, Ethiopia and Nepal. In fact, in terms of the general situation of children, even Bangladesh now seems to be doing better than India. This contrast is all the more striking as Bangladesh is poorer--much poorer--than India.

Some time ago I attended a conference in a village in Kerala. The conference was a little boring, and, as a diversion, I visited the nearest anganwadi (childcare centre). It was located in a tidy and spacious building, well furnished with toys, charts, cooking utensils, a medical kit, a ceiling fan, even a smokeless chulha. The children, I was told, were given a glass of milk on their arrival in the morning, a full meal at noon, and some upma before they left at around 3 pm. There were also well-rehearsed routines for immunisation, de-worming, growth monitoring, micronutrient supplementation and health checkups. Details of the age, weight, height and immunisation status of every child in the neighbourhood were neatly posted on the walls. The registers, including detailed 'minutes' of monthly meetings with the children's mothers, were in good order. When I asked the anganwadi worker how many anganwadis there were in the gram panchayat, she casually replied "twenty-five". She said that about 90% of children below 6 years of age were enrolled in these anganwadis.

It is perhaps not an accident that Kerala has the best indicators of child well-being among all the Indian states, by a long margin. In other states, early childcare and development services (hereafter 'child development services') are grossly neglected.

Against this background, there is an urgent need to re-examine what India is doing for the survival, well-being and rights of children under the age of 6. Ultimately, this involves addressing the structural roots of child deprivation, including mass poverty, social discrimination, lack of education, and gender inequality. However, there is also an immediate need to protect children under 6, by integrating them in an effective system of child development services that leaves no child behind. The best way of doing this is to universalise the Integrated Child Development Services (ICDS), the only major national programme addressing this age-group.

The quality of ICDS also needs to be radically enhanced. In other words, what is required is not just universalisation but "universalisation with quality". A more complete expression would be "universalisation with quality and equity". This stresses the need to prioritise underprivileged groups (for example, dalit and adivasi communities) in the process of universalisation, as well as to eradicate social discrimination of any kind in the implementation of ICDS.

A RIGHTS PERSPECTIVE ON ICDS

The value of a 'rights approach' to social development has been well demonstrated in recent years. Wider acknowledgment of elementary education as a fundamental right (recently expressed in the 86th constitutional amendment) has contributed to the rapid expansion of school education in the 1990s, evident in age-specific literacy data from the 1991 and 2001 censuses. The Right to Information Act 2005 has lifted the veil of secrecy from government documents, a major step towards restoring accountability in public life. Supreme Court orders on the right to food have forced the government to take major initiatives in this field, such as the provision of cooked midday meals in primary schools. Similarly, the National Rural Employment Guarantee Act has empowered rural labourers and reversed the long-standing neglect of rural employment in public policy.

In the light of these experiences, there is a case for more active use of the rights approach in the context of children's issues, including the survival and well-being of children under 6. Children's rights are not, of course, a new idea. The idea is conveyed in the Indian Constitution, notably Article 39 (f), which directs the State to ensure that "children are given opportunities and facilities to develop in a healthy manner and in conditions of freedom and dignity". This Article belongs to the Directive Principles, and should be read along with Article 37, which states that these principles are "fundamental to the governance of the country," and that "it shall be the duty of the State to apply these principles in making laws".

As Article 39 (f) illustrates, the Directive Principles (largely due to Dr Ambedkar) include a visionary emphasis on 'positive freedoms'. The government's formal commitment to child rights and positive freedoms was further affirmed in the international Convention on the Rights of the Child. In practice, however, little has been done to protect and promote the positive freedoms of children as a matter of right.

The primary role of the rights approach is to change public perceptions of what is due to Indian children. In particular, the rights approach can help to put children's issues on the political agenda, and to forge new social norms on these issues. To illustrate, the recent recognition of elementary education as a fundamental right of every child has helped to dispel the resilient notion that education is 'unnecessary' for some sections of society. A similar consensus needs to be built regarding the rights and entitlements of children under 6.

Aside from its political value, the rights perspective has practical implications for public policy on child development services. First, this perspective is the main foundation of the demand for 'universal' child development services. Indeed, one implication of the rights approach is that all children are entitled to certain "opportunities and facilities" (as the Constitution puts it) that do not have to be justified on a case-by-case basis, let alone submitted to cost-benefit tests. The main role of ICDS is to act as an institutional medium for the provision of these facilities.

Second, the rights perspective points to the need for strong monitoring and redressal mechanisms, so that people are able to claim their entitlements. There are few redressal mechanisms in the present scheme of things. In some states, for instance, nutrition programmes under ICDS have been interrupted for months at a time without any action being taken. One reason for this apathy is that these services are regarded as a form of state largesse, rather than as enforceable entitlements.

Last but not least, the rights perspective highlights the possibility of putting in place legal safeguards for children's rights. Many Indian laws, of course, deal with children's rights in one way or another. But these legislative provisions tend to be of a 'negative' kind, in the sense that they are aimed at protecting children from various evils (such as child labour or child marriage), rather than at guaranteeing the positive "opportunities and facilities" mentioned in Article 39 (f). The proposed Right to Education Bill, flawed as it may be, is an example of the sort of legislation required to guarantee positive freedoms to Indian children. More can be done in this respect, including similar legislation for children under the age of 6.

Needless to say, the protection of children's rights involves much more than better laws and policies relating to "child development services". It also calls for far-reaching action in fields such as elementary education, gender relations and even property rights. Nevertheless, the universalisation of ICDS has a crucial role to play in this context.

UNIVERSALISATION WITH QUALITY

In concrete terms, what does "universalisation with quality" mean? It means that (1) every settlement should have a functional anganwadi, (2) ICDS should be extended to all children under the age of 6 (and all eligible women), and (3) the scope and quality of these services should be radically enhanced.

ICDS is the only major national programme that addresses the needs of children under 6. It seeks to provide young children with an integrated package of services relating to nutrition, health and pre-school education. Because the needs of a child cannot be addressed in isolation from those of his or her mother, the programme also extends to pregnant women, nursing mothers and adolescent girls.

Basic ICDS include supplementary nutrition, growth monitoring, nutrition counselling, health education, immunisation, healthcare, referral services, and pre-school education. These services are provided through a vast network of ICDS centres, better known as anganwadis. Each anganwadi is managed by an anganwadi worker, assisted by an anganwadi helper. An anganwadi is supposed to cover a population of about 1,000 people--roughly 200 families.

The coverage of ICDS has steadily expanded since its inception in 1975. Today, the programme is operational in almost every block, and the country has more than 700,000 anganwadis. However, the effective coverage of ICDS remains limited: barely one-fourth of all children under 6 are covered under the supplementary nutrition component.

The basic premise of the demand for universalisation of ICDS is that all children have a right to nutrition, health, pre-school education and related opportunities. The anganwadi is an institutional medium to protect these rights, or at least to bring them within the realm of possibility. There are at least four other arguments in favour of universalisation: a legal argument, a political argument, an economic argument and an equity argument.

The legal argument is that, like midday meals in primary schools, the universalisation of ICDS is mandatory under Supreme Court orders. On November 28, 2001, the court directed the government to ensure that every settlement has a functional anganwadi, and that ICDS is extended to all children under 6, all pregnant or lactating women, and all adolescent girls. This order was reiterated and extended on April 29 and October

7, 2004, along with further directions on ICDS. The latest Supreme Court order on ICDS, dated December 13, 2006, goes even further. For instance, it states that an anganwadi should be created "on demand", within three months, in settlements where there are at least 40 children under 6 years of age.

The political argument is that the universalisation of ICDS is one of the core commitments of the Common Minimum Programme (CMP) of the United Progressive Alliance (UPA) government. The CMP clearly states: "The UPA will also universalise the Integrated Child Development Services (ICDS) scheme to provide a functional anganwadi in every settlement and ensure full coverage for all children." Thus, aside from being important in its own right, the universalisation of ICDS can be seen as an aspect of the need to hold the government accountable to its promises. It is in this spirit that the National Advisory Council formulated detailed recommendations on ICDS, in line with commitments in the CMP. These recommendations, unfortunately, have had little impact so far.

The economic argument is that providing health and nutrition services to children is a good 'investment', so to speak. Many recent studies indicate that the 'returns' on child nutrition programmes are quite high, or at least can be quite high. The methods underlying these estimates of economic returns have serious limitations, and the results are at best indicative. Further, one should guard against allowing economic criteria to become the arbiter of public policy in this field. Nevertheless, these studies strengthen the case for a major expansion of child development services in India.

Lastly, there is an equity argument for universalisation. Indeed, the universalisation of ICDS would curb the inter-generational perpetuation of social inequality, by creating more equal opportunities for growth and development in early childhood. It would also foster social equity by creating a space where children eat, play and learn together irrespective of class, caste and gender. This socialisation role of ICDS is very important in a country where social divisions are so resilient.

Taken together, these arguments add up to a fairly strong case for the universalisation of ICDS.

Two counter-arguments should be briefly addressed. One is that ICDS does not and cannot work. It is easy to provide superficial support for this claim by citing horror stories of idle anganwadis or food poisoning. These horror stories, however, are a poor reflection of the general condition of ICDS. Indeed, recent evidence suggests that ICDS is actually performing crucial functions in many states, and that there is much scope for consolidating these achievements.

The recent Focus On Children Under Six (FOCUS) survey sheds some useful light on these issues. The survey was conducted in May-June 2004 in six states: Chhattisgarh, Himachal Pradesh, Maharashtra, Rajasthan, Uttar Pradesh and Tamil Nadu. It involved unannounced visits to a random sample of about 200 anganwadis, and detailed interviews with about 500 mothers with at least one child under the age of 6, enrolled at the local anganwadi. It is encouraging to note that, according to a large majority of the sample mothers, anganwadis open regularly. This is, in fact, consistent with direct observation: nearly 80% of the sample anganwadis were open at the time of the investigators' unannounced visit. Similarly, 94% of the sample mothers stated that supplementary nutrition was being provided at the anganwadi. Even pre-school education, the weakest component of ICDS, was happening in about half of the sample anganwadis.

This is not to deny that the quality of ICDS services is low in many states, and needs urgent improvement. But there is no basis for the claim that ICDS is a non-functional programme. Aside from debunking this myth, the FOCUS survey draws attention to the enormous potential of ICDS. The sensible way to go is to make better use of this potential, given that the foundations of ICDS are already in place throughout the country. To put it another way, opposing the universalisation of ICDS on the grounds that there are serious quality issues in some states would be like saying that primary schools should be closed because schools are not working very well in Bihar, or Kalahandi.

Another counter-argument is that universalisation is unnecessary, even wasteful: instead, public provision of child development services should be "targeted" to disadvantaged children. This advice is based on the familiar case for targeting social services: targeted interventions are more "cost-effective" and also help to reduce inequality. Whatever its relevance in other contexts, this argument has little merit as far as ICDS is concerned.

For one thing, there is no reliable way of "targeting" children who are vulnerable to malnutrition or ill health. Indeed, undernourished children are found in all socio-economic groups. Even among relatively privileged households, a substantial proportion of children are undernourished. To look at this from another angle, the causes of malnutrition and ill health are diverse and these deprivations have no obvious, measurable "correlates" that could be used for targeting purposes. Thus, any targeted system is bound to leave large numbers of children exposed to malnutrition and ill health. It would effectively convert ICDS into a "hit-and-miss" programme. This is incompatible with the notion that nutrition, health and pre-school education are the fundamental rights of all Indian children.

(Jean Dreze is a leading development economist and Honorary Professor at the Delhi School of Economics and the Govind Ballabh Pant Social Sciences Institute. He has been closely associated with the Right to Food, Right to Information and NREGA campaigns. This article is based on excerpts from 'Universalisation with Quality: ICDS in a Rights Perspective', Economic and Political Weekly, August 26, 2006. The arguments and evidence are further developed in 'Focus on Children Under Six'(FOCUS), a recent report prepared by Citizens' Initiative for the Rights of Children Under Six.

What does the budget have to do with children?

Everything. Analysing trends in the government's allocation and expenditure on child-specific programmes and schemes is one way of holding the government accountable on its commitment to children. Though the percentage share of children in the Union budget has gone up from 1.2% in the 1990s to 4.91% in 2006-07, there is still quite a gap between need and allocation, and allocation and actual spending

The disparities in India are stark. Thirty-five per cent of Indians are illiterate and yet India produces millions of highly-skilled global knowledge professionals. The government is celebrating India's "unprecedented high rate of economic growth", huge Foreign Direct Investments (FDIs) and Foreign Institutional Investments (FIIs), and yet thousands of our children are dying of hunger. India has an estimated 440 million children (0-18 years) constituting over 40% of the country's population. Yet their rights continue to be neglected.

Why is this happening? Theoretically, government expenditure and investment are dependent on economic prudence and a vision of the nation's development. But it would appear that it is interest groups and lobbies that have a direct bearing on the vote banks of political parties and the dynamics of the global economy that manage to get their interests addressed. Tribals, women, farmers, unorganised labour in agriculture and various industries don't. But these marginalised groups can at least voice their concerns by virtue of adult franchise and their ability to form groups and associations. Children do not even have a voice and the right to be heard. Their rights are considered either subservient to the rights of other groups or at best part and parcel of adult rights.

When economic reforms were introduced in 1991, the Indian finance minister made it immediately clear that the government "was committed to adjustment with a human face". (1) Despite this, there were apprehensions that the reforms would lead to a decline in social welfare in general and child welfare in particular. Very few comprehensive studies have been done to assess the impact of the reforms specifically on children, (2) and therefore the relationship between reforms and welfare of children is not easy to establish.

The impact of the reforms on children received considerable attention in the late-1980s and early-1990s, especially after the publication of UNICEF's Adjustment with a Human Face (Cornia, Jolly and Stewart, 1987). Based on experiences in 10 countries, mainly in Latin America, Africa and East Asia, this study showed that adjustment often had very negative effects on the welfare of children. In many countries, there had been deterioration in most indicators of child development during the adjustment period. This was especially so because expenditure on health, nutrition and education had been reduced, and also because unemployment and loss of family income meant that families had less money to spend on their children.

Children have never received much explicit attention in India's economic policies. (3) They are hardly mentioned in the annual budget speeches, (4) or in other crucial policy documents. This, of course, does not mean that the policies do not affect them. Directly and indirectly, the survival chances, welfare and future of children are affected by macro-economic and policy changes.

How children are affected is, however, not always easy to ascertain. This is so for several reasons. Often policies do not all work in the same direction. In fact, even a relatively coherent set of policies that can be grouped together as 'structural adjustment' can have contradictory effects on children. The effects of policies can also be mitigated or reinforced by other developments. Finally, children themselves do not form a homogeneous group but are differentiated along lines of gender, class, caste, religion, age, etc; different policies may have a different impact on different categories of children.

BUDGETING FOR CHILD RIGHTS

Since India ratified the UNCRC it is obliged to submit periodic reports on its progress on realising the rights of all children to the Committee on the Rights of the Child. Based on its report that came up for review in January 2004, the Committee on the Rights of the Child, in its concluding observations, said:

> *Make every effort to increase the proportion of the budget allocated to the realisation of children's rights to the "maximum extent ... of available resources" and, in this context, to ensure the provision, including through international cooperation, of appropriate human resources and to guarantee that the implementation of policies relating to social services provided to children*

remain a priority; and Develop ways to assess the impact of budgetary allocations on the implementation of children's rights, and to collect and disseminate information in this regard.

In India, one out of 16 children die before they attain 1 year of age, and one out of 11 die before they attain 5 years of age. Thirty-five per cent of the developing world's low birth weight babies are born in India, and 40% of child malnutrition in the developing world is in India. Out of every 100 children, 19 continue to be out of school. Of those who enrol, many drop out.

This is a gloomy scenario, and there are many children who are not covered by the programmes/schemes of either the central government or the respective state governments. This sad state of affairs vis-à-vis children in India can be mainly attributed to a lack of State accountability. There are no functional mechanisms to monitor the formulation of programmes/schemes, their budgeting and implementation by the executive, though some avenues are provided for the people of India to monitor the functioning of the executive through elected representatives, that is, the legislature. The United Nations Convention on the Rights of the Child, 1989 (UNCRC, 1989), which India ratified in 1992, also provides avenues for NGOs to monitor State functioning to ensure the rights of India's children.

Realising the need for a mechanism to monitor the State and hold it accountable vis-à-vis its performance on the rights of children, HAQ: Centre for Child Rights developed a system of child budgeting in India and published its first research-based analysis, 'India's Children and the Union Budget', in 2001. This was an analysis of trends in allocation and expenditure on child-specific programmes/schemes of the Government of India in the post-reforms period spanning 1991-92 to 2000-01.

In an economy where government expenditure in a financial year is only around 12% of the total GDP for that given year, the budget is only a small player in the overall economy and economic policies. But the budget is not just an economic document; it's a reflection of the government's political will and direction. It is an indicator of the government's willingness to translate its commitments into reality. The manner in which the money allocated for programmes/schemes for children is spent also provides an indication of the government's commitment to child rights. In fact, it is a reflection of the whole governance system. Any political commitment, in the absence of adequate financial allocations, would be mere rhetoric rather than reality.

HAQ's 2001 study showed that the average expenditure on children in the '90s was a mere 1.2% of the total Union budget. And, as HAQ categorised expenditure on children into four sectors--child health, child development, child education and children in difficult circumstances--the sectoral spending projected an even grimmer picture. The share of expenditure on children in difficult circumstances was abysmally low, at 0.01% of the total Union budget expenditure (see Figure 1 and Table 2). (Note: The children's budget is not a separate budget. It is basically an attempt to disaggregate from the nation's budget what goes into programmes and schemes for the benefit of children.)

Figure 1: Share of Union budget spent on children (5) (1990-1998)

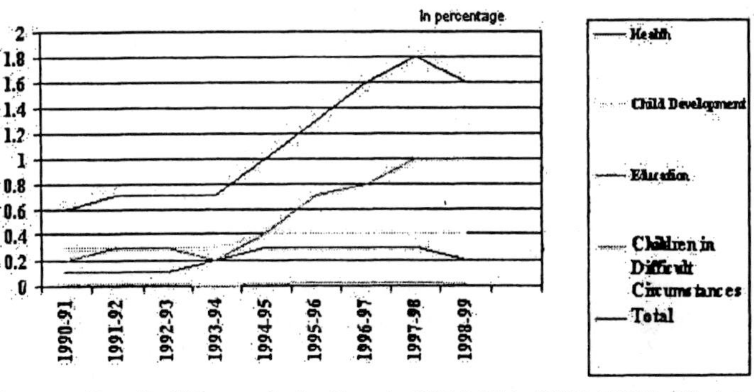

Source: Detailed Demands for Grants (1990-91 to 2000-2001), Ministry of Human Resource Development, Ministry of Social Justice and Empowerment, Ministry of Labour, Ministry of Health and Family Welfare

***Note:** Child development includes programmes on Early Childhood Care and Education (ECCE) and other miscellaneous programmes under the Department of Women and Child Development

Table 2: Sector-wise spending on children in the Union budget (6)

(1990-1998) In percentage

Year / Sectors®	Health	Child development	Education	Children in difficult circumstances	Total
1990-91	0.1	0.3	0.2	0.01	0.6
1991-92	0.1	0.3	0.3	0.01	0.7
1992-93	0.1	0.3	0.3	0.01	0.7
1993-94	0.2	0.3	0.2	0.00	0.7
1994-95	0.3	0.4	0.4	0.01	1.0
1995-96	0.3	0.4	0.7	0.02	1.3
1996-97	0.3	0.4	0.8	0.02	1.6
1997-98	0.3	0.4	1.0	0.02	1.8
1998-99	0.2	0.4	1.0	0.01	1.6
Average	0.2	0.4	0.6	0.01	1.2

Source: Demands for Grants (1990-91 to 2000-2001), Ministry of Human Resource Development, Ministry of Social Justice and Empowerment, Ministry of Labour, Ministry of Health and Family Welfare

Another startling revelation made in HAQ's 2001 study was about underspending in the various schemes for children.

In 1993-94, there was underspending in the elementary education and child development sectors, as well as in the sector relating to children in difficult circumstances (inter alia child protection).

Underspending in Elementary Education

There was under-utilisation in 12 out of the 17 elementary education schemes. Some of the important schemes, which show a high rate of under-spending, are:

- District Primary Education Programme (DPEP)--91.3% unspent

- Mahila Samakhya--80.6% unspent
- Teachers training programme--95.6% unspent
- Special schools for the disabled--93.3% unspent

Underspending in Child Development

o Integrated Child Development Services (ICDS)--11.6% unspent

Underspending in Child Protection

o National Child Labour Project (NCLP)--99.0% unspent

Source: HAQ: Centre for Child Rights, 'India's Children and the Union Budget, 2001'

Child Budgeting as Government's Mandate

The annual report of the Department of Women and Child Development (2002-2003) stated: "After gender, the next logical step for the Department of Women and Child Development as a nodal department for women and children is the analysis of public expenditure on children... A pioneering effort was made by HAQ: Centre for Child Rights, in their publication 'India's Children and the Union Budget'."

Since then, the Indian government has taken up child budgeting at the departmental level and, till date, has published three studies on child budgets in the annual reports of the Department of Women and Child Development (2002-03 and 2004-05) and in the annual reports of the Ministry of Women and Child Development (2005-06).

Even as the government took up child budgeting as its mandate and started analysing the budget allocations and expenditure on children, the allocation for children has seen a steady rise over the years (see Tables 3 and 4).

But there is still a huge gap between the money needed to fulfil the rights of India's children and the money promised through budgets, and between allocation and actual expenditure, thanks to incapacities in programme delivery mechanisms.

TRANSLATING OUTLAYS INTO OUTCOMES

In its annual reports of 2002-03 and 2004-05, the ministry has undertaken a series of analyses on child budgeting. In 2004-05, the ministry's report noted that an analysis of expenditure by the Centre and states on children's issues showed an increased commitment although actual expenditure "may however fall short of budgets for reasons like lack of capacity to spend/absorb funds, procedural delays, slackness in implementation" amongst other factors (Annual report (2005-06), Ministry of Women and Child Development, Pg 129)

Also, the increase in allocation for children is mainly on account of increased allocations on three programmes--Sarva Shiksha Abhiyan(SSA),the Midday Meal Scheme, and Integrated Child Development Services (ICDS).

Table 3: Percentage share of children in the Union budget (BE)

Year	Total Union budget (BE) (Rs crore)	Total child budget (BE) (Rs crore)	% share of child budget in Union budget
2003-04	438795.07	10264.23	2.33
2004-05	477829.04	11695.72	2.45
2005-06	514343.80	19841.01	3.86
2006-07	563991.13	27674.58	4.91

Source: GOI expenditure budget 2004-05, 2005-06, 2006-07 (Vols 1 and 2)

Table 4: Percentage share of sectoral allocation on children in Union budget

Year	% share of child development in Union budget	% share of child health in Union budget	% share of child education in Union budget	% share of child protection in Union budget	% share of total child budget in Union budget
2003-04	0.490	0.340	1.470	0.030	2.330
2004-05	0.422	0.423	1.567	0.033	2.445
2005-06	0.658	0.527	2.638	0.034	3.857
2006-07	0.830	0.556	3.487	0.034	4.907

Source: GOI expenditure budget 2004-05, 2005-06, 2006-07 (Vols 1 and 2)

Source: GOI expenditure budget 2004-05, 2005-06, 2006-07 (Vols 1 and 2)

Table 5: Percentage sectoral allocation in child budget

Year	% share of child development in child budget	% share of child health in child budget	% share of child education in child budget	% share of child protection in child budget
2003-04	21.30	14.60	62.70	1.30
2004-05	17.25	17.28	64.02	1.36
2005-06	17.40	13.66	68.40	0.89
2006-07	16.92	11.32	71.06	0.70
Source: GOI expenditure budget 2004-05, 2005-06, 2006-07 (Vols 1 and 2)				

Source: GOI expenditure budget 2004-05, 2005-06, 2006-07 (Vols 1 and 2)

Within the total allocation for children, the percentage share for education has gone up at the cost of allocations for child development, child health and child protection.

The reasons for this can be traced to politics and the politics of economics. Take the allocations for child education. With the inclusion of Article 21A in the Constitution of India in 2002, after the 93rd amendment, the Government of India was under pressure to increase allocations for elementary education. The government did increase the allocation, but compared to the actual requirement there was still a huge shortfall.

The allocation for elementary education in 2001-02 was Rs 3,801.00 crore. It increased to Rs 4,484.40 crore in 2003-04, and Rs 5,766.83 in 2004-05. When it increased substantially to Rs 11,219.75 crore it was mainly on account of collection from an education cess of 2% on all central taxes levied through the Finance (No 2) Act, 2004. To increase expenditure on elementary education the Government of India adopted the simplistic method of imposing an additional tax burden on the people instead of looking at other more viable options like collection of tax arrears. Income tax arrears to the tune of nearly Rs 99,000 crore and customs and excise arrears of another Rs 16,000 crore have piled up till 2005-06. On the one hand the finance minister has imposed an education cess to finance elementary education, and on the other hand he gifted corporates with a tax slash from 33% to 30% in the year 2005-06.

While the allocation on education increased, riding on resources generated from the education cess, child protection issues remained neglected as was evident from the fact that the allocation on child protection has stayed stagnant at 0.03% of the total Union budget allocations.

The Juvenile Justice Act covers children in need of care and protection and children in conflict with the law. The first category includes street children, child labourers, orphans and children of beggars and sex workers. The latter category consists of criminal offenders or children framed for criminal offences. The Act was altered in 2000. The upper age of 'children' covered has been increased from 16 to 18 years, the role of the police has been enhanced and the destination of preference is segregated institutions.

The government's programme for such children is a 'Programme for Juvenile Justice'. The money needed to run homes for children comes from this programme and allocation for this programme in the year 2006-07 is just Rs 23.00 crore, when there is a requirement of 280 children's homes, 308 observation homes, 258 special homes, 101 after-care homes, 410 child welfare committees, 596 shelter homes, 315 juvenile justice boards and 704 special juvenile police units, according to the Working Group for Children Living in Difficult Circumstances, set up under the Tenth Five-Year Plan. The State, already under pressure to reduce and off-load social sector spending, is withdrawing from the provision of social security and is eager to have its institutions privately run.

THE BATTLE FOR SURVIVAL

The declining sex ratio was pointed out as far back as 1974. But it was only taken seriously after the shocking revelations of Census 2001. How can the female foetus and the girl-child be protected? Preventing sex-selective abortion by law is one way. But it cannot be the only way

June is the month of school admissions, a trying and testing time for most parents and teachers. However, apart from the usual hassles that characterise this period, a new problem has apparently emerged in places such as Sangli district in Maharashtra. Schools, or divisions run exclusively for girls, are now apparently facing a shortage of admissions. Considering that the kanyashalas (girls' schools) were inspired by the social reform movement led by Mahatma Jyotiba and Savitribai Phule, Maharshi Karve, Gopal Ganesh Agharkar and others who pioneered women's education in Maharashtra, this is a sorry state of affairs. While the evidence may still be anecdotal, it reinforces the gravity of the situation in no uncertain terms--the number of girls/women in the state is declining steadily, and that too in a state where the question of gender equality was firmly and squarely a part of social reform.

The continuous decline in the proportion of women in the country has been a matter of concern for the women's movement for a very long time. As far back as 1974, 'Towards Equality', the report of the Committee on the Status of Women in India, noted that the "decline in the sex ratio ever since 1901 is a disturbing phenomenon," and pointed out that the lowest ratio had been recorded in Punjab, and in the metropolitan cities of the country. But it was only the publication of the 2001 Census report that forced the Government of India to acknowledge that the phenomenon was reaching alarming proportions.

The census report indicated that there had been the sharpest-ever decline in the child sex ratio (0-6 age-group) between 1991 and 2001. The decline was greatest in the relatively prosperous states of Punjab, Haryana, Gujarat and Maharashtra, and in urban areas. Significantly, Delhi, India's capital, recorded a decline from 915 in 1991 to 865!

It was clear that apart from the traditional means of neglect of the girl-child, which include undernourishment, lack of medical attention, lack of education, early marriage, etc, purposive sex selection using modern methods such as ultrasonography was contributing heavily to the decline. It also meant that the Pre-Natal Diagnostic Techniques (PNDT) Act that had been legislated in 1994 following the efforts of women's organisations and health groups to prohibit sex selection and the consequent abortion of female foetuses, had been pretty much useless.

The report prompted a sharp response from women's organisations that demanded urgent strategies to protect the girl-child. The Supreme Court also issued interim orders in a Public Interest Litigation (PIL) that had been filed earlier by

Dr Sabu George, CEHAT and MASUM to seek directions for the implementation of the Act and explicitly include pre-conception tests within its ambit. In February 2003, the Act was amended and is now called the Pre-Conception and Pre-Natal Diagnostic Techniques (Prohibition of Sex Selection) Act. Meanwhile there has been some effort by government agencies to put in place the administrative structures necessary to implement the Act, and some sort of media campaign to highlight the issue.

But mid-term data for a state like Maharashtra indicates that the decline, far from being arrested, continues unabated (the child sex ratio further declined from 922 in the 2001 to 898 in 2005) and calls for far more serious measures in the future.

THE LAW IS NOT ENOUGH

While it is absolutely necessary to have laws that support the struggle for women's equal status in society, it is equally true that the existence of a law by itself does not prevent anti-women practices, whether it is sex selection, dowry or bigamy. There have to be simultaneous social campaigns to create awareness amongst women and the public at large in order to bring about a change in attitude. This, in turn, requires a proper analysis and understanding of the various factors that contribute to such anti-women practices being upheld by people.

Son-preference in India is rooted deep in religious and cultural practices, as is evident from the various rituals in different communities. Despite women's contribution to the economy and family, there has always been a traditional patriarchal perception that women are a burden, and therefore a liability. They are considered temporary residents of the natal family, biding their time before they enter into matrimony. On the other hand, sons are seen as bringing pride and honour to their families. They are also the source of inheritance of property, and therefore security in old age.

The challenge before the women's movement is the continuation of these perceptions even in the current context, when women have obviously made their mark in all fields in modern Indian society. In the case of sex selection, traditional son-preference has become intertwined with a slew of other reasons that effectively combine to devalue women and the girl-child. This calls for a multi-faceted strategy by the women's movement to deal with what is really a basic struggle for existence.

IMPACT OF MARKET-DRIVEN GLOBALISATION

The current policies of market-driven globalisation are responsible for a further devaluation of women's labour. With shrinking employment opportunities, more and more women are forced to take up poorly paid work in the unorganised sector, much of which is invisible. The economic insecurity of women also increases the vulnerability of women to various forms of social and domestic violence. The presence of young girls in the family becomes a source of parental worry. In stark contrast to the fact that women are actually taking on greater and greater economic burdens in increasingly adverse circumstances, the cultural perception that they are a burden is being reinforced.

Globalisation is not just about economic issues but also the values it promotes in the process. Market-driven consumerism has resulted in the practice of dowry, once confined to upper-caste and prosperous families, extending across all classes, castes and communities. The exchange of gifts is no longer restricted to the time of marriage; the girl's parents are expected to provide a steady stream of cash and/or other items to her matrimonial family. Bollywood cinema and television companies that need constant fodder for their 24x7 channels systematically fuel ostentatious marriages. Corrupt politicians provide the social sanction for such vulgar display of wealth. Hapless parents are forced to borrow at exorbitant rates of interest. This in turn leads to the specious argument that it is better to spend money to illegally abort a female foetus than be burdened for life with a girl.

The same market values have taken over the medical profession; some doctors have no qualms about informing parents of the sex of the child, and, in turn, justify it as a matter of 'choice'. Others argue that they are doing society, and particularly women, a service by helping get rid of unwanted girls. It is the same set of values that makes people believe that if the number of women in society goes down, their 'price' will increase, as if women are sacks of potatoes or onions!

THE NEED FOR A SOCIAL CAMPAIGN

Therefore, as noted by the Seventh National Conference of All-India Democratic Women's Association (AIDWA), held in Bhubaneshwar in 2004: "The fight to save the female foetus and the girl-child from elimination is a political struggle linked to the discriminatory policies and cultures that strengthen patriarchy." AIDWA's struggle against sex determination is not confined to implementation of the PNDT Act but has been expressed in multiple forms.

For this national mass organisation of women, the problem of declining numbers of women in the country has been an issue of concern for a long time. For example, in Tamil Nadu, the AIDWA state unit was at the forefront in exposing the prevalence of female infanticide in the districts of Salem and Madurai. Eventually, the state government adopted what is now known as the Cradle Baby Scheme, which is basically an incentive scheme to protect the girl-child. As far back as 1993, the Haryana unit of the organisation held a demonstration against a clinic in Sirsa that was displaying female foetuses preserved in jars in its window with a view to attracting potential clients, and was successful in having it closed down. In Maharashtra, AIDWA was part of the sustained campaign that led to the passage of the Maharashtra Regulation of Pre-Natal Diagnostic Techniques Act, in 1988. Calling for a ban on sex selection, AIDWA also presented a detailed memorandum to the parliamentary committee that examined the draft legislation proposed by the government.

Starting with a countrywide survey of the practice of dowry conducted by its own activists, national and state-level conventions have been conducted to bring out the pernicious nature of dowry and its consequences. At all these conventions, the organisation has also stressed the importance of AIDWA members taking a firm stand on the practice in their own families. In Haryana, the state unit has highlighted the plight of 'bought wives', a phenomenon that is the direct result of the shortage of girls in many villages, and which belies the perception that the value of women will improve if their numbers decline! In Maharashtra, the organisation has conducted an awareness campaign in the four districts that have shown the sharpest decline in sex ratios, particularly Pune, Satara, Sangli and Kolhapur.

Linking the campaign to the rich tradition of social reform in the state, the campaign has highlighted the changing values in a state that espoused the cause of women's equality as a central theme of its renaissance. Inspired by the campaign, activists in Pune city went on to use a decoy to nab a doctor carrying out sex selection using sonography. The case provided an opportunity to examine the various aspects of implementation of the PNDT Act. It brought to light the fact that the state government had not notified appropriate authorities that are legally responsible for implementing the Act, showing up the nexus between the private medical sector and the public establishment.

Simultaneously, AIDWA has been reiterating the issues of economic vulnerability of women and growing devaluation of their labour, demanding the implementation of the National Rural Employment Guarantee Act and comprehensive protective legislation for the unorganised sector, including agricultural workers, of whom women make up substantial numbers.

The campaign has thrown up many challenges. It is our experience that while there is a willingness to recognise the value of women, especially their economic contribution and supportive role within the family, there is resistance towards taking concrete steps to end dowry, or son-preference rituals. The wider struggle for the economic rights of women, including equal property rights, has to be linked with the struggle against sex selection. The depiction of women in the media, and the role models that are played out have a deep influence on the youth of the country, and there have to be effective strategies to counter it.

There is a need to initiate debate amongst doctors, who prefer to ignore the fact that illegal practices are rampant within their community. This is, in turn, linked to the regulation of the private health sector. Implementation of the PCPNDT Act is vested with the Health Ministry, and there is a reluctance to expose members of their own fraternity. Most importantly, there is a need to bring the question of declining sex ratios on the agenda of the ruling parties. Unless there is the political will, strategies to combat sex selection will remain only on paper. To build that political will is the major challenge facing us.

Important human development indicators for the girl-child

Indicator	Males	Females	Persons
Population (0-6)1	81,911,041	75,952,104	157,863,145
Sex ratio (0-6)2	-	-	927/1,000
IMR (April 2006)3	-	-	58
MMR4	-	407	-
Child mortality rate			
(0-4)5 (2000)	18.6%	20.6%	19.5%
Anaemia (15-19)6	-	56%	-
Literacy rate	75.26	53.67	64.84
Gross drop-out rate7	-	-	-
Class I-V	35.85	33.72	34.89
Class 1-VIII	52.28	53.45	52.79
Class I-X	60.72	64.97	62.58

Source: 'Girl-child in the 11th Five-Year Plan', Ministry of Women and Child Development, India

Problems faced by the girl-child in India

Years	Problems faced
Before birth to 1 year	• Foeticide and infanticide • Infant mortality • Discrimination in breastfeeding and infant food • Neglect of health (immunisation)

1 to 11 years (this includes specific problems faced by age-groups 1-5 years and 6-11 years)	• Discrimination in access to food and healthcare • Malnutrition and anaemia • Health problems like polio and diarrhoea • Iodine, Vitamin A and Micronutrient deficiency • Low school enrolment and school drop-outs • Vulnerable to trafficking, child labour, child marriage • Abuse, exploitation and violence • Domestic chores • Looking after siblings • Restrictions on mobility and play • Discrimination in overall treatment and parental care
11 to 18 years (adolescents)	• Poor health • Low literacy level • Restrictions on mobility and play • Frequent illness due to malnutrition, anaemia and micronutrient deficiency • Child marriage • Early childbearing morbidity and mortality • Poor access/denial to information and services • Early and frequent pregnancy, coupled with abortions • Marital and domestic violence • Dowry harassment, desertion, polygamy, divorce • Child labour, trafficking • STDs and HIV/AIDS

- Heavy domestic work, including commuting long distances to collect firewood/ drinking water
- Unpaid and unrecognised work and drudgery
- No voice either in the home or in society

Source: 'Girl-child in the 11th Five-Year Plan', Ministry of Women and Child Development, India

MISSING

According to statistics compiled by the Institute of Social Sciences, a staggering 45,000 children go missing in India every year. Of these, 11,000 are never found

The macabre killings of young children in Noida's Nithari village have brought the plight of India's missing children into focus. According to statistics compiled by the Institute of Social Sciences (ISS), a staggering 45,000 children go missing in India every year. Of these, 11,000 are never found.

The most shocking revelation of this two-year study, titled 'Trafficking of Women and Children in India', compiled by Shankar Sen and P M Nair, with a team of ISS researchers, is that the graph of missing children continues to rise. In Delhi, in 2004, 6,227 children were reported missing, according to police reports; in 2006 the number of missing kids had climbed to 6,683.

Providing a break-up of the missing children, the ISS report highlights how in Maharashtra the number of missing kids in 2001 was 13,881, in Madhya Pradesh 4,915, in Karnataka 3,600, in Andhra Pradesh 2,007, and in Gujarat 1,624.

In the Andaman and Nicobar Islands, the number of missing kids has gone up by 1,000% within a five-year period, in Arunachal Pradesh it has risen by 883%, in Andhra Pradesh by 78%, in Assam by 151%, in Chhattisgarh by 83%, in Gujarat by 80%, in Haryana by 142%, in Tamil Nadu by 194%, and in Tripura by 300%.

Statistics provided by state police agencies show that in Rajasthan the number of children reported missing in 1996 was

154; in 2001 the number had shot up to 278. In Orissa, for the same period, the number of missing children was 419; by 2001 it had risen to 541. In Haryana, the figures are equally alarming. In 1996, the number of missing children was 64, but by 2001 the figure had gone up to 155.

CSOs working in the field estimate that this is only the tip of the iceberg, as only 10% of all cases are registered with the police. They say the numbers are much higher. Kiran Bedi, Director General, Bureau of Police, Research and Development, conceded that "the numbers of missing children who were being reported on child helplines were much more than the figures in police records".

The report also highlights how the percentage of untraced persons continues to increase every year. In other words, the chances of locating missing people are steadily diminishing.

The metros continue to report the largest number of missing children. Delhi heads the list with the highest number of untraced kids, followed by Mumbai, Hyderabad, Kolkata and Bangalore. But while Kolkata and Hyderabad are not meeting with much success in tracing missing children, one exception has been Chennai, in terms of both numbers of missing kids and also ability to trace them. In a serious indictment of the state governments of West Bengal and Delhi, the report questions why 75% of missing children in Kolkata and 65% in Delhi "continue to remain untraced".

The report adds that trafficking of women and children is also increasing in the states of Jharkhand and Chhattisgarh. Trafficking is a profitable business, with traffickers targeting low-income families. Kailash Sathyarthy of the NGO Bachpan Bacchao Andolan points out: "The maximum number of children being trafficked today belong to dalit, tribal and poor Muslim families that do not have the economic strength to put pressure on the police or political leaders."

The survey involved interviews with 510 trafficked children who had been rescued by the police and NGOs and were living in homes. Forty per cent of the children said they had been trafficked when they were less than 10 years old; the rest were trafficked between the ages of 11 and 14. Half of these children had never been to school. The children had been trafficked by family members or people who knew the family. Only 7% said they had been trafficked by total strangers. The children admitted that they had seen their parents or relatives accept money for them. In most cases, the traffickers had paid Rs 5,000 or less to acquire their human cargo.

TRAFFICKED

A recent study of 412 brothel owners from 12 states revealed that there were six girl-children on average per brothel. One-hundred-and-sixty traffickers interviewed admitted that young girls were their main target. In 35% of cases, it is families that sell their women into the flesh trade for as little as Rs 1,000-Rs 5,000

Thousands of women and children are being trafficked every year. Trafficking of women and children has emerged as the third largest industry, after the arms and drugs trade. Researchers estimate that Kamathipura in Mumbai alone generates over $ 400 million annually, with 100,000 prostitutes servicing six customers a day, at Rs 100 a customer. Transactions in prostitution are reported to gross Rs 40,000 crore per annum, with revenues being shared between procurers, pimps, brothel keepers and the police.

A two-year study by the Institute of Social Sciences (ISS) and the National Human Rights Commission (NHRC), published in 2005, tracked down the "merchants of the flesh trade", including brothel owners and traffickers.

Assured of anonymity, 160 traffickers spoke at length about their modus operandi. A fifth of them were from Andhra Pradesh while the rest came from Bihar, Karnataka, Tamil Nadu, Rajasthan, West Bengal and Uttar Pradesh. Most of those interviewed were in their mid-20s and early-30s, though researchers came across two traffickers from Maharashtra and Goa who were just 18 years old.

At the top of the hierarchy are the 'master' traffickers whose identity remains largely unknown. They are assisted by field-level purchasers, transporters, master operators, pimps and procurers and the crime syndicate that involves brothel owners and brothel managers where most of the trafficked women and children end up being forced to live.

Young girls continue to be the main target of the traffickers, especially since clients are eager to have sex with virgins. The majority admitted to trafficking children in order to sexually exploit them.

Sixteen-year-old Chaya, rescued recently from a G B Road brothel in New Delhi, was picked up by a trafficker from her village when she was very young. She was forced to entertain customers for over 12 hours a day; the first customer came in at 10 am and the last customer would come into her cabin after midnight. "By the time I finished with my last customer I did not have the strength even to breathe. But the 'madam' would keep pushing in more and more customers so that she could make more profit out of me," said Chaya. She was rescued by the police and has been living in a rescue home in Nirmal Chhaya for the last four years.

Ten-year-old Priti from Anori village in Karnataka was sold by her father and stepmother for Rs 12,000. A trafficker took her by train to Mumbai where she was forced into the sex trade. "I had not even begun menstruating when I was compelled to entertain around 60 customers every day," she says. "Each customer paid Rs 400 to the brothel owner. When I attained puberty, at the age of 13, I was expected to entertain 30 customers. But my rate went down to Rs 300 per customer which, again, was taken by the brothel owner. She even took the tips." Priti revealed this to the police when she was rescued seven years after being inducted into the sex-trade.

In a majority of cases, the traffickers admit they first develop a relationship with members of the family. The study highlighted how, in 35% of the cases, it was the family members and relatives, including parents and husbands, who helped facilitate the deal for a financial consideration.

While the majority of women/girls were sold out of poverty, in approximately 10% of cases, the traffickers claimed, women were sold out of greed. There are some upper class women too; many are lured under the guise of being helped to gain a foothold in the glamorous Hindi film industry.

Trafficking, they admitted, was a low-investment, high-profit business. Girls were being bought for as little as Rs 1,000 per girl, though the majority said they spent around Rs 5,000 to purchase a girl. Only in exceptional circumstances did they fork out as much as Rs 10,000-Rs 20,000 for a girl, with payments being made on a commission basis.

The study cited the example of 'AM', a well-known trafficker from Muzaffarpur, who is presently supplying women in Siliguri, Darjeeling, Kishanganj, Katihar, Purnea and Ataria. On average, 'AM' trafficks 40 women and children every month, earning around Rs 10 lakh just from the sale of these women.

During the festival season, the number of women can go up to 60. 'AM' is reported to own several houses in Siliguri and other cities.

On average, each trafficker interviewed had bought/sold over 42 women and children. They also said they had sexually assaulted their victims. Forty-two per cent of them admitted to having abused between three to 10 of their victims, while 37% said they had abused more than 10 victims. Only then did they hand the women over to a brothel for them to start soliciting clients.

Many traffickers admit to exploiting women and children for pornographic reasons too. Children from Karnataka, Andhra Pradesh and Madhya Pradesh are being trafficked out of the country to the Middle East, UK, Korea and the Philippines for these purposes.

The study also interviewed 412 brothel owners from 12 states. Each of them had at least seven to 10 girls/women working for them.

Despite the government's assurances about ensuring that children are not part of the sex trade, the brothel owners candidly admitted that they had over 245 girls below the age of 16, and another 615 girls between 16-18 years of age. "This works out to a minimum of six children per brothel. Bihar had the largest number of girls, followed by Maharashtra and Uttar Pradesh," says Dr George Mathew, Director of ISS.

The Missing Face of AIDS

Yesu Babu of Vambay Colony in Vijayawada is 12. He has lost both his parents to AIDS. His younger brother is positive. There are almost 2 million AIDS orphans like him in India. But the national and global response to the HIV/AIDS crisis in India has virtually ignored children.

Imagine you are a 12-year-old boy. You live in India, on the outskirts of a town called Vijayawada. Your name is Yesu Babu.

Your home is a tiny two-room concrete block, approximately 200 square feet, in a slum known as the Vambay Colony. Imagine that you share this small home with your grandmother, Durgamma, and your 9-year-old brother. You live with your grandmother because your parents died of AIDS-first your father, who brought the infection home, in 2001; then your mother in 2004. There was no one left to take care of you and your brother except your elderly grandmother, who never expected to be raising two more children at this age.

Soon you learn that although you are HIV-negative, your young brother is HIV-positive. He begins to grow ill. He battles many infections. He cries in the night when he's sick and calls for his mother. There is no one else to provide an income for this new family that has formed. So you let your brother go to school, although for what future is painfully unclear, while you go to work.

You are 12 years old. You know you should be in school. You should have a childhood, but it has been traded in far too soon for adult work and worries, for hardships that no 12-year-old should ever have to face. But what can you do? There is no one else. There is no other way. From a normal life with a mother and father, school, a childhood, possibilities-to this previously unimagined reality.

This is your new normal. Imagine.

The children are everywhere in India. They fill the streets, the railway stations, the villages. Many of them are homeless, overflowing the orphanages and other institutional homes to live on the streets. Amidst the growing prosperity of India, there is an entire generation of parentless children growing up-25 million in all, with nearly 4 million more being added each year. Many are trafficked into prostitution or child labour in conditions amounting to slavery. They are invisible children, shunned by society and often their own families. Left to fend for themselves, they are virtually unnoticed by the world.

Nowhere is this more true than among the nearly 2 million children who have lost their parents to AIDS, the most AIDS orphans of any country and expected to double within five years. India is now home to the largest HIV-positive population in the world with 5.7 million infected, accounting for 15% of all cases globally. In May 2006, the Joint United Nations Programme on HIV/AIDS (UNAIDS) reported that India had overtaken South Africa to become the first non-African country to report such alarming numbers. The disease is silently spreading and reaching critical proportions. Almost 1% of people in India's six most populous states are HIV-positive, and 20 out of 37 states show high-prevalence areas. The sheer size of India's population-more than 1 billion-makes a widespread AIDS pandemic almost unimaginable. The one percentage figure is deeply disturbing to health officials because it is regarded as the tipping point, at which a smoldering health crisis can explode into an epidemic of vast magnitude.

Sitting in her small house, Grandmother Durgamma spoke to me about her life. "It is very hard taking care of my two grandchildren. I have leg pains, I cannot run with them. I want to take care of them but it is hard. I am only one. I am always thinking about their futures. If something happens to me, when I die, what will happen to them? I don't need anything for myself. I am living only for my grandsons."

Hers is a familiar story in Andhra Pradesh, the epicenter of the crisis with the highest infection rates in the country. The pandemic has created a secondary human rights crisis-the orphaning of children on a massive scale. UNAIDS reports,"Orphaning remains the most visible, extensive, and measurable impact of AIDS on children."

The trend of grandparents raising grandchildren has become so prevalent-as many as 40% of these orphans live with their grandparents-that VMM (Vasavya Mahila Mandali) and similar organisations have started what they call Granny Clubs. These are social and educational networks of women (and some men) like Durgamma who are caring for orphaned grandchildren. The granny clubs generally have 10 to 15 members who meet once a month, with social time and education about various topics. At one meeting, they might learn about HIV medications and treatment; at another, the subject might be nutrition. The time is also used to make friendships, share problems, and offer solutions.

"Sometimes we play games or sing," Durgamma told me about her club. "We have become friends, like sisters, and we support each other. We are older people who have watched our children die. We share our joys and our sorrows."

Ramulamma is another active granny club member in Vambay Colony. She lives with her granddaughter and great-grandson Krishna, who is HIV-positive. Krishna was so tiny I would have guessed him to be a boy of four or five years old; when I inquired I was told that he is nine. Krishna's mother, the breadwinner of the family, was at her job as a hotel maid in Vijayawada the day I visited. She earns Rs 40 per day, although it costs her Rs 10 to travel into town and back. They are a family with three generations affected by HIV: Krishna's father died two years ago, and his grandfather died just the month before my visit, both from AIDS. Krishna and his grandmother gazed at me listlessly as we spoke, both of them with the same vacant, hopeless eyes. In Vambay, it seemed death was not a feared stranger but a constant, familiar companion.

VMM provides doctor care and medicine every month for Krishna, as well as a local physician who is available for immediate needs, but he is not on ART therapy currently because he is not deemed sick enough. In India, CD4 blood count levels must be 200 or below to qualify for ART drugs-the level at which HIV is medically considered to have become full-blown AIDS. Only 7% of HIV-positive people were receiving any Anti-Retroviral Treatment in 2005. In the United States, ART is started well before this time to prevent AIDS, generally at CD4 levels of 300 to 350. Krishna continues to have regular blood tests so that ART drug treatment can be started as soon as his condition qualifies.

In spite of their plight Krishna and Yesu are among the lucky children because they have family to live with. For every child fortunate enough to live in a family home there are a thousand more who have nowhere to turn. Those without any kinship ties-or whose families refuse to take them in because of the stigma of AIDS-often end up in institutional homes, forming child-headed households, or simply on the streets. They are the missing face of AIDS, these children left behind.

India's crisis is acute in part because the country has done little to protect children affected by HIV/AIDS, and has no provisions at all for those orphaned. At the VMM office before my visit to Vambay Colony, Keerthi Bollineni said that the national and global response to the HIV/AIDS crisis in India has virtually ignored children. It is a sentiment I heard over and over, from every organisation and social worker I talked to. Resources for orphans and other children made vulnerable by HIV/AIDS have increased in recent years, but funding for these programmes is nevertheless small. An enormous gap exists between what is needed and what is actually being done to address the needs of children affected by AIDS.

The response to AIDS in India has focused primarily on high-risk target groups: the sex trade, truckers who spread the infection from town to town, and drug users. 80% of AIDS funding goes toward prevention in the high-risk populations, and only 20% to caring for children and families living with HIV. Kanika Singh, Executive Director of Heroes Project India, confirmed this. "Young people and women are the two vulnerable groups today. One out of every three people infected with HIV is a woman, and 80% of these women are housewives. That has a direct link to children. They unknowingly pass on the infection to their child." Mother to child transmission is the most common source of infection in children at a rate of 30,000 per year, but they are also acquiring HIV through blood transfusions, syringe injections, and consensual or non-consensual sexual contact. But, added Kanika, "Nobody talks about HIV-positive children."

Stigmatised through no fault of theirs, these children are far more vulnerable to abuse and exploitation. A Human Rights Watch investigation uncovered discrimination on a constant basis: segregation and expulsion from schools, refusal of treatment by doctors, rejection from orphanages and even their own family homes. "Children are being turned away from schools, clinics and orphanages because they or their family members are HIV-positive," reported Zama Coursen-Neff, a senior researcher with Human Rights Watch. "If the Indian government is serious about fighting the country's AIDS epidemic, it should stop ignoring children affected by AIDS and start protecting them from abuse."

Becoming orphaned is not the only way children are affected by this epidemic. There is also a devastating impact on their emotional and psychological well-being. "They are missing their entire childhoods," said Dr Deeksha Pillarisetty, Medical Director of VMM. "They go immediately into adulthood at a very young age." VMM estimates that 25% of children affected by AIDS live in child-headed households, a trend of particular concern. Dr Pillarisetty described the trauma these children face with no adult support. They are the most common caregivers for sick parents and eventually watch those parents die-after which they all too often must step into adult roles themselves, becoming the guardians of younger siblings or working to support their remaining family. They may be denied their property and inheritance rights, often face discrimination from their neighbours, and must deal with fears for their own health. Alarming new evidence by UNAIDS found that orphans and vulnerable children have a higher risk of exposure to HIV than non-affected children.

Girls are especially vulnerable. They are more likely to be removed from school to care for sick parents or other family members and are often the last in the family to receive medical care. Loss of family income can push them into the sex trade and inability to control safe sex, even within marriage, puts them at a disadvantage. Less access to education, sexual abuse and child marriage all place girls at higher risk of becoming infected. Many families marry daughters off at increasingly young ages so the girls will have someone to care for them after their parents die. Parents are also afraid of HIV rendering them unmarriageable, a finding that the Human Rights Watch investigation corroborated. This has the added effect of creating a lot of very young widows. Dr Pillarisetty sees a lot of girls widowed by the age of 18. One of them was married at the age of 13, widowed at 14, and is now 15 years old and living with HIV. Often these widows are blamed for the husband's death and outcast by his family.

On the flip side, the potential impact these children will have on the epidemic as they grow up is also an area of concern. As they become sexually active, the lack of education about transmission and prevention and poor role models are likely to contribute to the spread of the infection. Missing family ties, they often form unhealthy attachments in which they are vulnerable to abuse. "They just want a relationship-it doesn't matter what kind it is," Dr Pillarisetty said. "There is nobody for them, nobody wants them. They are very traumatised."

There are more children living in India today with HIV-positive parents than children already orphaned. If those parents are not treated and continue to die the worst impact on children is still to come, and scarcely comprehensible.

The face of India's future if it fails in the battle against HIV lies in a small village called Cherlopalem in rural Andhra Pradesh. Cherlopalem is home to 30 families of dalits, a farming community surrounded by lush green fields that now stand empty. Three-fourths of the residents have been affected by AIDS. Seven people have died within the past eight months and dozens more are in the last stages, leaving many children behind without any sort of supervision. On April 8, 2007 the Eenadu newspaper reported, "The village, known for its hardworking lifestyle, is now ravaged by a cureless malady." The article accused officials of doing nothing. The remaining residents confessed that they knew nothing about the "dreaded disease". They do not know how it transmits or what precautions will protect them.

Cherlopalem is a microcosm of the ability of AIDS to unravel the social fabric of entire communities. It is clear that a failure to address the looming crisis in India will have dire consequences for the country, its children and the world for generations to come. A childhood cannot wait for the AIDS epidemic to subside, for poverty to be eradicated, for adults and governments to act, for the world to notice them.

'Enrolment is cause for celebration, quality is cause for concern'

According to the 2006 ASER survey, 93.2% of India's children in the 6-14 age-group are now in school. Farida Lambay of Pratham believes that the challenge is now keeping children in school and finding out why even after four years of schooling children cannot read

There are an estimated 140 million children in the 6-14 age-group in primary schools. Of these, 30 million cannot read, 40 million can recognize only a few alphabets, 40 million can read some words, and 30 million can read paragraphs. Over 55 million of these children will not complete four years of schooling, eventually adding to India's vast illiterate population.

Pratham, which began in the slums of Mumbai in 1994 as an endeavor by a few committed individuals to tackle the problems of education, has grown into an organisation whose activities reach across 18 states.

Pratham's mission has been 'Every child in school and reading well'. In pursuit of this it has launched the Read India campaign aimed at achieving reading and arithmetic proficiency among all children in India, within and outside school.

The campaign, phased over two years, has a March 31, 2009, deadline for achieving its goal. The phasing will be both geographical (about 300 districts in the first year, the rest in the second year) and sequential within each district (there will be a summer campaign followed by a low-intensity school campaign during the academic year).

Pratham has also facilitated the Annual Status of Education Report (Rural) (ASER) 2005 & 2006 which examines the status of primary and secondary education for India's children, and has extensively recorded data on enrollment, dropout rates, quality of education and other criteria like mothers' literacy, etc.

Farida Lambay, vice-principal of Nirmala Niketan and founder trustee of Pratham, spoke about the findings of ASER, various government policies, and why gauging children's reading abilities and quality education is so important.

So the major finding of ASER 2006 which calls for celebration is the rise in enrollment?

A cause for celebration is enrollment; a cause for concern is of course, quality. Specifically, I would say this with regard to reading. In spite of going to school for four years children are not reading. That is a great cause for concern. Personally I am not so worried about out-of-school children--they'll come back. The challenge is whether children in school are actually learning.

What are Pratham's plans to meet the Millennium Development Goals with regard to child rights?

We started with a perspective of child rights in terms of basic education--that every child should learn, and every child should think. That is the basic right of every child. But now we are talking not only about enrollment but also quality. By quality we mean every child should be able to comprehend and compete with other schoolchildren.

We are also looking at the rights of children not just from stable families but vulnerable groups-i.e. the basic rights of children who cannot make it to school, child labourers and workers. This is in keeping with the Millennium Development Goals.

We had also said that by 2005, in Mumbai, we would make sure that every child got an education. We have partly done that. As far as child labour is concerned, we are looking at having no child working. We have done that, to a great extent. We are now looking at this for all of India.

Pratham has always said that whatever we do we will work with the government, and whatever we do will be replicated. We are goal-oriented and community-based. People--whether it is the community or those providing support--all must be brought together.

Is 2015 a reasonable deadline for the Millennium Development Goals? How much do you plan to achieve by then?

For Pratham the goal is 2009, because we are going by the goals of the Sarva Shiksha Abhiyan (SSA), which has fixed 2009 as the deadline. I think we can make it. Every child must get to read. That is our mandate right now with the launch of the Read India campaign. Because of the ASER report, Pratham has been able to work in all states and with their respective governments, and that should make achieving the goals possible.

What are the education policies that have worked?

I think the midday meals scheme has worked in some places. The programme is doing very well in the south. Also, free girls' education and incentives for girls like transport and conveyance have helped.

The Sarva Shiksha Abhiyan has given a strong focus to primary education, especially in terms of creating a movement. Yet we can do a lot more.

The Sarva Shiksha Abhiyan is the State's effort to realise guarantees enshrined in Article 21 A of the Constitution, and to have a non-discriminatory delivery system for primary education. How do you rate the SSA vis-a-vis Pratham's work?

In the seventh standard, the SSA mentions Pratham as a model. The SSA came afterwards. Also I think Pratham is the only urban model that looks at education for all.

The other good thing that happened is that Dr Madhav Chavan (Programme Director, Pratham) is part of the national-level advisory council and commission headed by the prime minister. I am on the SSA committee at the national level. The presence of Pratham's members on such bodies helps translate our practices into policies.

What are the main gaps with regard to education?

The major gap right now is vulnerable children, in terms of visibility. We do not have proper data on this issue. Also, vulnerable in terms of them being street-children, working children, child labourers...

Another gap is in higher education, from the seventh standard onwards. The gap here relates to both general dropout cases and girls' education. Then there are patches or areas in states like the northeast, Orissa, parts of Maharashtra, Uttar Pradesh and Bihar. What's interesting in Bihar is that children's learning abilities are good; those children who do go to school and stay in school do well.

Then there is the Muslim minority. Higher education and girls' education are still problems here. Also, in terms of early childhood care, there is no Integrated Child Development Services (ICDS) or anganwadis in Muslim localities.

What role does Pratham play in supporting the Integrated Child Development Services scheme (ICDS)? What ails the ICDS?

I personally think that as a scheme the ICDS is very good. Maharashtra, according to our report, is doing quite well with a coverage of 80%, which is not bad at all. The problem is in the implementation stage... the anganwadi worker is one among many in that remote village. If she doesn't get recognition from her superiors there are bound to be problems. I also feel that if other schemes like, say, the Public Distribution System, don't do well it has a direct impact on the anganwadi and children. There are problems of convergence. There should be more convergence between, say, the anganwadi and healthcare services.

Is there a concerted child rights movement in India or is work being done in a fragmented fashion by non-government organisations?

There is a child rights movement but there are many different mandates--child labour, right to quality of education, etc. Also, there are many different funding organisations and different campaigns. I think now there must be convergence.

How does Pratham incorporate a rights-based approach in India? How does Pratham conceptualise the meaning of child rights?

The mission 'Every child in school and reading well' is itself rights-based. We are saying 'No' to child labour. We are saying every community has the right to participate. When we work with the government we focus on the issue of rights. We have been able to advocate policies both on child labour and education at the national level.

What are Pratham's fundamental strategies for guaranteeing full access to primary education?

Pratham's strategy is that we work with the government. We work with the entire hierarchy--with schools, with parents. I think we have had much more success working with the community. We create an enabling environment within the community; and we are working with parents. We hope, ultimately, that schools feel the pressure.

Pratham's strategy is to make the government more accountable. Everything we do is to make it more effective.

THE ASPIRATION FOR EDUCATION

There is unimaginable poverty and hunger in the picturesque Doars region of West Bengal. Still, the people here feel that education is more important for their children than nutrition. How is this aspiration for education being met in these remote villages?

The children were shivering. They had nothing but cheap woollen rags to protect themselves from the January cold. Still, they arrived early in the morning to attend the ICDS (Integrated Child Development Services) centre in Ranagapani Nepaliline village of Madarihat block, Jalpaiguri district, West Bengal. Visibly malnourished, they came to eat the food served at the centre, whose quality--boiled rice and pulses, or khichdi--was more abominable than palatable. It consisted mainly of stale leftovers of rice and dal. Life in the Doars region of this part of West Bengal is bleak. The lush green tea gardens and dense woods are picturesque, but only from a distance. Amidst the greenery are unimaginable poverty and a terrifying hunger that forces people to accept whatever they are offered: "Jo mileyo," as a mother, Nimi Thapa, told us.

Yet the people here are uncomplaining; it would seem they have accepted the hardships of their life as their fate. There is, however, an undercurrent of dissatisfaction against the State's basic service delivery system. To our surprise Nimi, barely able to manage two square meals a day, says the ICDS centre should give priority to education. "Feeding is important, but more important is education," she says. "If the children can acquire a basic education then they will be able to understand society and the system and be able to change them." Clearly, she understands the importance of education and wanted her child to start learning even before going to primary school (pre-schooling, besides child nutrition, is actually an important component of the ICDS programme that has been designed to focus on children under 6).

Nimi's views are echoed by thousands of parents, especially mothers, of children attending ICDS centres and primary schools throughout West Bengal. This aspiration for education was fuelled by the launch of the midday meal scheme in primary schools, which has pushed up enrolments and attendance. While the rate of never-enrolled children has radically declined to near-zero, the rate of attendance for primary school children, according to several studies, has shot up between 5-40%.

As part of a research team constituted by the Pratichi Trust, an organisation set up by Professor Amartya Sen from his Nobel Prize money, I visited more than 300 villages to study the delivery of primary education, basic health, and child nutrition. Although our geographical focus has largely been West Bengal, we have expanded our studies to include parts of neighbouring Jharkhand.

This overwhelming aspiration among people to give their children an education is not restricted to West Bengal and Jharkhand. Wider studies, such as PROBE (Public Report On Basic Education) suggest that it is a pan-Indian phenomenon.

Still, the state of education in many parts of the country remains bleak, with the delivery of education uneven in different states and areas. West Bengal is marked by some unfortunate contradictions. The state has achieved remarkable progress in terms of radical pro-people agendas like land reform and decentralisation of power through local governments (panchayats). It has unquestionable political stability: the ruling coalition that assumed power in 1977 is still in office. West Bengal has a long history of leading political and social reform. It has made several advances in higher education. And yet, almost every third person in Bengal is denied the right to literacy.

The illiterate are mainly from the socio-economically backward communities--scheduled castes (SCs), scheduled tribes (STs) and Muslims. While the average level of illiteracy in the state, according to Census 2001, is around 31%, the figures for SCs (41%), STs (57%) and Muslims (43%) are substantially higher than the state average. The level of illiteracy among women is extremely low in general; among the socio-economically weaker communities in particular it is appalling.

POLICY FAILURES

West Bengal's problems with education begin with its outright neglect of primary education. In spite of several declarations on universalising primary education, the funds allocated to primary education have been consistently low. There has been greater emphasis on the superstructure than on the base, and this has exacted its penalty: the primary education sector suffers severe deficiencies in infrastructure facilities and the availability of teachers, though, of late, these problems have begun to be addressed.

A single example would make the point. In 2002 there was an average of one teacher for 54 primary school children in West Bengal, placing it as the third worst state in an all-India pupil-to-teacher ratio ranking. The school inspection system, till date, is not properly functional; measures to free policy formulation and major implementation procedures from bureaucratic centralisation are inadequate; the formulation of syllabi, testing methods, modes of governance in schools, etc, remain centralised.

ORGANISATIONAL PROBLEMS

If bad policies are harmful, weakness in implementation is sometimes worse. The shortage of teachers is well known; what is less known is the miserable organisational failure in allocating available teachers. Marginal areas are marred by unjust distribution of teachers. In a semi-urban area of South 24 Parganas district, that has comparatively better accessibility and connectivity, the local primary school had six teachers, including four females, to look after around 100 children. On the other hand, a primary school in a geographically remote village had only one teacher for 232 children. Single-teacher schools formed about 6% of the total in West Medinipur district (same as the state average). But Belpahari, a marginal block in the district, had 23% (21 out of 91) single-teacher schools when we visited the area in November 2005. In Gopiballavpur East and West Circles of the same district the single-teacher primary schools formed 21% and 16% respectively. When such discrepancies are the norm rather than the exception, there is reason to be concerned about the state of affairs of primary education in the state. West Bengal has a general deficit of female teachers (female teachers constitute only 25%; figures for Kerala and Tamil Nadu are 70% and 66% respectively).

Often geographical patterns have a strong correlation with demographic patterns: geographically backward areas are generally inhabited by socio-economically backward populations--adivasis, scheduled castes and Muslims. A list of backward villages prepared by the Panchayat and Rural Development Department of the West Bengal government amply proves this connection: areas with high concentrations of SC, ST and Muslim populations share the majority of backward villages. How does this connection affect primary education? With the general paucities--shortage of teachers, lack of infrastructure, etc--schools face various irregularities, including teacher absenteeism, poor learning achievement, etc. Parents from underprivileged backgrounds can neither raise their voice against the poor functioning of the school nor can they provide extra inputs for their children's education.

One of Pratichi Trust's most disturbing findings is the embedding of private tuition with primary education: most children have to take paid assistance outside the school (private tuition at the primary school level is unheard of everywhere except in the Indian sub-continent). It is, according to Amartya Sen "an evil" and a "regrettable necessity" that causes multiple damage: poor children who cannot afford private tuition learn very little, and the relatively richer parents find it safer to resort to private tuition rather than raise their voices against the frailties of school functioning.

While government channels for inspection of primary schools are limited, the scope for initiating a process of social auditing through the parents' participation is also limited. In spite of their keenness to take part in the governance of schools, the government system does not allow much space for this extremely important input into primary education. An innovative programme by the West Bengal government called Sishu Siksha Karmasuchi shows how effectively schools can be run when local communities are involved in school governance. These schools, which are under community management (called Sishu Siksha Kendra) have shown greater operational regularity. It is another matter, however, that this programme too suffers from gross neglect, particularly in terms of teacher salaries and infrastructure.

But in the case of government primary schools, the opportunity for community participation has seemingly been unutilised. There are of course committees to involve local people, but these so-called 'participatory committees' are not school-specific; rather a village education committee is based at the gram sansad level (the lowest level of the panchayat system), despite the fact that a gram sansad may have more than one school or no school at all. And the deep-rooted divisiveness prevalent in society keeps all but the most influential parents out of such committees.

VOICE, PARTICIPATION AND ACTION

Yet, it's not an entirely one-sided story. True we do not often hear the voices of the poor, but, at certain times, the collective grumblings of the underprivileged and their democratic allies do make a real difference.

West Bengal has seen one such struggle between the rich and the poor. This was best manifested during the launch of the midday meal programme which the West Bengal government was initially reluctant to implement. The media, bureaucracy, rural and urban, affluent and poor--everyone opposed the programme. In spite of this opposition, however, the government had to launch the programme following a Supreme Court order. The midday meal programme gained strong support from the underprivileged. And now we can see the results: the bottom 30%, who could never attend school, now have the opportunity to step into the school arena.

At the same time there has been rapid expansion in building and repairing school infrastructure (classrooms, toilet facilities, water, etc) and the recruitment of teachers. This would not have been possible without the raising of voices.

Without the voice of the people being heard there cannot be any constructive participation. The experiences of Pratichi Trust, which has not only been carrying out research but is also engaged in building public debate and advocacy, show that public participation can remedy many operational problems. The Trust's collaborative work with the Birbhum District Primary School Council, for instance, has resulted in a number of positive changes. This joint intervention that incorporates parents, villagers, teachers and local and state government offices has, to a large extent, improved the quality of schooling (regular attendance by children and teachers, punctuality, improvements in teaching and learning). Again, teachers' unions have started showing better motivation in streamlining the education system. The All-Bengal Primary Teachers' Association (ABPTA), in association with Unicef and Pratichi Trust, has taken up 150 primary schools in Kolkata city where the basic agenda is to ensure enrolment, attendance, teaching and learning and greater public participation. The organisation plans to extend the scheme to other areas.

These positive interventions, nevertheless, have their limitations. While they have the potential to remedy some of the organisational problems, it would be naïve to expect local initiatives to change things by themselves, particularly when a lot of constraints originate at the policy level. The required policy changes include both budgetary allocation for primary education, greater attention to teachers' recruitment, and overhauling the system through a democratic process (initiating school-specific parent-teacher committees with legal power to govern schools, involving teachers in the process of making the curriculum, formulating teaching and evaluation methods, making the Sarva Shiksha Abhiyan, midday meal and other programmes more transparent, etc).

As Nimi says: "Sarkarko bhanne ke hamiheruko naniko parhaiko lagi ali bandovast garne." ("Please tell the government to do something in order to provide education to our children.") Although clearly dissatisfied, she has not given up hope in the government's capacity to provide that education.

GETTING CHILDREN INTO SCHOOL

All government interventions in education are based on the assumption that child labour cannot be abolished and that the poor do not wish to send their children to school. In fact, the poor make enormous sacrifices to do just that. It is time the administration responded with strategies that help children enrol and stay in school

Today, millions of Indian children are joining the labour market where they are subject to exploitation and drudgery with little hope of ever realising their dreams and aspirations. They are engaged mostly in unpaid domestic work and in the unorganised sector. Girls succumb to the pressures of early marriage, which harms their overall growth and development. Being out of school, they lose their childhood early, are denied basic rights and live in a world of fear and anxiety.

Even children who are physically and mentally challenged are badly neglected and face enormous difficulties in getting any kind of schooling.

At the same time there is a growing demand for education, and the past decade has witnessed many poor parents making huge sacrifices to send their children to school.

This important fact goes largely unnoticed by the authorities whose planning is based on the understanding that the poor cannot and will not send their children to school, and that it is impossible to abolish child labour. This attitude fuels the government's indifference in providing the necessary infrastructure to enable every child to go to school and to continue to do so without disruption. And so, in spite of six decades of independence, an estimated 100-120 million children between the ages of 5-15 have either never been to school or have dropped out.

Although the Indian education system is one of the largest in the world, it is wasteful and inefficient. Almost 54.6% of children (56.9% are girls) drop out before they finish Class VIII, and 66% (68.6% are girls) drop out before reaching Class X (GoI, MHRD website, provisional data for academic year 2001-02). (1) The percentages in tribal areas, backward districts and among scheduled castes and scheduled tribes are appalling. What's worse is that even after five years of being in school, only 60% of children are able to read, write and do basic calculations.

The system is structured on the premise that almost one-third of children entering primary school will drop out before they reach the upper primary level, and another one-third before they reach high school. Indeed, given the situation on the ground, a child entering Class I in a rural government school or urban municipal school reaches Class X more by accident than by design. Even a marginal increase in the number of students passing Class VI or VII and Class X would expose the incapacity to absorb them at the next level.

The government must make a concerted attempt to ensure that every child enjoys the right to education. This would mean:

- Making institutional arrangements to cater to 100 million more children in the school system, preparing not just the education system but the welfare, labour, police, development and revenue bureaucracy to ensure that they coordinate to make it possible for every child to be take out of work and allowed to join school.
- Making arrangements for older children to join school and get into age-appropriate classes.
- Ensuring that first-generation learners and poor children are treated with respect and supported to overcome barriers in accessing and staying in school.

- Preparing all sections and classes of society to join the campaign for universalisation of school education, and ensuring that their areas are free of child labour. Simultaneously, the government must recognise such achievements and provide all the necessary infrastructural support.
- Investing in building a social norm that children must not work and should instead be in school, in places where social mobilisation is weak and where there is no clear support for a child's right to education. The role of gram panchayats and local bodies must be seen as indispensable to all government efforts.

There are many barriers in a child's access to and continuance in school until Class X. Although the solutions lie at the macro level, in terms of policies and investments, there is also a need to address day-to-day issues that the child confronts at the micro level.

GETTING CHILDREN BACK TO SCHOOL

Over the past decade, of taking around 400,000 children out of work and getting them into schools in Andhra Pradesh, the following points were highlighted.

It is important to understand that the main responsibility of ensuring that children learn and are put into classes appropriate for their age is that of the school. No other institution can take the place of the school. It is the school that has qualified teachers, infrastructure, an atmosphere for disciplined learning and a system of evaluation to help children improve and grow. Therefore, schools must be prepared to accept children from Residential Bridge Courses (RBC) without insisting on standards of performance. Once children are mainstreamed into regular schools, it should be the responsibility of the school to prepare them for an age-appropriate class.

Identification of Children for Eligibility to Residential Bridge Courses (RBC)

Only those children who have been identified under a survey conducted by the education department are deemed eligible for

RBCs. Further orders have been issued to the effect that "only those children listed as 'out-of-school' may be admitted". Any other admissions of "out-of-school children may be done under proper certification by the concerned headmaster and Mandal Education Officer".

Most attendance records kept by the school authorities are linked to issues like the provision of midday meal schemes, teacher recruitment, maintenance of teacher-to-pupil ratios (TPR) and other structural necessities of the school system. Under these circumstances, it is cumbersome and impractical to get an 'out-of-school' certificate.

School surveys show that many children recorded as enrolled have never been to school or have dropped out of school and been absent for two-three years. Some of these children's names appear in the attendance registers because of enrolment drives. Some, whose names are in the register, attend private schools; some are married; some may even have left their village.

There are also anomalies in the out-of-school list, especially with regard to girls. Several names are missing and do not appear either in the school-going or non-school-going lists.

Typically, children are identified as a consequence of social mobilisation and intense campaigning. Several conflicts, either of bonded labour or child marriage, have been resolved before the child decides to join school. It is unfair to deny such children admission to RBCs on grounds that their names are already on the school list. Instead, we should try to send such children to school because they are already on the list of enrolled children.

Besides, our schools are ill equipped to deal with children who are 9+ (Standard IX?) and have never been to school. The child is therefore at risk of dropping out. Also, many children who are 12+ and willing to join RBCs are discouraged from doing so. They are told they are too old to be in school.

Admission to Regular Schools is Non-negotiable

All RBCs are closed by June 30. Children are to be admitted to schools and residential programmes based on eligibility tests conducted by schools. But what happens to a child who does not pass the test? Where do these children go? And what are the arrangements for the continuance of the bridge programme?

Several children are denied the right to take the Class V and VI examinations because they are 'over-age', that is, above the age of 13. We need a grievance cell to take up such specific issues and provide practical solutions in favour of the child.

First-generation Learners: Need for Appreciation of Language, Social and Cultural Barriers

Children speak different dialects and need time to adjust to a standardised language. They are not dull because they do not speak the language of the texts in the classroom. They cannot be insulted or excluded because their cultural expressions do not match those of the school system. Given time, and a little patience, they will be able to master the language and culture of power and authority. These issues must not act as barriers when children are being mainstreamed or subjected to scrutiny through eligibility tests and subsequent unit tests and examinations.

FLEXIBILITY IN ADMISSIONS

Children must be allowed to enter school at any time during the academic year; they cannot be denied admission on any grounds. This must be true for all classes, not just for primary school. There must be provision for a Class VI, VII, VIII or IX dropout to rejoin school.

Need to Orient Upper Primary Schools and High Schools

There is a lack of sensitivity among upper primary and high school teachers regarding older children who seek admission to schools from Class VI onwards. Under tremendous pressure to show a good pass percentage and good examination results, even under normal circumstances, teachers are compelled to exclude a many children from the school system. Further, lack of infrastructure, number of teachers and adequate classrooms add to the teachers' unwillingness to admit children aspiring to enter the school system. It is necessary to integrate schools into the entire planning process. In the transitional phase, a good school must be gauged by the number of children it has been able to retain, not by the number of children who have passed out of it.

There must also be a re-look at the internal evaluation system so that children who have been mainstreamed are given enough time to adjust to the academic sessions before they are subjected to the rigours of assessment.

Payment of school fees, examination fees and other school-related expenditure

The government must issue strict instructions to the school authorities against charging school fees and other maintenance charges. If a school has insufficient facilities, it must be encouraged to bring this to the notice of the government and quickly resolve the problem.

Putting the pressure on poor students contributes towards pushing them out of school. Also, children who enter schools through the process of social mobilisation and RBCs, tuitions and coaching classes must be exempt from payment of examination fees as private candidates. They simply cannot afford it.

Conclusion

- Provision must be made to ensure that children are integrated into the school system and not excluded.
- If children are not up to the required standard, it is the responsibility of the school to ensure that they are.
- Adequate flexibility must be allowed to help children overcome all barriers in order to participate in school as students.
- Children must be enrolled as students at regular schools even as they study in RBCs on a full-time basis. The RBC programme must not be seen as a substitute or even an alternative to school. The bridge is meant to enable an 'out-of-school' child to become a student. It is also meant to enable schools to set up facilities for all such children, and get prepared for the backlog of children who are waiting to be mainstreamed.

- Schoolteachers in middle and high schools must be oriented to accept children and establish systems at each level of governance within the education department to make it easy to include every child in school.
- Officials at the state and district level must listen to the children's voices on the ground and respond to them by creating flexibility in governance at schools.

We have failed to universalise education because of a lack of political will. Consequently, in planning for education there is no sense of urgency that children must not work, and that every child should be in school and remain there until Class X. It is almost as if the system were designed to cater to a small percentage of children who come in at Class I and get to Class X. This half-hearted approach determines all our policies and programmes, as a result of which millions of children who aspire to join schools are neglected. Those who have gained the most from the system are often blind to the conditions of a vast majority of children in our country and to the aspirations of their parents. It is by building a social norm in favour of the child's right to education, and providing every support to the poor in their fight to get into school, that education can become a reality for every Indian child.

MAINSTREAMING DISABILITY INTO THE CHILD RIGHTS AGENDA

One in every 10 children is born with or acquires a disability. While the pulse polio drive and immunisation against diphtheria, pertusis and tetanus have been quite successful, the State's efforts to prevent conditions such as blindness, deafness and neurological disabilities have been dismal

One in every 10 children is born with or acquires a physical, mental or sensory disability (Government of India estimates). So India is probably home to millions of disabled children. More than 75% of disabilities are preventable. Although there has been some improvement in the status of children in the areas of health, nutrition and education in general, the situation of children with disabilities remains deplorable, particularly in rural areas and among the lower socio-economic strata. Also, gender-discriminatory feeding and healthcare practices within the home render the girl-child more vulnerable to ill health and acquired disabilities compared to her male counterparts.

The first six years in a child's life are crucial. It is in these years that the physical, cognitive, language and social development of the child is at its peak. Investment in early childhood health and education is therefore essential.

Although various horizontal and vertical health programmes of the State, such as the National Health Policy, Integrated Child Development Services (ICDS) scheme and National Iodine Deficiency Control and Vitamin-A Supplementation Programmes do focus on prevention of childhood disability, their impact on overall decline in the incidence of disability remains minimal. For instance, more than 210,000 children are born cretins, or turn blind every year. High levels of childhood malnutrition and little over 50% immunisation coverage further increase the vulnerability of millions of children to death, disease and disability.

Disability continues to fall in the area of 'social welfare'. While efforts are on to bring it into the 'rights' arena, there is still a long way to go. Various groups of children, including those physically and mentally challenged, juvenile offenders, destitute children and minor drug addicts, etc, are particularly disadvantaged because of their social, economic, physical or mental condition.

Such children are placed under the category of 'children under special or difficult circumstances' by the Indian State. Government policies, legislative action, schemes and provisions for the disabled give the impression of a State that is committed to human rights and equal opportunities. But the ground realities are quite different. While the pulse polio drive and immunisation against diphtheria, pertusis and tetanus have been quite successful, efforts aimed at the prevention of other conditions such as blindness, deafness and neurological disabilities have been dismal. The incidence of developmental disability such as mental retardation and autism has increased to an alarming level.

Children with disabilities must cope with all the physical changes, emotional anxieties and social conflicts of their non-disabled counterparts, in addition to those produced by their disability. Along with the physical and communication-related limitations that their disability places on their daily activities, they constantly face discrimination--economic, educational, architectural, legal, health.

When poverty, physical neglect and social marginalisation intersect, the impact on the disabled girl-child can be devastating. Since women embody family honour, disabled girls are kept hidden away at home by families and denied the basic rights of mobility, education and employment. They are viewed as asexual and dependent.

Sexual identity is a critical component of overall personality development and self-esteem, which crystallises during adolescence. Children with disabilities are at a particular disadvantage in this regard as well. There is a strong attitude of overprotection towards the disabled child. Parents infantilise disabled children and imply that sex is only for the able-bodied and of no relevance to the disabled. These parental attitudes are transmitted to the child in subtle ways making him/her feel that s/he is inferior and unworthy of love. Parents of children with disabilities encourage dependence and share in a general societal perception of disabled persons as essentially child-like, innocent and by extension asexual. To make matters worse, these attitudes also colour the perceptions of teachers.

Key terms in disability discourse are dignity and respect, inclusion, participation, equalisation of opportunities and empowerment. However, if the underlying negative attitudes and cultural representations of disability in society are not challenged through vigorous awareness-generation and attitudinal change strategies, such words will remain empty slogans. Throughout the ages the disabled have been looked upon with disdain, almost as if they were sub-human. Even in literature, negative characters were attributed some form of deformity, be it Manthara, the hunchback, in the Ramayana, or Shakuni the lame, in the Mahabharata. Whether in folk tales or contemporary comic strips, the heroine is invariably fair, slim and beautiful, and the hero, tall, smart and handsome. Rarely is a person with an impairment conferred a positive or heroic role. Most people continue to believe that disability is either an irremediable medical condition or an act of fate. In both cases the onus of care devolves upon the family of the disabled and not on the community.

Myths and misconceptions about disability abound, causing the disabled to be ostracised, isolated and marginalised. From a very young age, children with disabilities internalise such perceptions undermining their innate potentialities and self-esteem.

Disability and the disabled have to be integrated into everyday life. Segregation in special schools and institutions must be minimised; the issue of disability must consciously move beyond issues of special education and medical rehabilitation and be mainstreamed into other discourses such as the economy, polity, entertainment, sports, fashion and lifestyle. The language of special needs and vulnerable groups has to be replaced with less stigmatising and more empowering terms like human rights and specific needs. Families have to be helped to overcome feelings of shame at having a disabled child. And, most important of all, children with disabilities have to be helped to acquire a positive sense of self, self-confidence and self-respect. Only when these are achieved will there be total inclusion and empowerment, and having a disability will mean as much or as little as having black hair or brown eyes.

CHILDREN AND THE CRIMINAL JUSTICE SYSTEM

The Juvenile Justice Act 2000 lays down a non-penal protective juvenile justice system for children alleged to have committed an offence. While the legislation itself is well-intentioned, there are many stumbling blocks in its implementation, chief among them the difficulty of establishing whether an offender is a child or not, in a country where millions do not have birth certificates or other records

The Criminal Justice System (CJS) consists of the legal provisions defining offences, providing punishment for those offences, procedures for investigation of those offences, prosecution and trial leading to conviction or acquittal of accused persons. Initially, CJS dealt with all persons committing offences. However, since 1920, special laws have been made for children committing offences and presently it is the Juvenile Justice (Care and Protection) Act, 2000 that prescribes different procedures for investigation and trial of cases where children are alleged to have committed an offence.

JJA 2000 is applicable to the whole of India, except the state of Jammu and Kashmir, and lays down a non-penal protective juvenile justice system for them. JJA 2000 applies to all children who have not completed the age of 18 years who may have committed an offence or may be in need of care and protection. This legislation was passed to bring the law in conformity with international legal provisions contained in the UN Convention on the Rights of the Child, the Beijing Rules for Administration of Juvenile Justice System, Riyadh Guidelines and the Rules Relating to Children Deprived of Liberty. While the Indian Penal Code (IPC), the primary penal law in India, contains two special provisions in relation to children, and declares that nothing done by a child below the age of 7 is an offence and that all children above the age of 7 but below the age of 12 are presumed to have the mental capacity that makes a person liable for commission of an offence, JJA 2000 provides for no punishment but only corrective measures for all children found to have committed an offence. There are a few crucial aspects about the operation of this Act that need to be understood clearly.

The most important among them is to prove that the person in question was below the age of 18 on the date of the event. While there are many judgments declaring that in the absence of a birth certificate, the age as is recorded in the school registers before the occurrence should be taken as the true age of the person, there are problems where different ages are recorded in different schools or if the child has never been to school. In the absence of documentary proof, a court may send the accused for a medical examination to determine the age. The problem with medical examination is that it can at best provide only an approximate age within the range of 6 months, give or take a few days. In the case of Rajinder Chandra v State of Chhattisgarh, ([2002] 2 SCC 287), the Supreme Court held that in case of doubt about the accused being a child or not on the date of offence, the benefit of doubt should be given to the accused child. It is crucial therefore that advocacy for children emphasise the importance of birth certificates that are important for so many other purposes too.

Another important question relating to children committing offences has been which legislation will apply in case of children committing serious offences. Long ago, in the cases of Rohtas (AIR 1979 SC 2037) and Raghubir (AIR 1981 SC 2037), the Supreme Court held that the juvenile courts alone would have jurisdiction to deal with cases of children committing offences punishable with death penalty or life imprisonment. Subsequently, similar questions arose in view of special legislations like the Narcotics Drugs and Psychotropic Substances (NDPS) Act or the Prevention Of Terrorism Act (POTA) which provide for special courts to deal with offences under these legislations. While different high courts had taken different positions on the applicability of JJA 2000 to cases where the accused is a child, the Supreme Court has clearly held that JJA 2000 will apply to children alleged to have committed offences under those special penal legislations too (Madan Singh v State of Rajasthan, SC DOJ 2.4.05; Raj Singh v State of Haryana, [2000] 6 SCC 759).

Children arrested for any offence must be released on bail, unless the release will bring the child into contact with known criminals, expose the child to moral danger, or the release is against the interests of justice. It is also necessary to separate the cases of children from adults, in the event that they are charged with the offence together. The child's case is to be dealt with by the Juvenile Justice Board (JJB), which consists of a magistrate and two social workers and decides the case by majority. Members of the JJB exercise the powers of a magistrate but are empowered to deal with all offences committed by children, including those triable only by a sessions judge.

In case the JJB finds that the child has committed an offence, it may pass any of the following orders: release after due admonition and counselling to him/her and the family;

keep the child under the supervision of parents/guardian/ probation officer/fit person/fit institution; impose a fine; send for community service; order group counselling; send to a special home. No child may be sent to death or imprisonment under any circumstance, or to prison in default of payment of fine or producing sureties. In case the child is above 16 years of age and commits a very serious offence, he/she may be ordered to be kept in safe custody. A child dealt with by the JJB does not suffer any disqualification attached to conviction for an offence.

JJA 2000 establishes another body, namely the Children Welfare Committee (CWC), to deal with children in need of care and protection. Members of the CWC also exercise the powers of a magistrate, while all of them are non-judicial persons. The CWC gives the appropriate orders for care, protection and rehabilitation of children in need of care and protection. There are numerous categories of children in need of care and protection, including children without parents, or without sufficient means of livelihood or a permanent place to live, the terminally ill, victims of natural disasters, war or civil strife, etc. The CWC may send such children to a children's home, or place them with a fit person/institution.

JJA 2000 also prescribes that each police station should have a special police officer to deal with children--whether arrested for committing an offence or in need of care and protection. These police officers should have special training to deal with children in a friendly manner.

JJA 2000 contains provisions for sponsorship of children to promote their care within family and institutional structures. It also makes provisions for the adoption and foster care of children covered under it, to ensure family care to children. Provisions for adoption of children under JJA 2000 are much wider than those under the Hindu Adoption and Maintenance Act. Under JJA 2000, any person can adopt any child irrespective of religion and the number or sex of natural-born children the adoptive parent may already have. Adoption under JJA 2000 was implemented as a measure to provide for the welfare and care of children and not as a religious act. The JJA also provides for shelter homes for temporary reception of children in need of urgent care.

The CRC has laid down the basic principles of decision-making to promote the best interests of children, and all decisions relating to children need to be guided by this consideration. The Beijing Rules direct that institutions should be used only as a last resort and only until community measures become available for children. As JJA 2000 was specifically made to implement India's obligations under these and other international instruments, it is incumbent upon the authorities implementing this legislation to ensure protection and promotion of these principles.

While the legislation has been made with the best intentions, it has been criticised for its unprofessional and tardy drafting. Its implementation, also, has been piecemeal. The biggest problem faced in implementation is the absence of all-India data relating to the status of children in India. While Unicef provides some figures about the number of children below 18 years of age in India, such information is missing from the Census of India. There certainly are no figures available on the number of children in need of care and protection as defined under JJA 2000. In the absence of basic data relating to children, proper planning is not possible.

The largest number of cases that come before the high courts and the Supreme Court under this legislation and its predecessors has been for determination of age. In the absence of a birth certificate, a child may easily be excluded from the operation of the JJA and denied its care and protection. In 1990, Delhi police conducted a raid in the red-light area and took custody of around 111 children. They claimed that they were child prostitutes, children of prostitutes or children working in brothels. The next day, under pressure from NGOs working for the welfare of prostitutes, and opposition from the personnel of observation homes, the Child Welfare Board released all but seven of the children by determining their age through 'facial examination'. Ameena, the minor girl from Hyderabad married to a 60-year-old Arab, rescued by airhostess Amrita Ahluwalia, remained in the observation home in Delhi for over seven months before being sent back to Hyderabad.

But her age was never properly determined and different courts kept referring to her as 10, 11 or 12 years old. In the case of Ramdeo Chauhan ([2001] 5 SCC 714 &2000 II AD [Cr] SC 801), the Supreme Court refused to determine the age of the accused on the basis of entries in the school register or medical evidence, both of which indicated him to be a child on the date of the offence, and confirmed the death penalty for the offence of murder even though one judge expressed a doubt as to whether the boy was a child on the date of commission of offence. The governor later commuted his sentence to life imprisonment on the recommendation of the National Human Rights Commission. India is a young nation, with about 40% or more of its 1 billion people being children. Way back in 1974, the National Policy for Children declared that the nation's children were its most important asset. We need to lobby for the allocation of necessary resources to develop this national asset to its full potential.

ABBREVIATIONS

AIDS	Acquired Immuno Deficiency Syndrome
ARI	Acute Respiratory Infection
ARWSP	Accelerated Rural Water Supply Programme
BCG	Bacillus Calmette Guerin
CARA	Central Adoption Resource Agency
CLASP	Child Labour Action and Support Programme
CRC	Convention on the Rights of the Child
CRSP	Central Rural Sanitation Programme
DPT	Diptheria, Pertussis and Tetanus
ECCE	Early Childhood Care and Education
ECE	Early Childhood Education
FNB	Food and Nutrition Board
HUDCO	Housing and Urban Development Corporation
IWY	Indira Awaas Yojana
ICDS	Integrated Child Development Services
ILO	International Labour Organisation
IMR	Infant Mortality Rate

IPEC	International Programme for Elimination of Child Labour
MCH	Maternal and Child Health
MMR	Maternal Mortality Rate
NFE	Non-Formal Education
NGO	Non-Government Organisation
NIN	National Institute of Nutrition
NIPCCD	National Institute of Public Cooperation and Child Development
NNMB	National Nutrition Monitoring Board
NNT	Neonatal Tetanus
NPCL	National Policy on Child Labour
NPE	National Policy on Education
NREP	National Rural Employment Programme
OPV	Oral Polio Vaccine
ORT	Oral Re-hydration Therapy
PEM	Protein Energy Malnutrition
PHC	Primary Health Centre
PHED	Public Health & Engineering Department
PIL	Public Interest Litigation
RBD	Registration of Births and Deaths
RGNDWM	Rajiv Gandhi National Drinking Water Mission
RLEGP	Rural Landless Employment Guarantee Programme
SAARC	South Asian Association for Regional Cooperation
TT	Tetanus Toxoid
UN	United Nations
UBSP	Urban Basic Services for the Poor
VCA	Voluntary Coordinating Agencies

BIBLIOGRAPHY

Archavanitkul, K. and Havanon, N.: *Situation, Opportunities and Problems Encountered by Young Girls in Thai Society*, Bangkok, Terre des Hommes, 1990.

Bandman, B.: *Children's Right to Freedom, Care, and Enlightenment*, New York, Garland Publishing, 1999.

Banerjee, S.: *Child Labor in India*, London, The Anti-Slavery Society, 1979.

Bell, L.: *Good Girls/Bad Girls: Feminists and Sex Trade Workers Talk Face to Face*, Toronto: The Women's Press, 1987.

Beth, S. : *Voices From The Fields: Children of Migrant Farmworkers Tell Their Stories*, Boston: Little Brown & Co., 1993.

Bremner, H.: *Children and Youth: Social Problems and Social Policy Series*, New York, Arno Press, 1974.

Burja, J.: *Crime, Justice and Underdevelopment*, London, Heinemann, 1982.

Cole, S.: *Working Kids on Working*, New York, Lothrop, Lee, and Shepard, 1980.

Dodge, C.: *War, Violence, and Children in Uganda*, Oxford, Oxford University Press, 1987.

Dunford, Madeleine: *Tackling the Symptoms or the Causes?: An Examination of Programmes by NGOs for Street Children in Nairobi, Kenya*, Edinburgh, Centre of African Studies, Edinburgh University, 1996.

Ennew, J., & Milne, B.: *The Next Generation: Lives of Third World Children*, London, Zed Books, 1989.

Ennew, J.: *Sexual Exploitation of Children*, Cambridge, Polity Press, 1986.

Enos, Njeru: *Street Children in Kenya: Voices of Children in Search of a Childhood*, Westport, Connecticut: Praeger, 2001.

Fallon, P. : *Child Labor: Issues, and Directions for the World Bank,* Washington, World Bank, 1998.

Fernand-Laurent, J.: *Report of the Special Rapporteur on the Suppression of the Traffic in Persons and the Exploitation of the Prostitution of Others,* Geneva, United Nations, 1983.

Fozzard, S.: *Surviving Violence: A Recovery Program for Children and Families,* Geneva, International Catholic child Bureau, 1995.

Fuller, C. J.: *The Nayars Today,* New York, Cambridge University Press, 1976.

Fyfe, Alec: *All Work and No Play: Child Labor Today,* London, Trade Unions Congress, 1985.

Gabriel, Marie Cruz: *Children of the Street,* New Delhi, Penguin Books, 1994.

George, K. K.: *Limits to Kerala Model of Development: An Analysis of Fiscal Crisis and Its Implications,* Thiruvananthapuram, Centre for Development Studies. Monograph Series, 1993.

Goldberg, Vicki: *Children at Work,* Prestel, USA, 1999.

Grant, James P.: *The State of the World's Children: 1988,* Oxford, Oxford University Press, 1988.

Harris, Marvin: *America Now: The Anthropology of a Changing Culture,* New York, Simon and Schuster, 1981.

Haspels, Nelien: *Action Against Child Labor,* Washington, DC: Brookings Institution, 2000.

Hiew, C. C.: *Child Prostitution: Social and Psychological Factors,* Sukhothai University, Bangkok, 1992.

Hitchcock, K.: *Globalization, Child Labor, and Children's Rights,* Lincoln, Nebraska: Nebraskans for Peace, 2002.

Holland, P.: *What Is A Child,* London, Virago, 1992.

Jeffery, Roger: *The Politics of Health in India,* Berkeley, University of California Press, 1988.

Joseph, M.: *The Children's Rights Movement: A History of Advocacy and Protection,* Boston, Twayne Publishers/ Division of G.K. Hall & Co., 1991.

Judith, E.: *The Sexual Exploitation of Children,* Cambridge, Polity Press, 1986.

Kevin, Major: *Free the Children: A Young Man's Personal Crusade Against Child Labor*, New York, HarperCollins, 1998.

Lim, Anne Siew Kum: *Face to Face: the Street Children of Bukit Ho Swee*, Singapore, Landmark Books, 1991.

McIntosh, Robert: *Boys in the Pits: Child Labour in Coal Mines*, Montreal, McGill Queens University Press, 2000.

Miller, Barbara: *The Endangered Sex: Neglect of Female Children in Rural North India*. Ithaca, Cornell University Press, 1981.

Muntabhorn, V.: *Sale of Children, Report submitted by the Special Rapporteur on the Sale of Children*, New York, United Nations, 1992.

Murray, A.: *No Money, No Honey A Study of Street Traders and Prostitutes in Jakarta*, OUP, Singapore, 1991.

Nardinelli, Clark: *Child Labor and the Industrial Revolution*, Bloomington, Indiana University Press, 1990.

Narvesen, O.: *The Sexual Exploitation of Children in Developing Countries*, Oslo, Redd Barna, 1989.

Noble, Christina: *Nobody's Child: a Woman's Abusive Past and the Inspiring Dream that led to Rescue the Street Children of Saigon*, New York, Grove Press, c1994.

O'Grady, R.: *The Child and the Tourist*, Bangkok, ECPAT, 1992.

O'Grady, R.: *The Rape of the Innocent*, Bangkok, ECPAT, 1994.

Pandey, Rajendra: *Street Children of India: a Situational Analysis*, Allahabad, Chugh Publications, 1991.

Perkins, Eugene: *Home is a Dirty Street: the Social Oppression of Black Children*, Chicago, Third World Press, 1991.

Phillips, W. S. K.: *Street Children in India*, Jaipur, Rawat Publications,1994.

Rane Asha J.: *Street Children: a Challenge to the Social Work Profession*, Bombay, Tata Institute of Social Sciences, 1994.

Robert, H.: *Children and Youth: Social Problems and Social Policy Series*, New York, Arno Press, 1974.

Rone, Jemera: *Children in Sudan: Slaves, Street Children and Child Soldiers*, NewYork, Human Rights Watch, c1995.

Rozario, Sr. R. M.: *Trafficking in Women and Children in India*, Uppal Publishing House, New Delhi, 1988.

Sanders, Thomas Griffin: *Brazilian Street Children*, Indianapolis, Universities Field Staff International, 1987.

Shner-Nishmit, Sara: *The Children from Mapuh Street*, Jerusalem, World Zionist Organization, 1968.

Sittitrai, W. and Brown, T.: *The Impact of HIV on Children in Thailand*, Bangkok, Thai Red Cross Society, 1994.

Sturdevant, S. P. and Stotzfus, B.: *Let the Good Times Roll: Prostitution and the Military in Asia*, CIIR, The New Press, 1993.

Thitsa, K.: *Providence and Prostitution: Women in Buddhist Thailand*, Change International, London, 1980.

Trattner, I., *Crusade for the Children: A History of the National Child Labor Committee and Child Labor Reform in America*, Chicago, Quadrangle Boos, 1970.

Truong, T. D.: *Virtue, Order Health and Money: Towards a ComprehensivePerspective on Female Prostitution in Asia*, United Nations, Bangkok, 1986.

Tzannatos, Z.: *Child Labor: Issues, and Directions for the World Bank*, Washington, World Bank, 1998.

Vittachi, A.: *Stolen Childhood*, Cambridge, Polity Press, 1989.

West, Morris L: *Children of the Shadows; the True Story of the Street Urchins of Naples*, Garden City, N.Y., Doubleday, 1957.

White, B.: *Child Workers. Special Issue of Development and Change*, London, Sage Publications, 1982.

William, James: *The World's Exploited Children: Growing Up Sadly*, Washington, Bureau of Labor Affairs, 1980.

Zelizer, R.: *Pricing the Priceless Child*, Princeton: Princeton Univ. Press, 1994.

INDEX

D

I

J

L

M

N

T

U

V

W

Y

❑❑❑